Chapter 7: Your Name

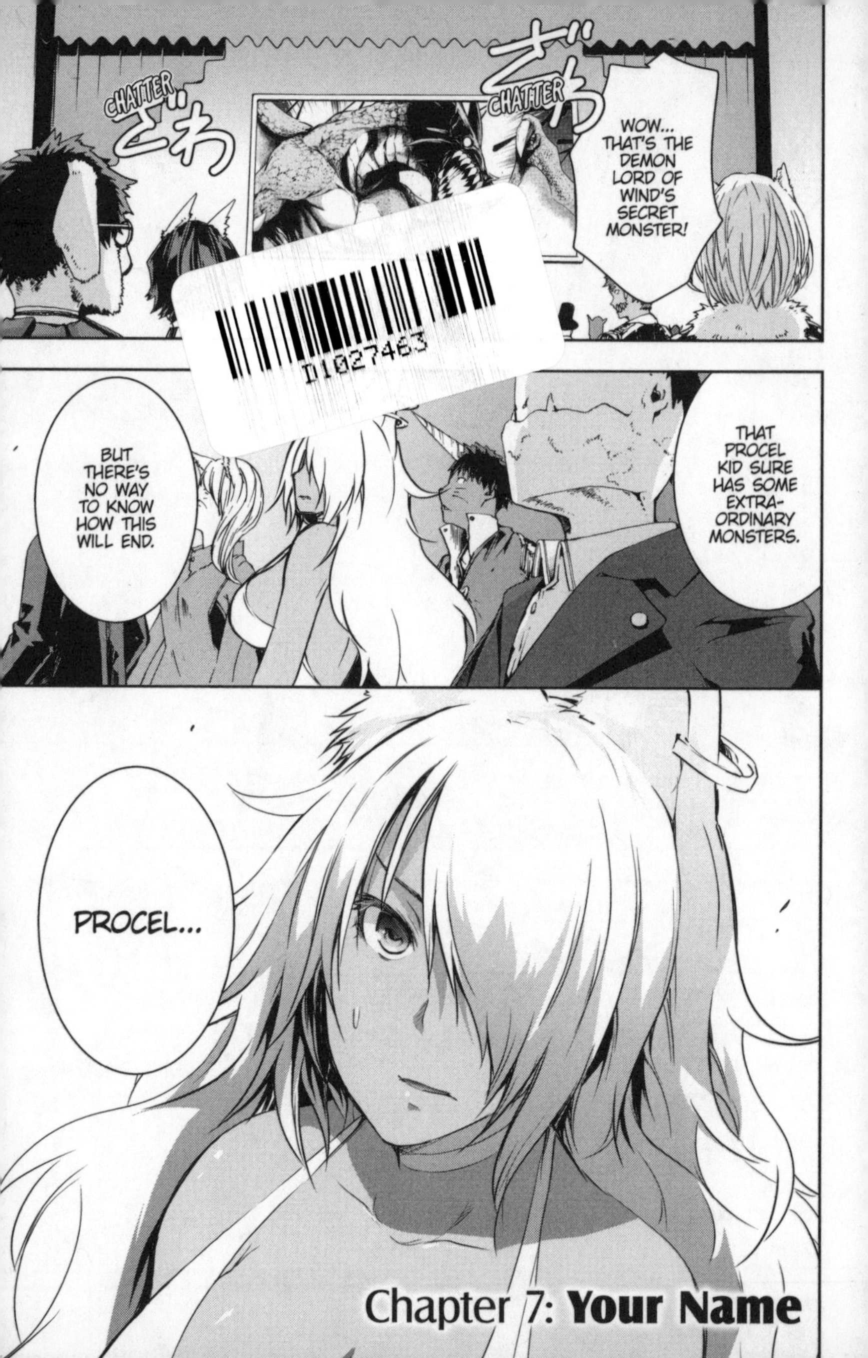

ざわ
CHATTER
ざわ
CHATTER
WOW... THAT'S THE DEMON LORD OF WIND'S SECRET MONSTER!
THAT PROCEL KID SURE HAS SOME EXTRA-ORDINARY MONSTERS.
BUT THERE'S NO WAY TO KNOW HOW THIS WILL END.
PROCEL...

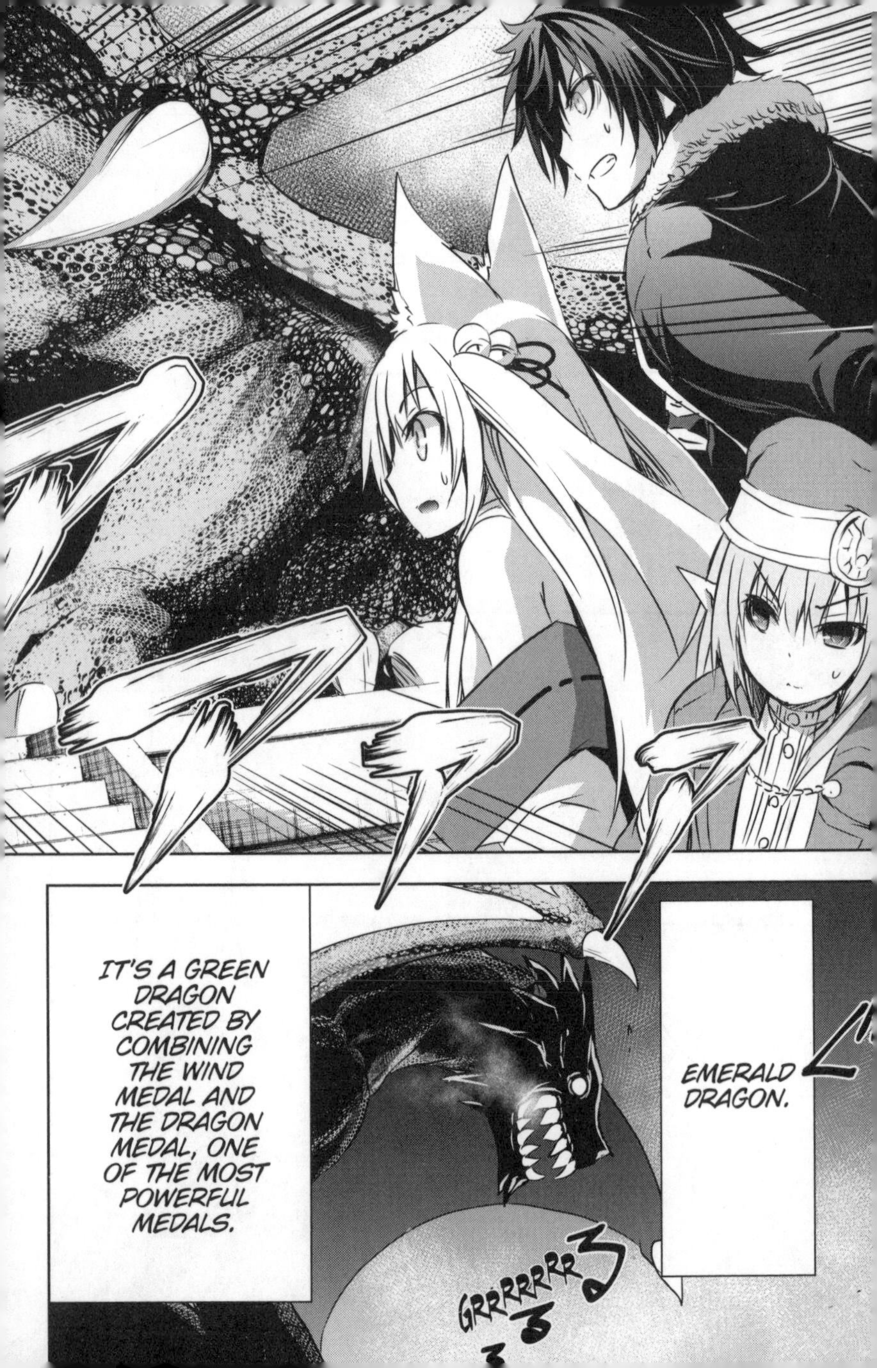

EMERALD DRAGON.
IT'S A GREEN DRAGON CREATED BY COMBINING THE WIND MEDAL AND THE DRAGON MEDAL, ONE OF THE MOST POWERFUL MEDALS.
GRRRRRRR

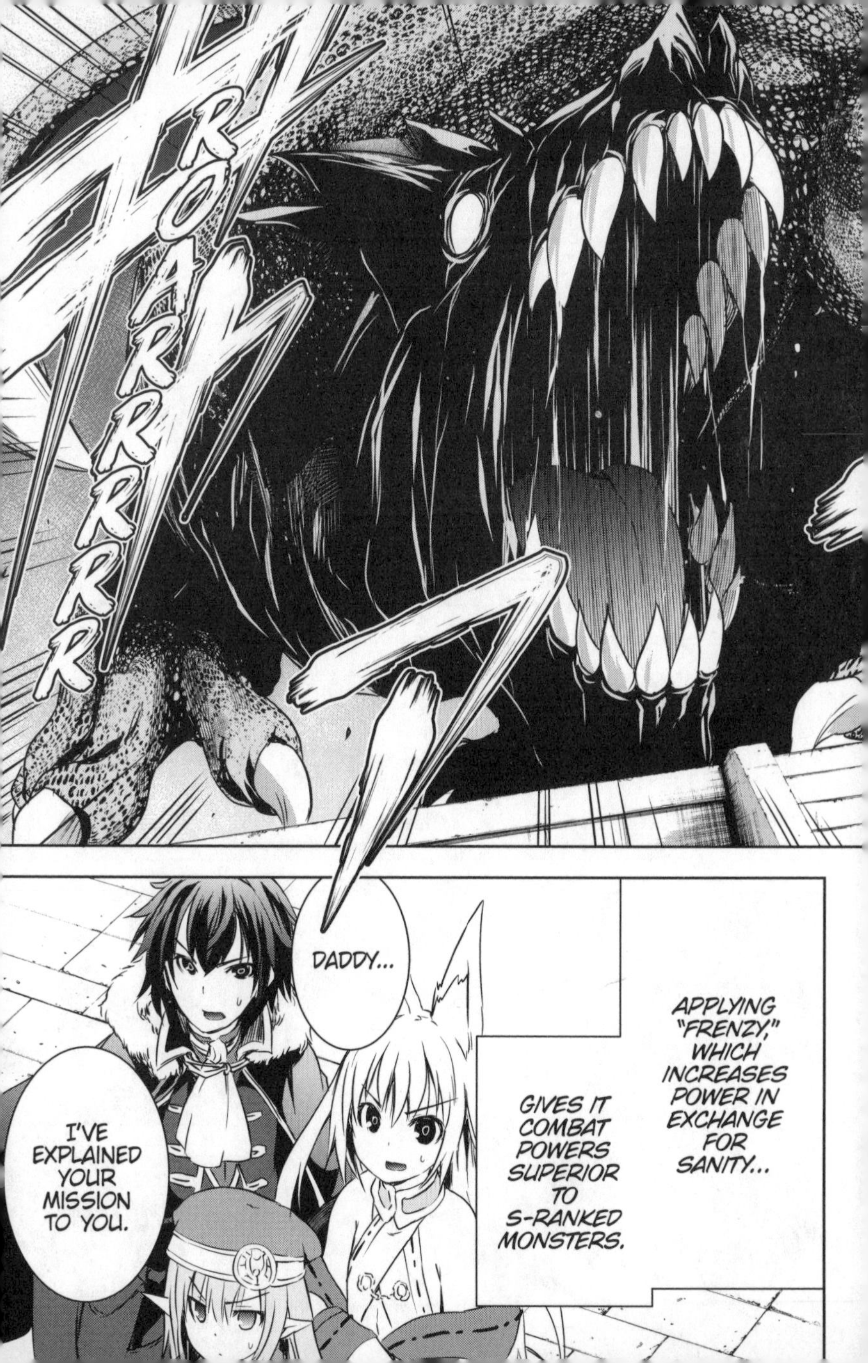
ROARRRRRRR
APPLYING "FRENZY," WHICH INCREASES POWER IN EXCHANGE FOR SANITY...
GIVES IT COMBAT POWERS SUPERIOR TO S-RANKED MONSTERS.
DADDY...
I'VE EXPLAINED YOUR MISSION TO YOU.

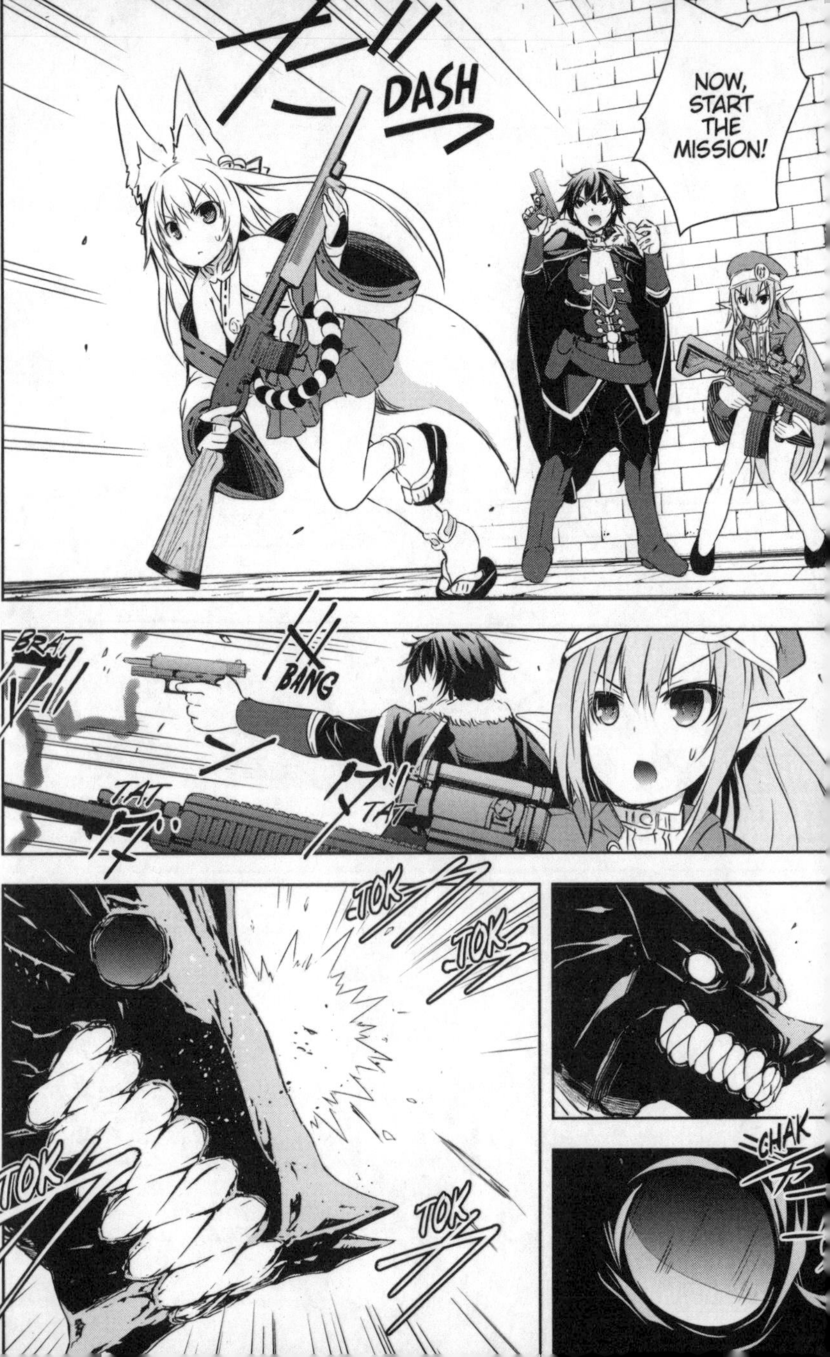
NOW, START THE MISSION!
DASH
BANG
TAT
BRAT
TAT
CHAK
TOK
TOK
TOK
TOK

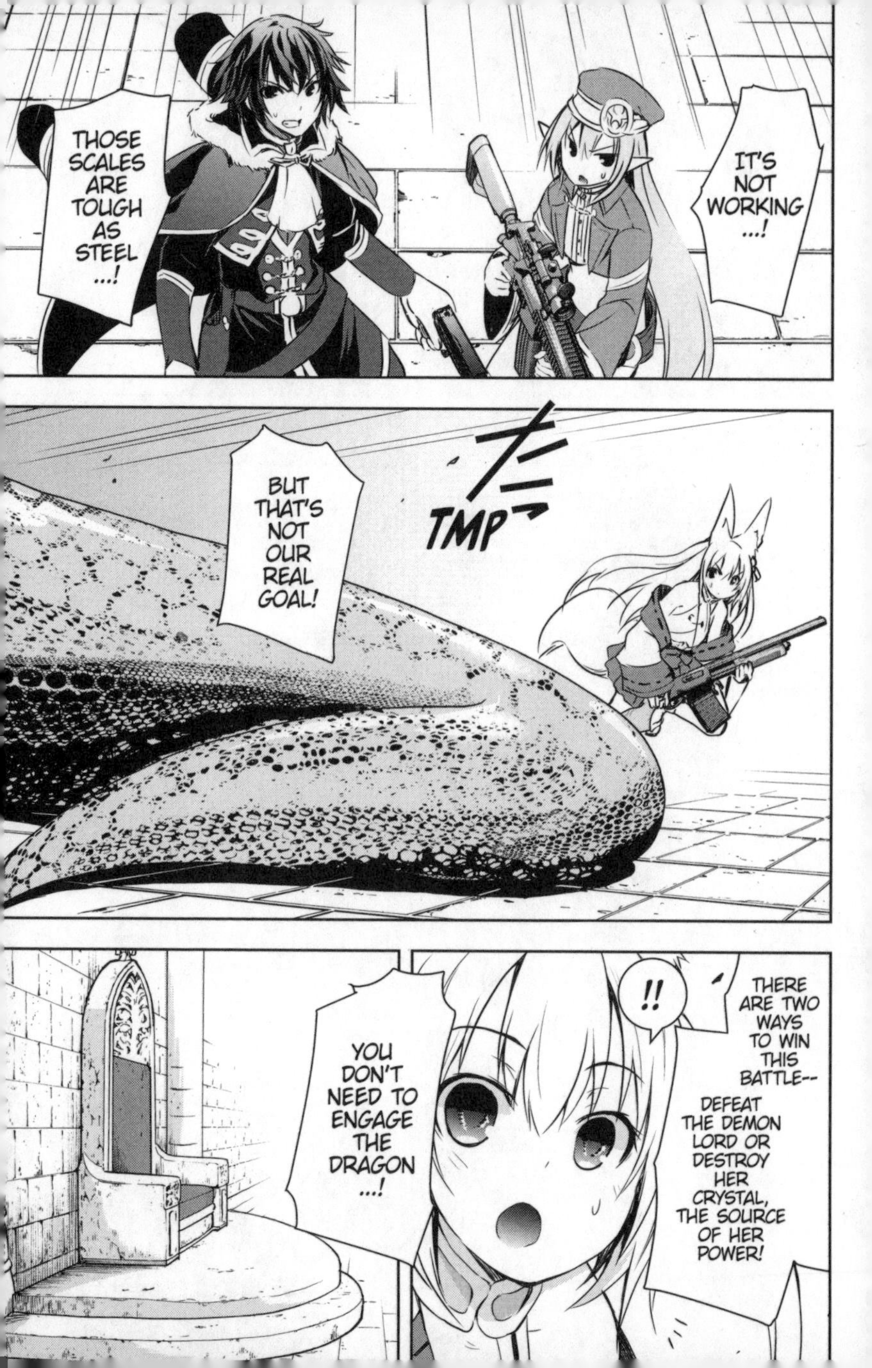
IT'S NOT WORKING...!
THOSE SCALES ARE TOUGH AS STEEL...!
BUT THAT'S NOT OUR REAL GOAL!
TMP
THERE ARE TWO WAYS TO WIN THIS BATTLE--
DEFEAT THE DEMON LORD OR DESTROY HER CRYSTAL, THE SOURCE OF HER POWER!
!!
YOU DON'T NEED TO ENGAGE THE DRAGON...!

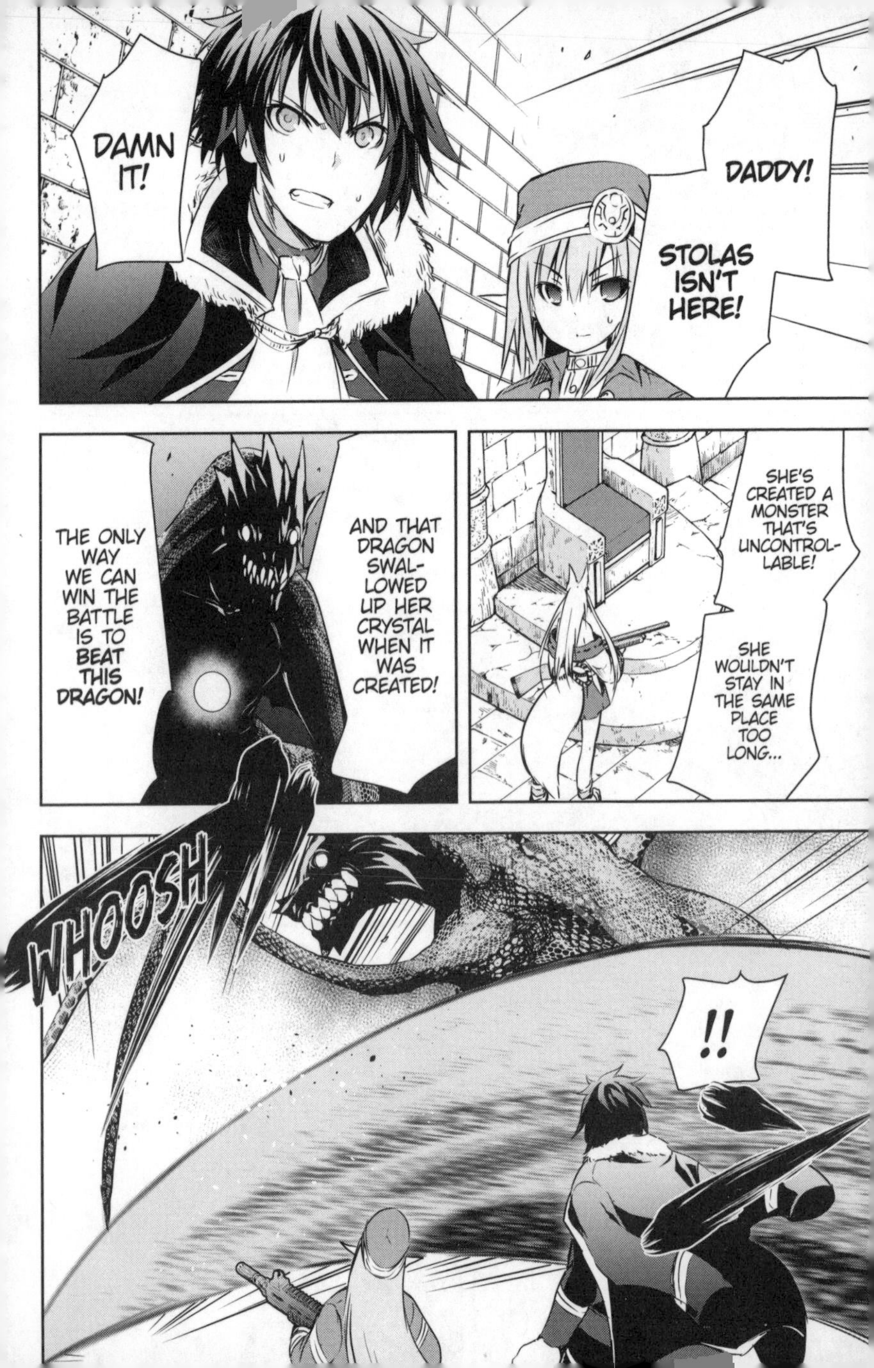
DADDY!
STOLAS ISN'T HERE!
DAMN IT!
SHE'S CREATED A MONSTER THAT'S UNCONTROL-LABLE!
SHE WOULDN'T STAY IN THE SAME PLACE TOO LONG...
AND THAT DRAGON SWAL-LOWED UP HER CRYSTAL WHEN IT WAS CREATED!
THE ONLY WAY WE CAN WIN THE BATTLE IS TO BEAT THIS DRAGON!
!!
WHOOSH

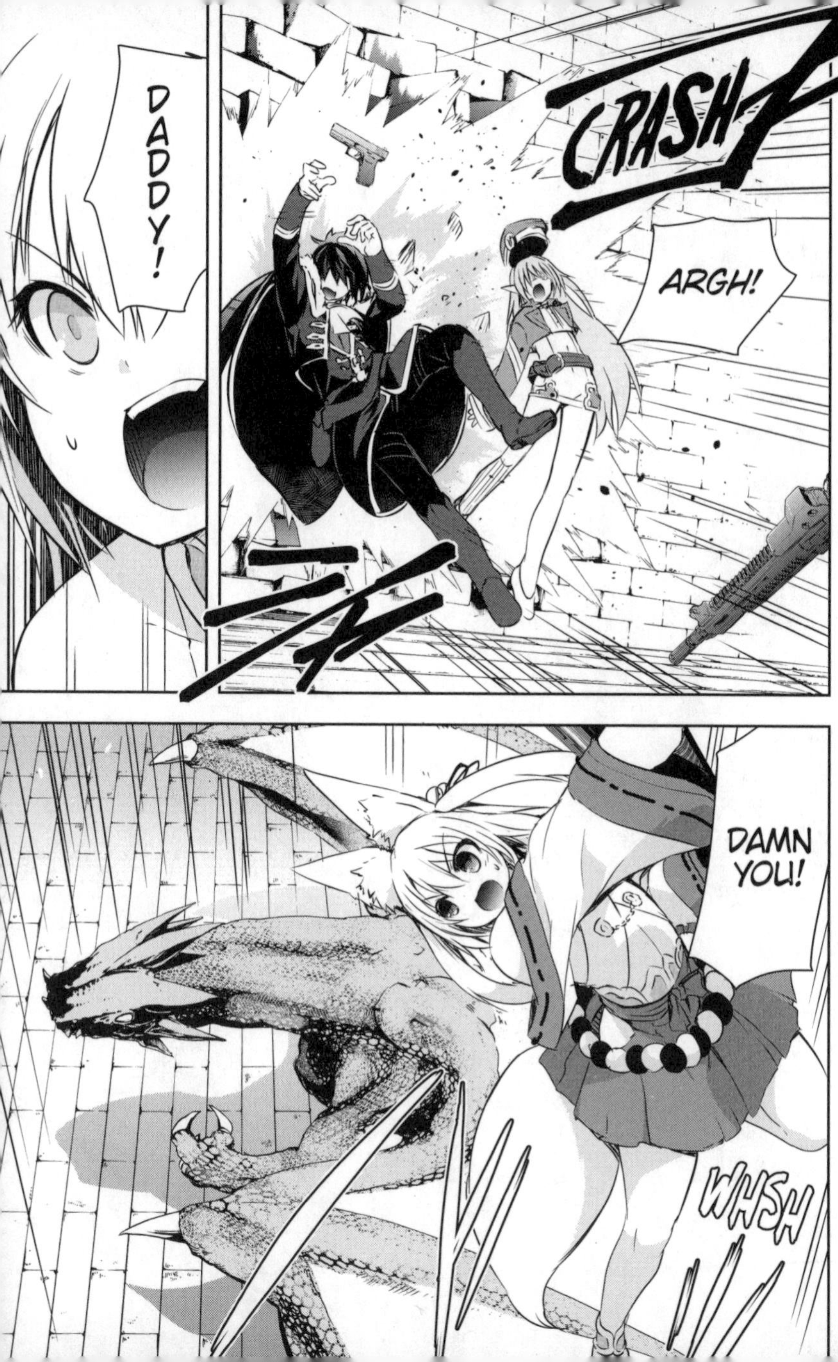
CRASH
ARGH!
DADDY!
DAMN YOU!
WHSH

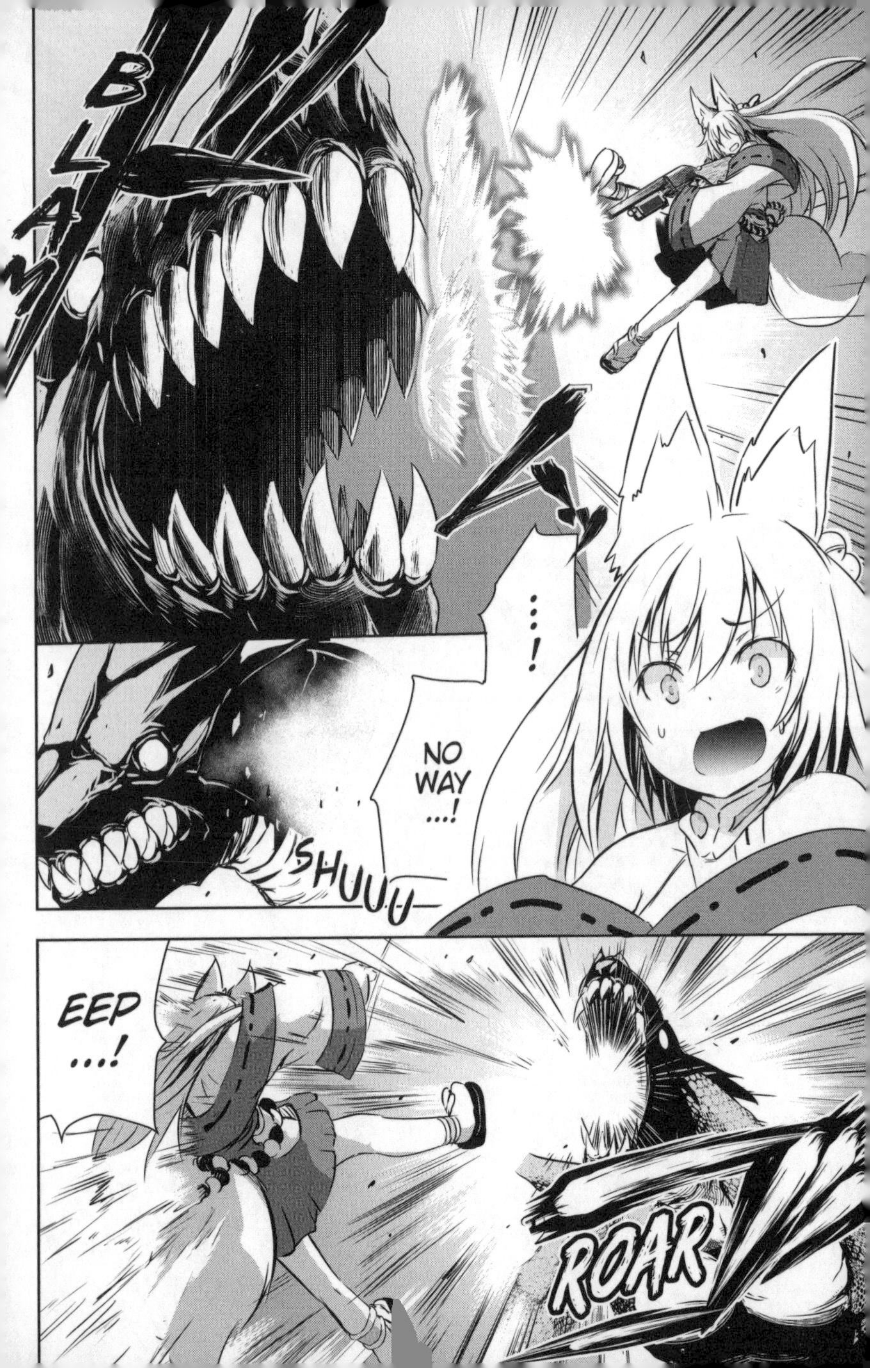
BLAM
...!
NO WAY ...!
SHUUUU
EEP ...!
ROAR

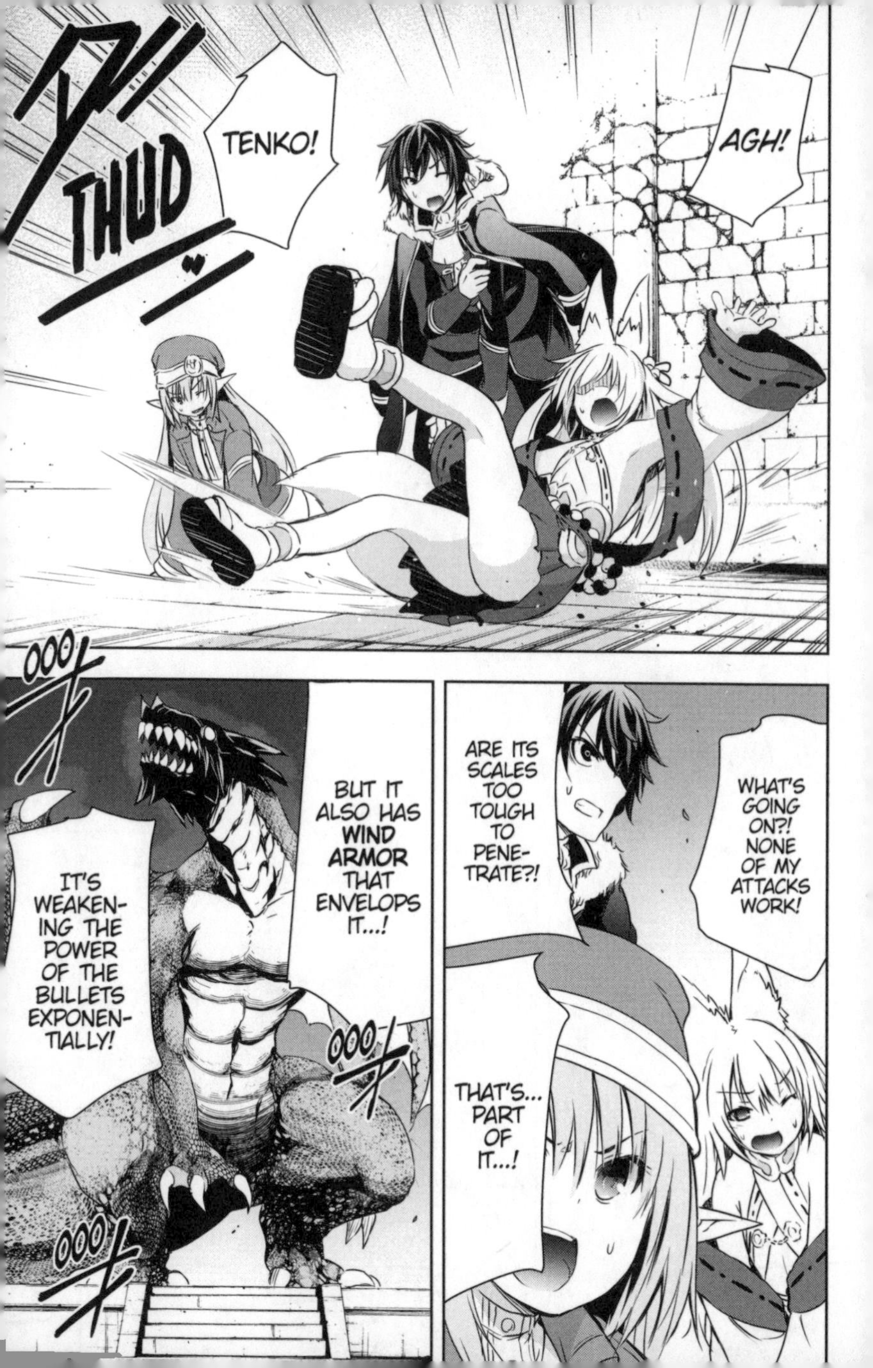
AGH!
TENKO!
THUD
WHAT'S GOING ON?! NONE OF MY ATTACKS WORK!
ARE ITS SCALES TOO TOUGH TO PENETRATE?!
THAT'S... PART OF IT...!
OOO
BUT IT ALSO HAS WIND ARMOR THAT ENVELOPS IT...!
IT'S WEAKENING THE POWER OF THE BULLETS EXPONENTIALLY!
OOO
OOO

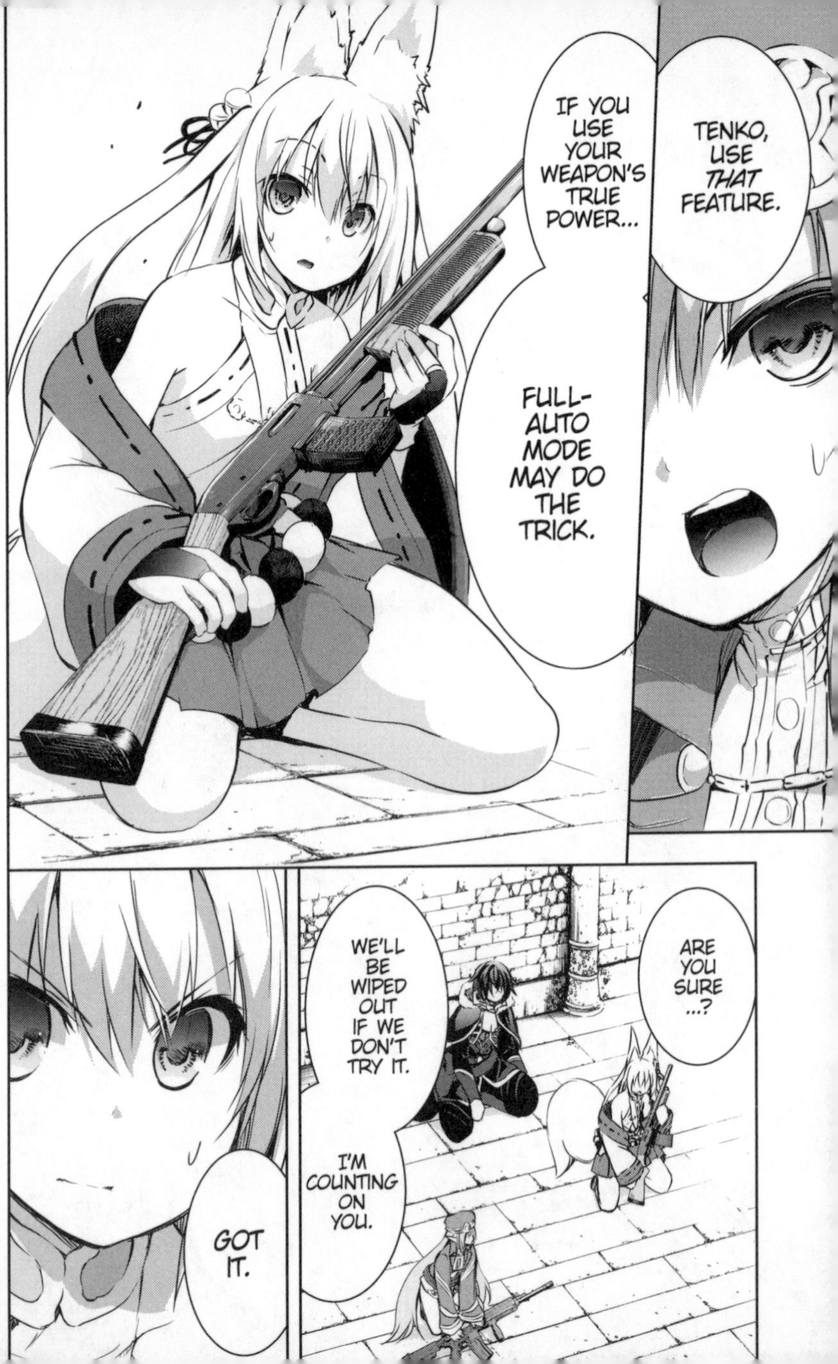
TENKO, USE *THAT* FEATURE.
IF YOU USE YOUR WEAPON'S TRUE POWER...
FULL-AUTO MODE MAY DO THE TRICK.
ARE YOU SURE ...?
WE'LL BE WIPED OUT IF WE DON'T TRY IT.
I'M COUNTING ON YOU.
GOT IT.

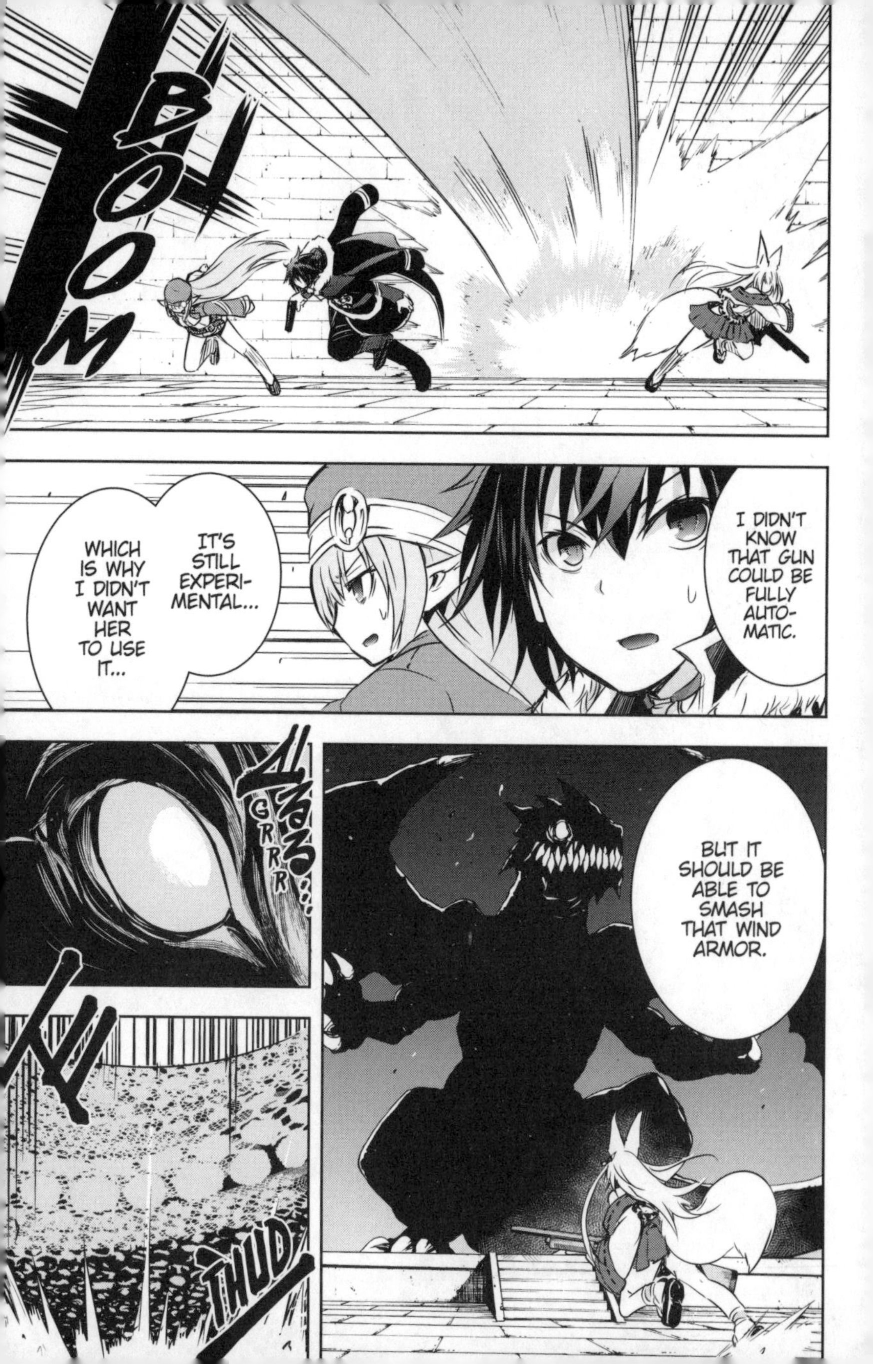
BOOM
I DIDN'T KNOW THAT GUN COULD BE FULLY AUTO-MATIC.
IT'S STILL EXPERI-MENTAL...
WHICH IS WHY I DIDN'T WANT HER TO USE IT...
BUT IT SHOULD BE ABLE TO SMASH THAT WIND ARMOR.
GRRR
THUD

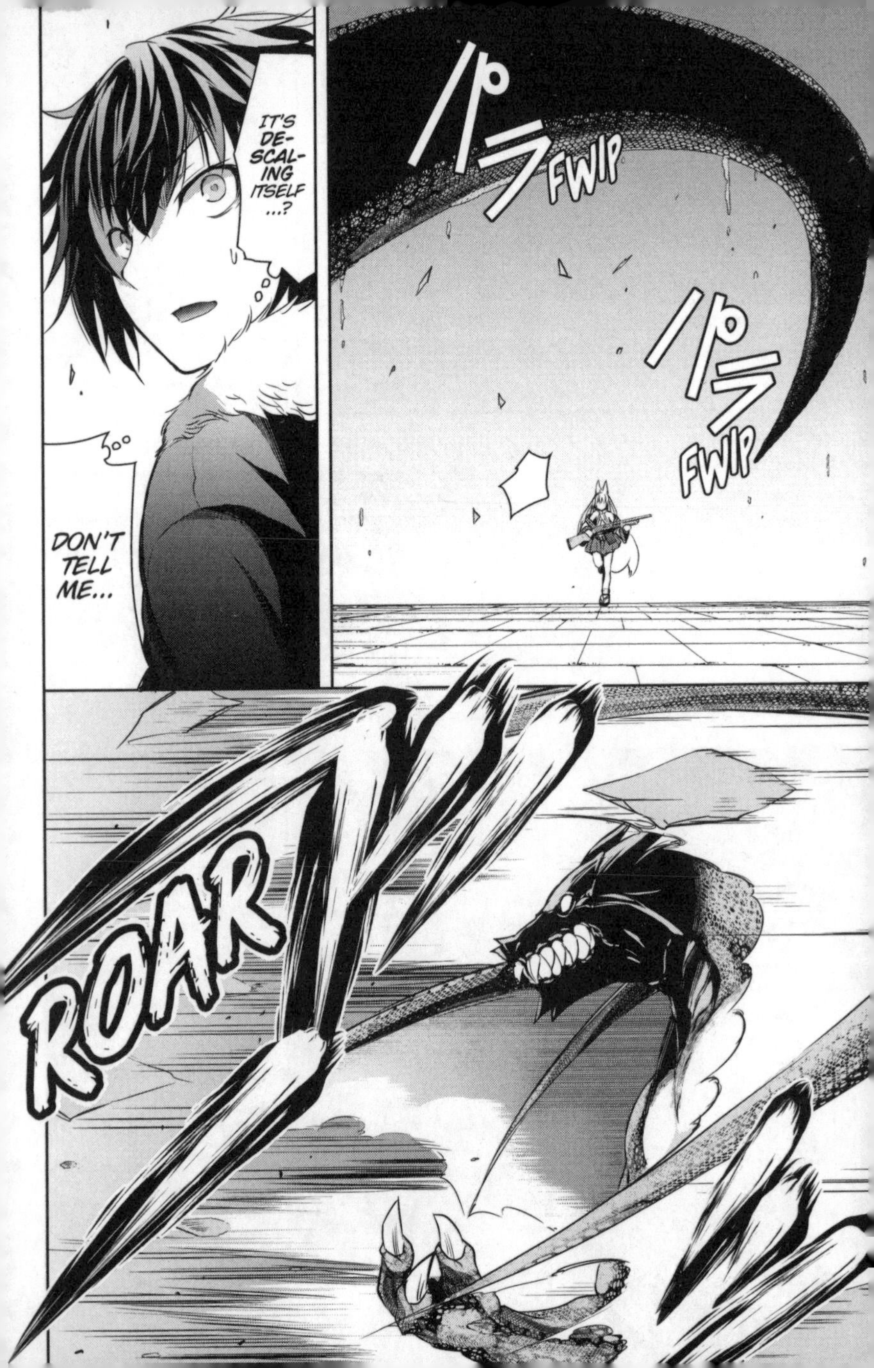
パラ
FWIP
パラ
FWIP
IT'S DE-SCALING ITSELF ...?
DON'T TELL ME...
ROAR

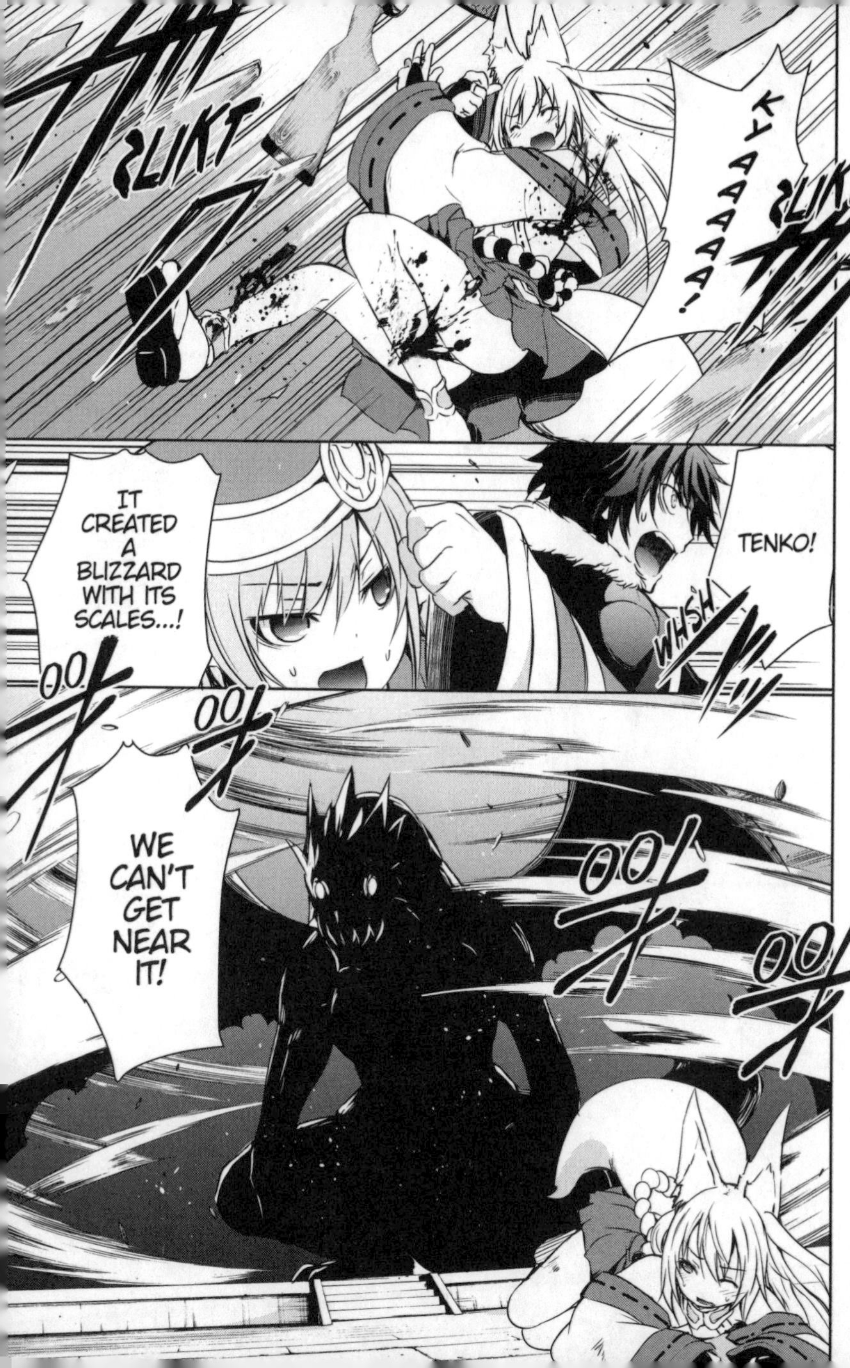
KYAAAAAAA!
ZLIKT
ZLIKT
TENKO!
WHSH
IT CREATED A BLIZZARD WITH ITS SCALES...!
WE CAN'T GET NEAR IT!

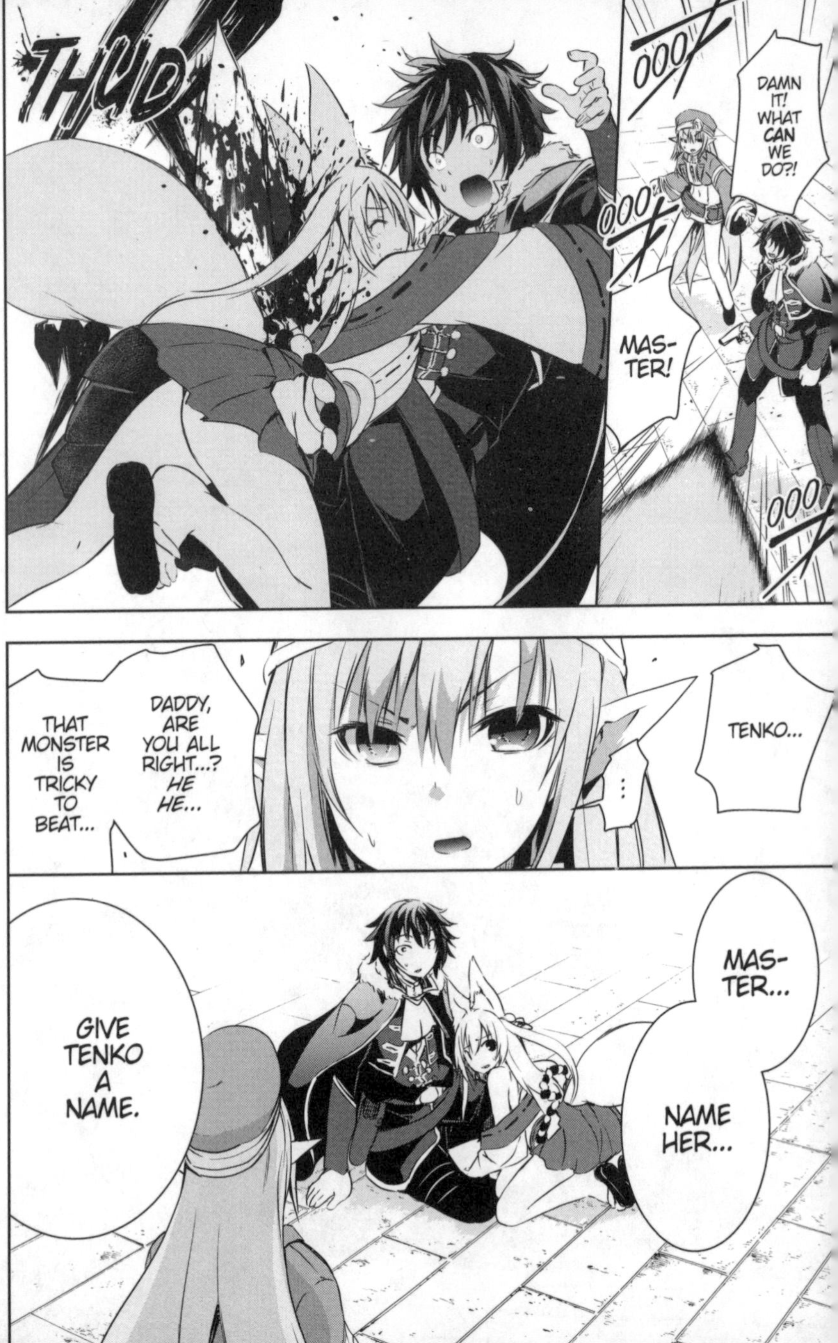
OOO
DAMN IT! WHAT CAN WE DO?!
OOO
MAS-TER!
OOO
THUD
TENKO...
...
DADDY, ARE YOU ALL RIGHT...? HE HE...
THAT MONSTER IS TRICKY TO BEAT...
MAS-TER...
NAME HER...
GIVE TENKO A NAME.

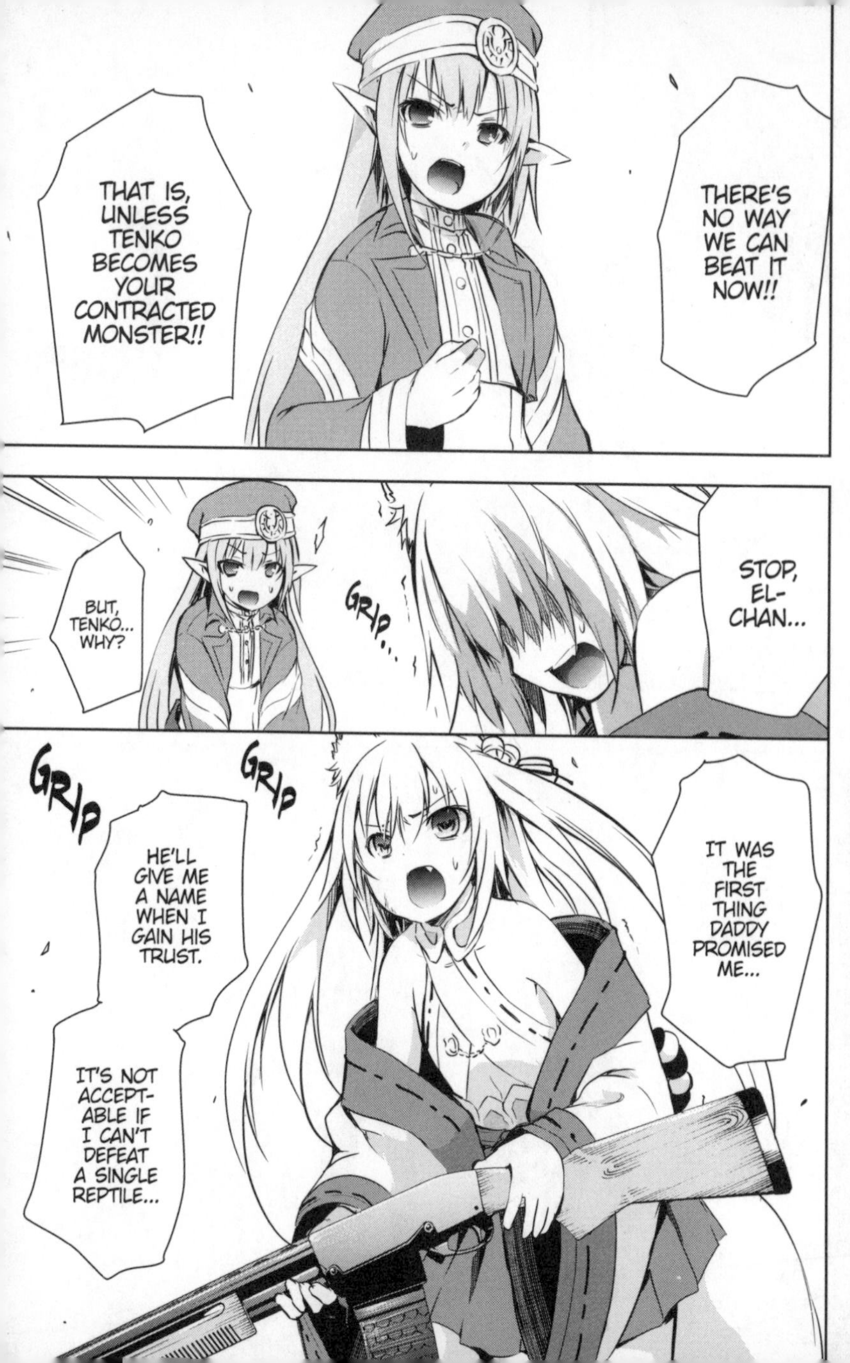
THERE'S NO WAY WE CAN BEAT IT NOW!!
THAT IS, UNLESS TENKO BECOMES YOUR CONTRACTED MONSTER!!
STOP, EL-CHAN...
GRIP...
BUT, TENKO... WHY?
GRIP
GRIP
IT WAS THE FIRST THING DADDY PROMISED ME...
HE'LL GIVE ME A NAME WHEN I GAIN HIS TRUST.
IT'S NOT ACCEPT-ABLE IF I CAN'T DEFEAT A SINGLE REPTILE...

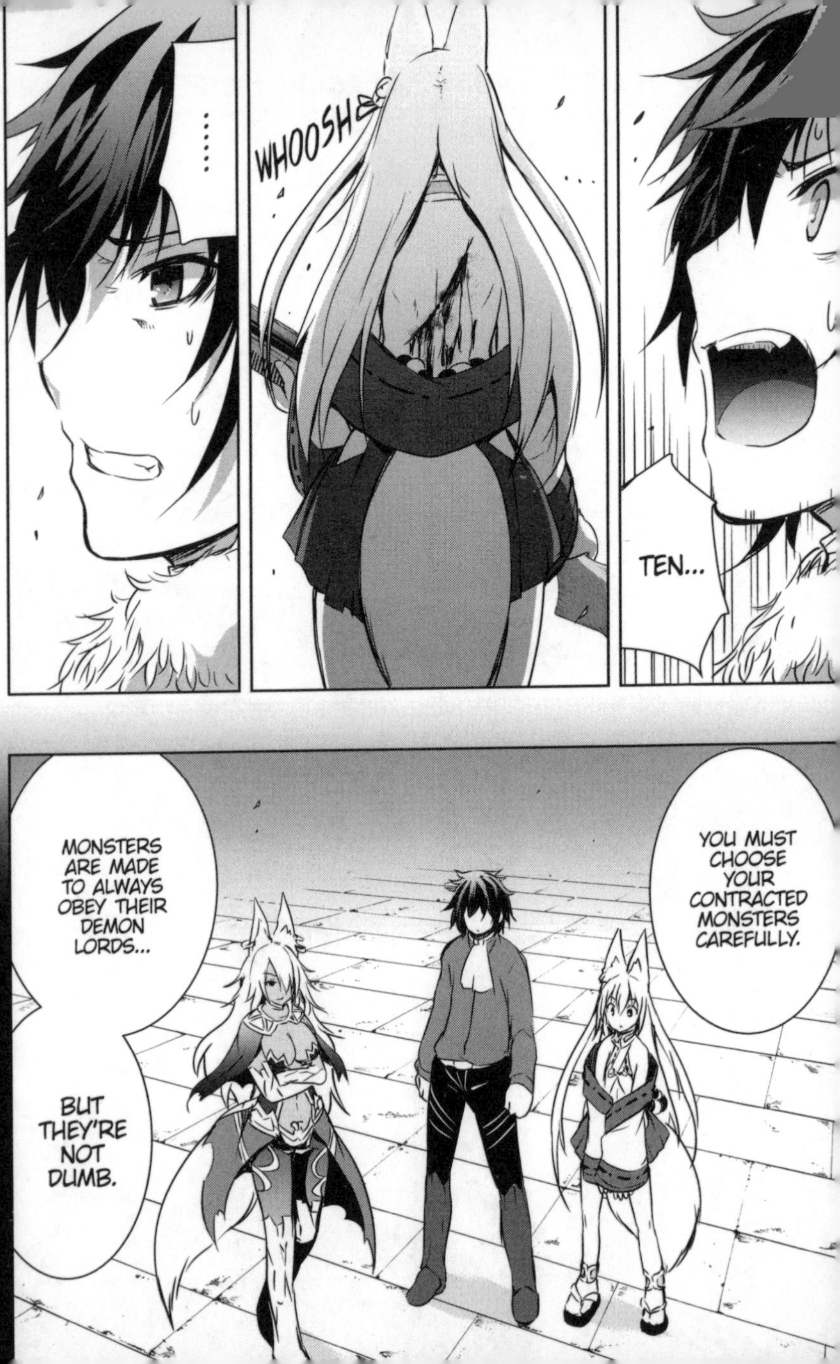
TEN...
WHOOSH
...
......
YOU MUST CHOOSE YOUR CONTRACTED MONSTERS CAREFULLY.
MONSTERS ARE MADE TO ALWAYS OBEY THEIR DEMON LORDS...
BUT THEY'RE NOT DUMB.

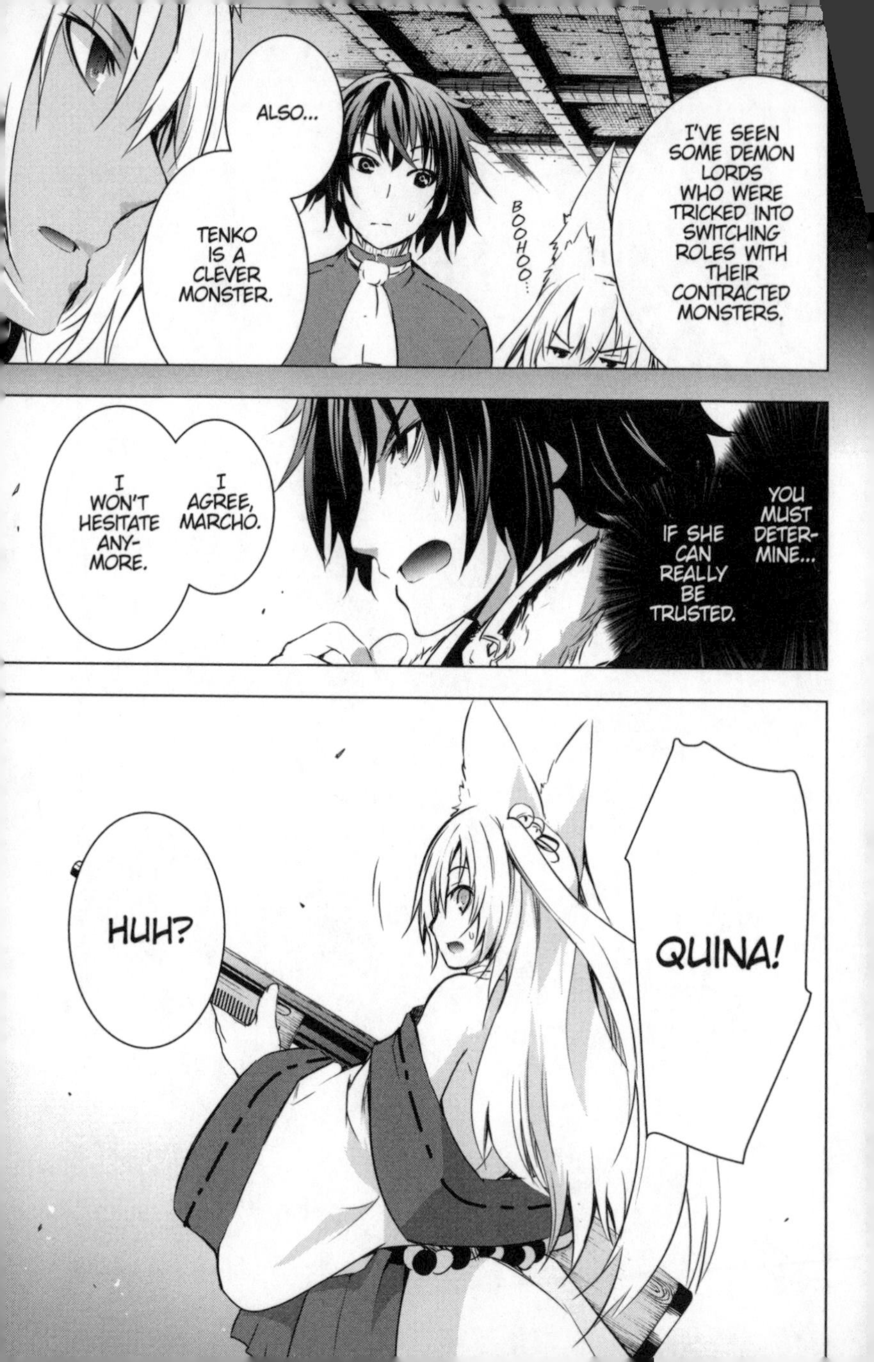
I'VE SEEN SOME DEMON LORDS WHO WERE TRICKED INTO SWITCHING ROLES WITH THEIR CONTRACTED MONSTERS.
BOOHOO...
ALSO...
TENKO IS A CLEVER MONSTER.
YOU MUST DETERMINE...
IF SHE CAN REALLY BE TRUSTED.
I AGREE, MARCHO.
I WON'T HESITATE ANYMORE.
QUINA!
HUH?

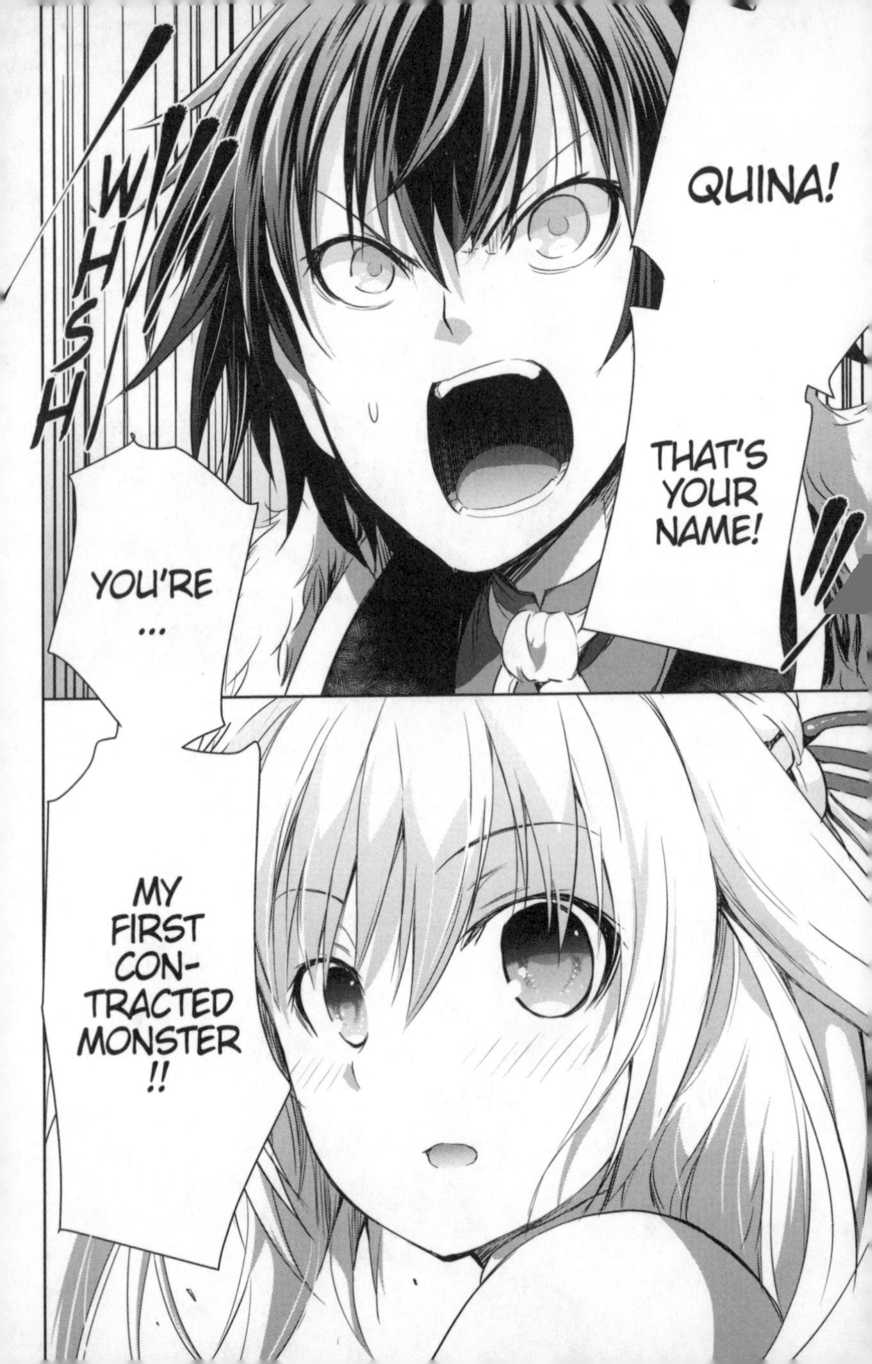
QUINA!
THAT'S YOUR NAME!
WHSH
YOU'RE ...
MY FIRST CON-TRACTED MONSTER!!

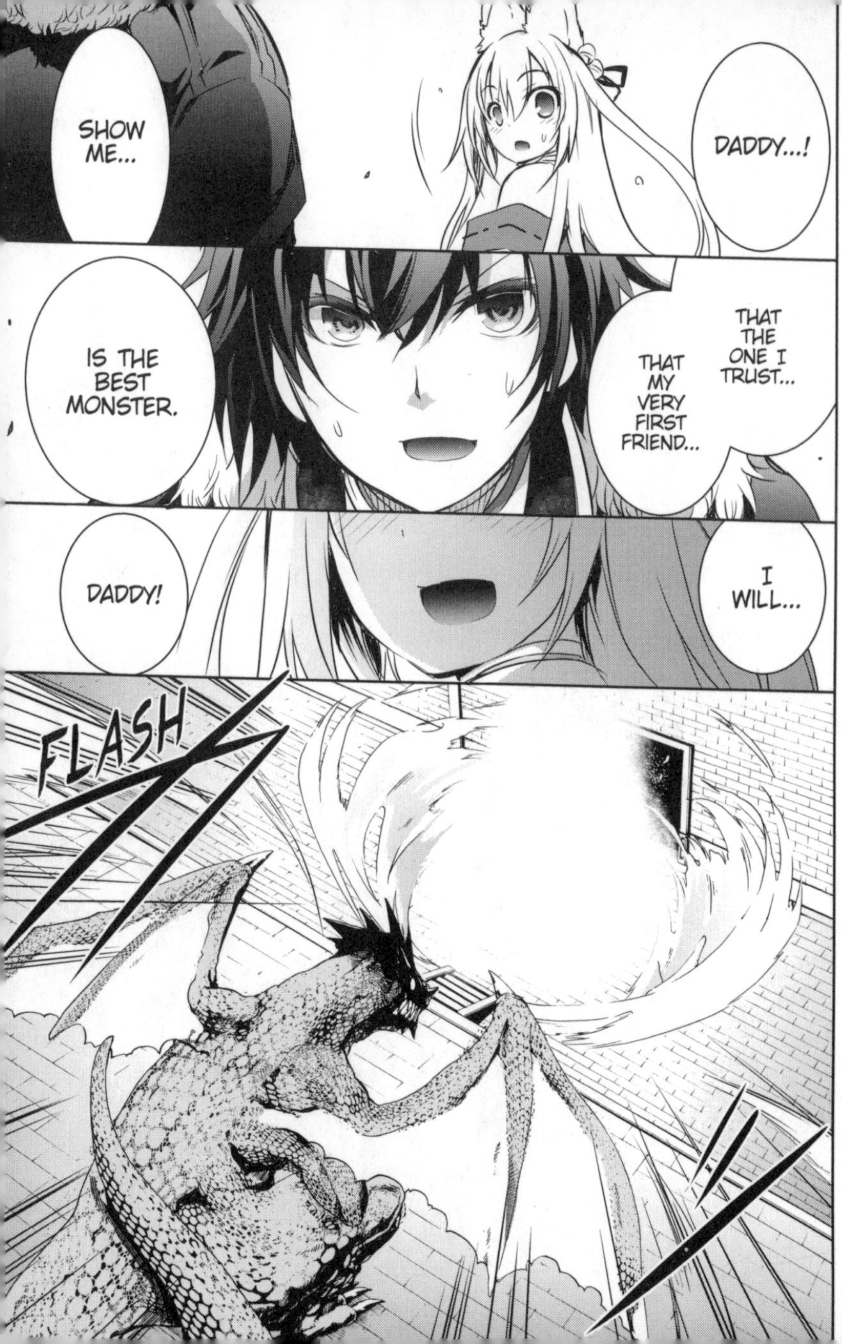
DADDY...!
SHOW ME...
THAT THE ONE I TRUST...
THAT MY VERY FIRST FRIEND...
IS THE BEST MONSTER.
I WILL...
DADDY!
FLASH

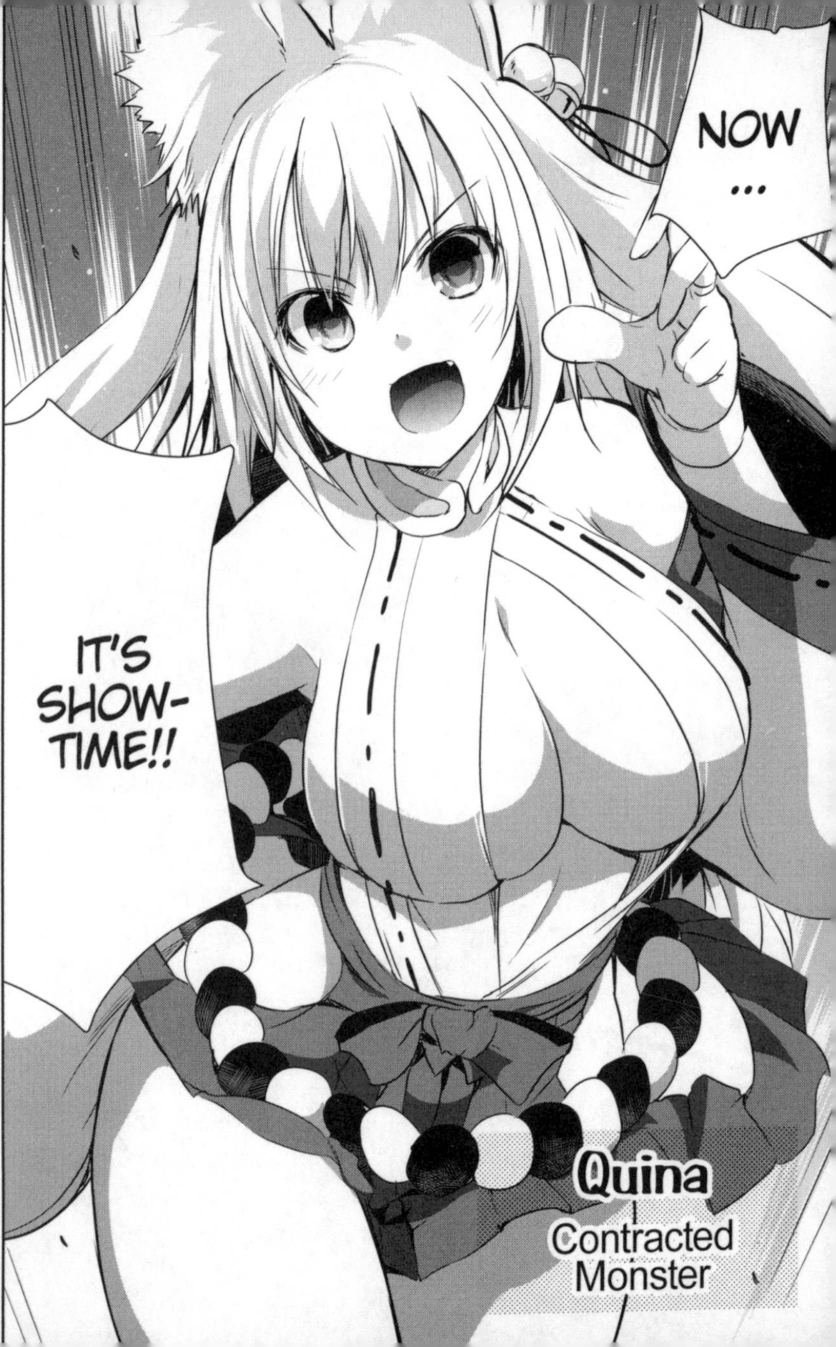
NOW ...
IT'S SHOW-TIME!!
Quina
Contracted Monster

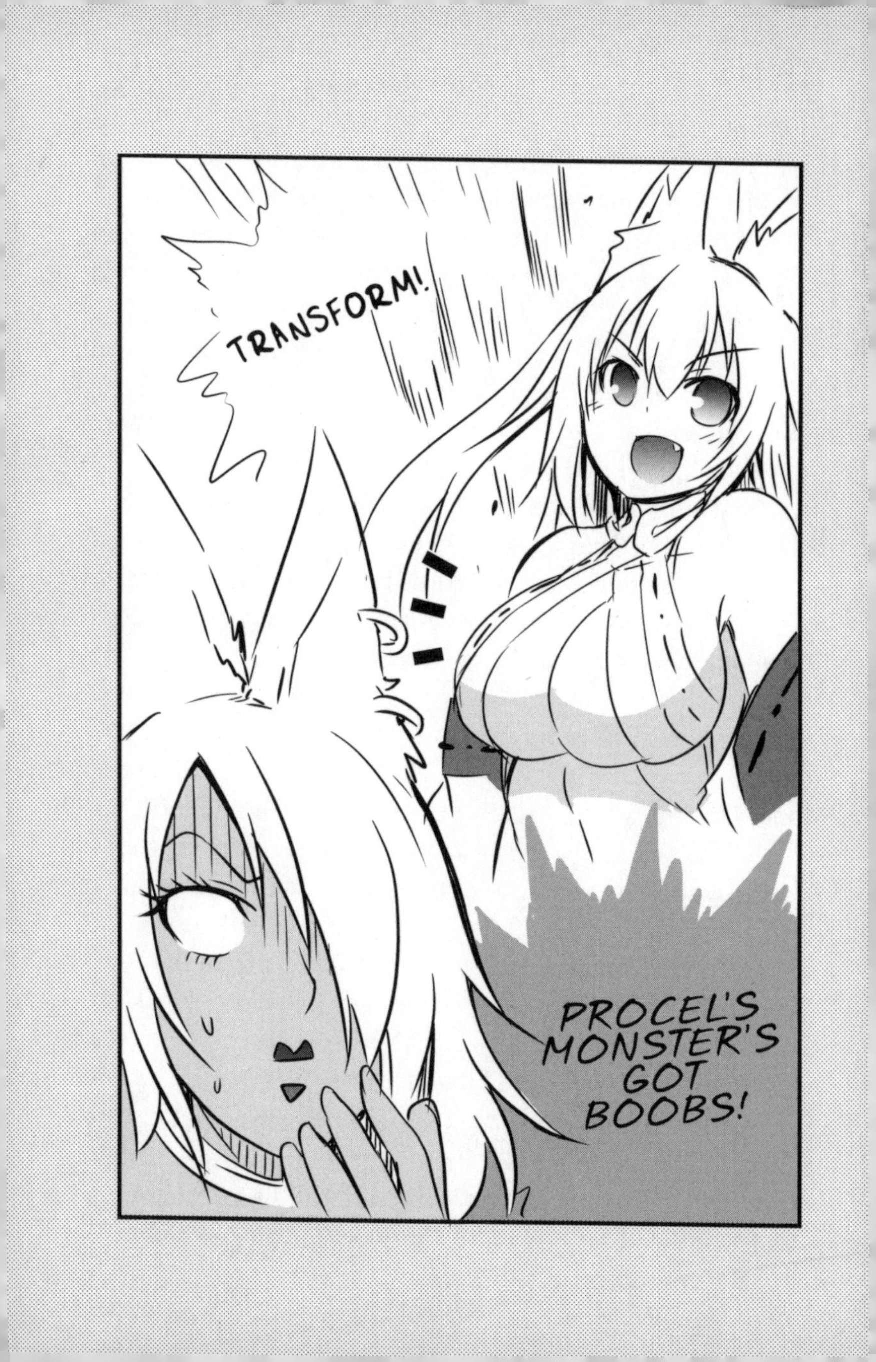
TRANSFORM!
PROCEL'S MONSTER'S GOT BOOBS!

DUNGEON BUILDER:
THE DEMON KING'S LABYRINTH IS A MODERN CITY!

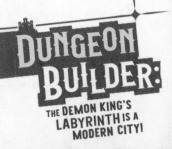

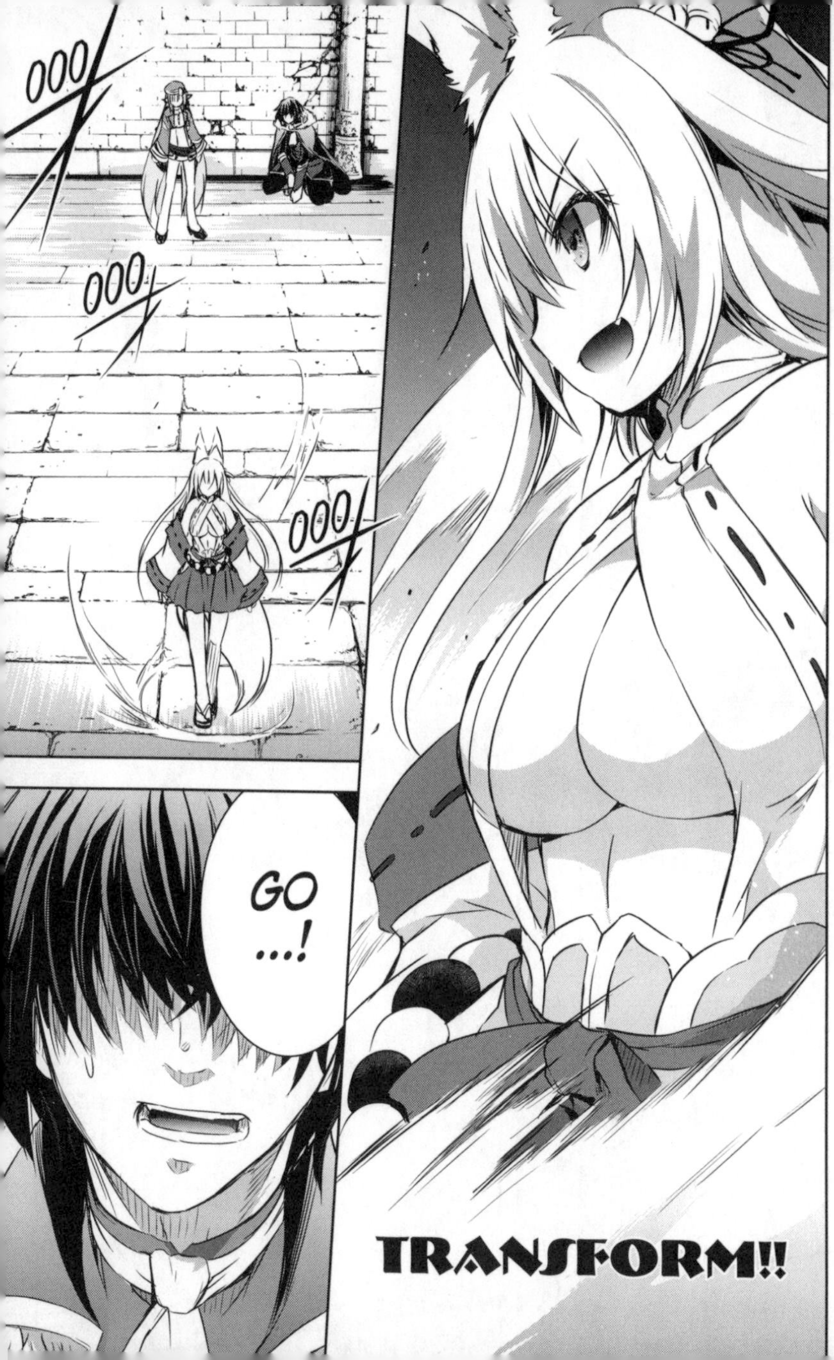
TRANSFORM!!
OOO
OOO
OOO
GO
...!

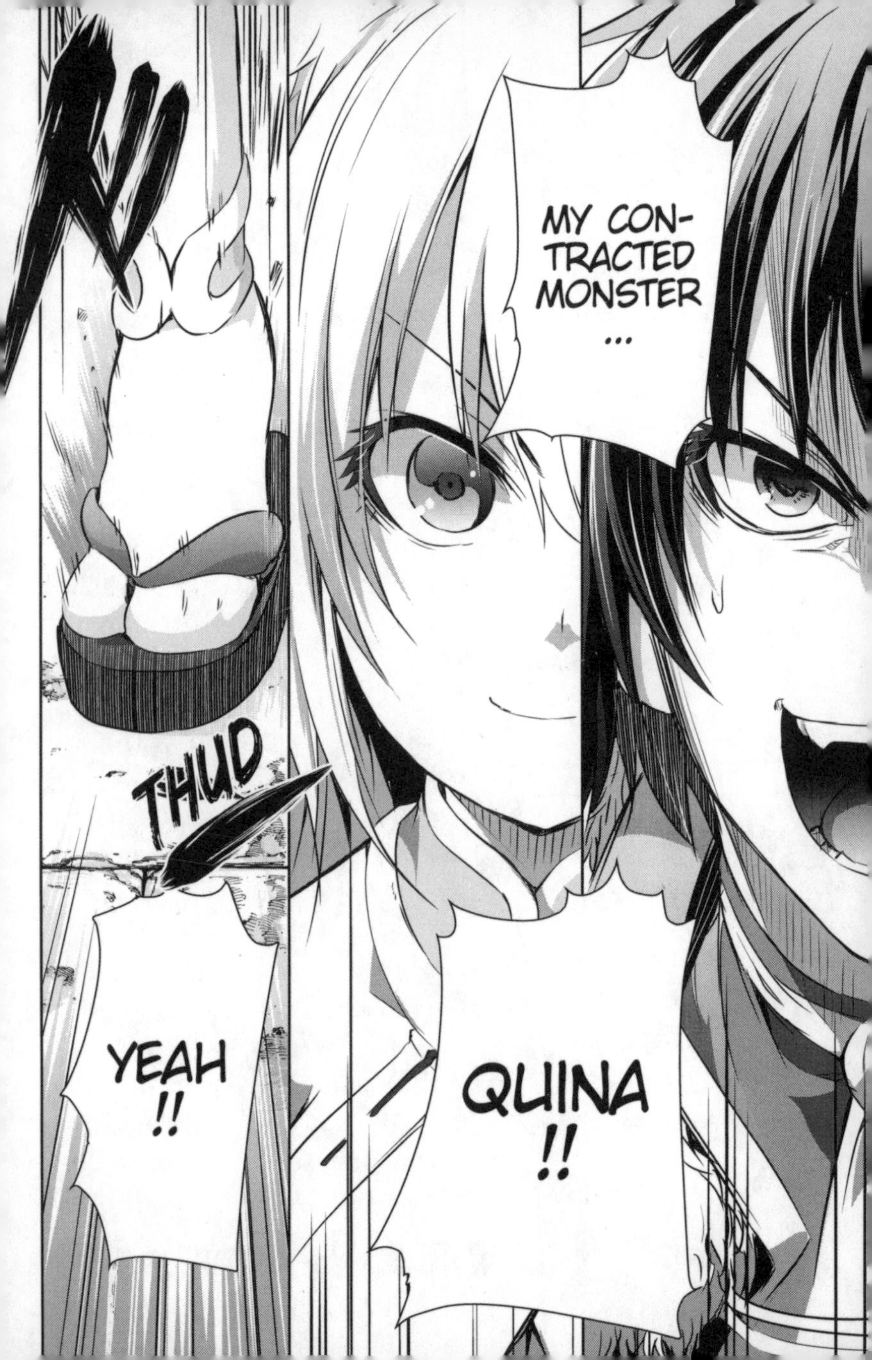
MY CON-
TRACTED
MONSTER
...
QUINA
!!
THUD
YEAH
!!

Chapter 8: The Demon Lord Plans a City!

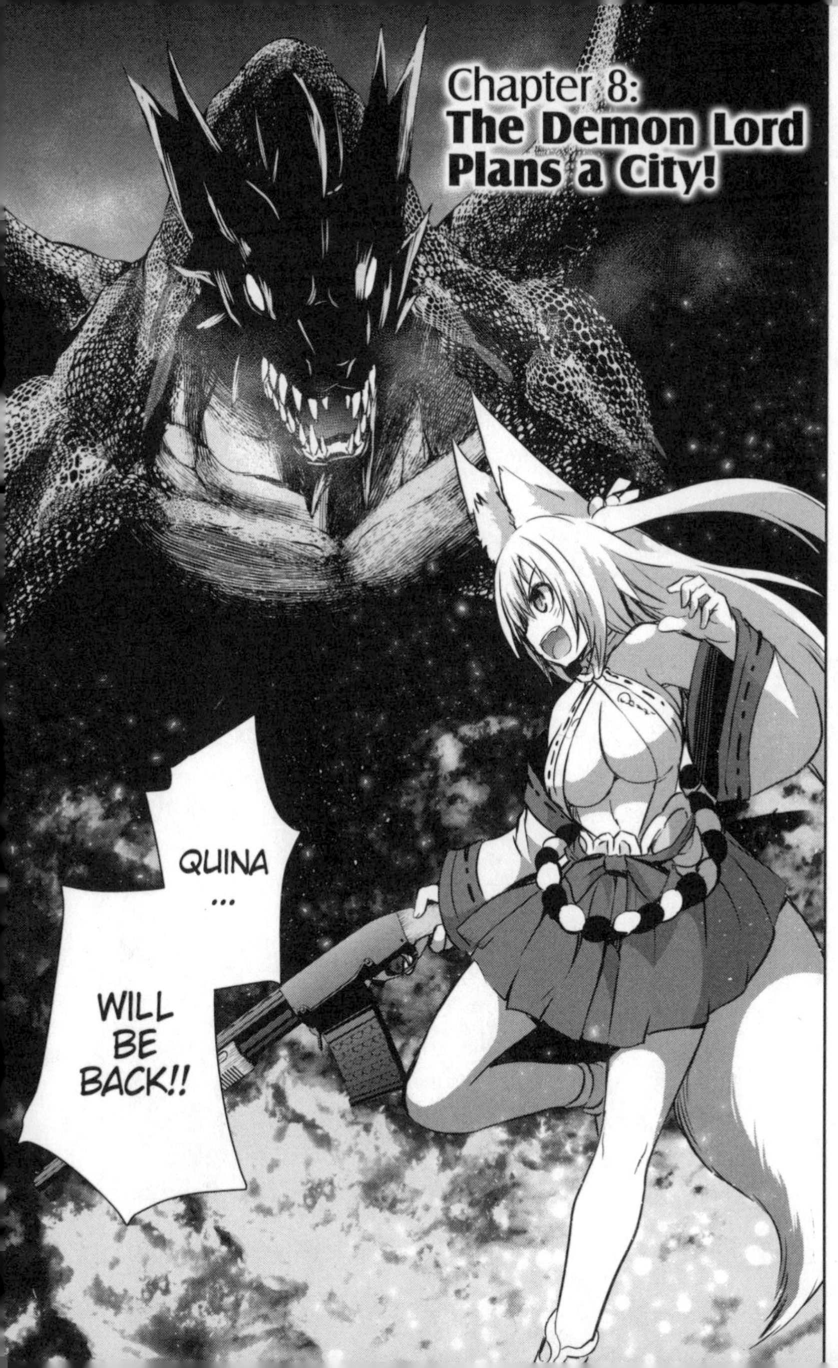
QUINA ... WILL BE BACK!!

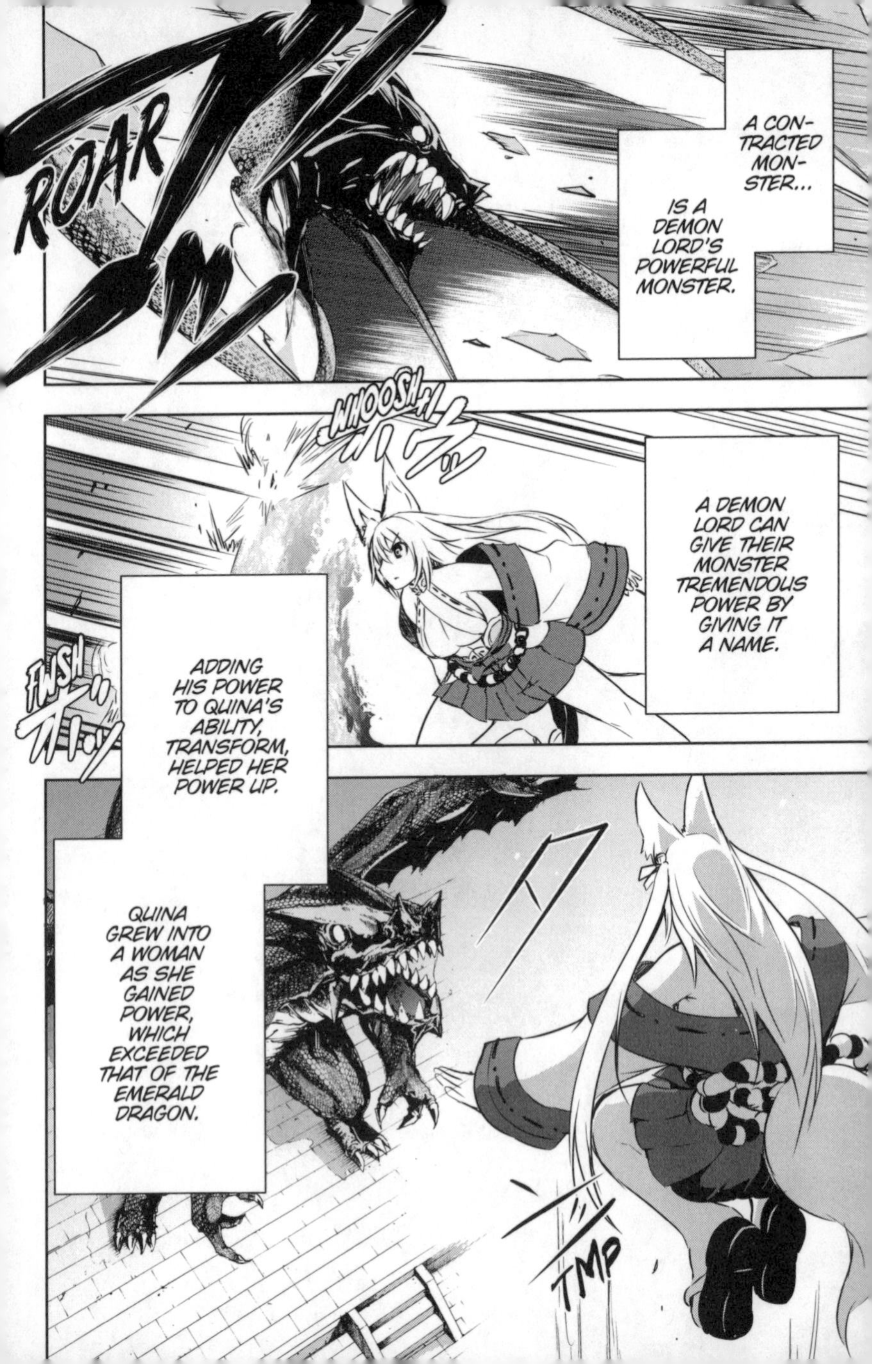
A CON-TRACTED MON-STER...
IS A DEMON LORD'S POWERFUL MONSTER.
ROAR
WHOOSH
A DEMON LORD CAN GIVE THEIR MONSTER TREMENDOUS POWER BY GIVING IT A NAME.
ADDING HIS POWER TO QUINA'S ABILITY, TRANSFORM, HELPED HER POWER UP.
FWSH
QUINA GREW INTO A WOMAN AS SHE GAINED POWER, WHICH EXCEEDED THAT OF THE EMERALD DRAGON.
TMP

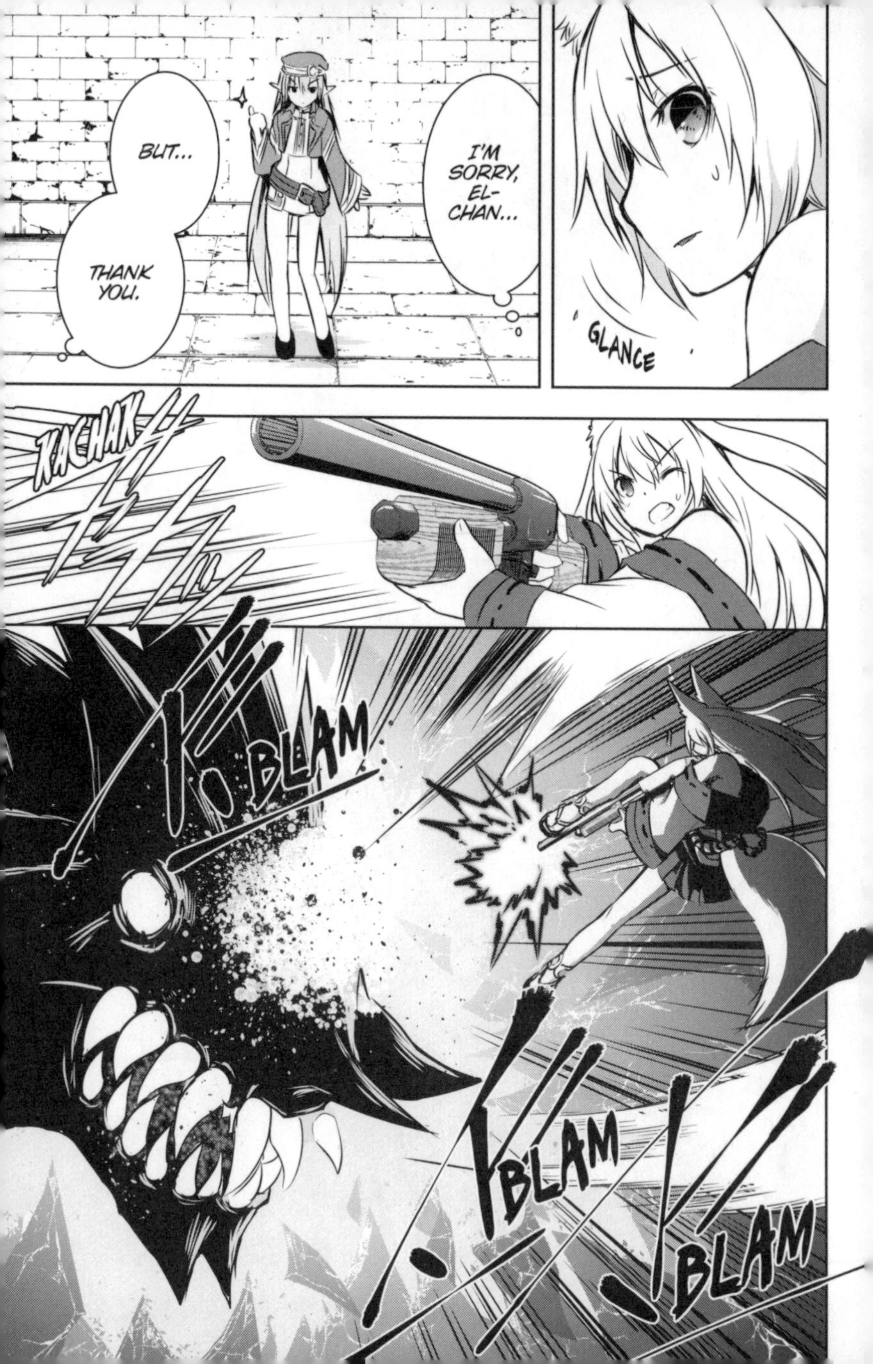
GLANCE
I'M SORRY, EL-CHAN...
BUT...
THANK YOU.
KACHAK
BLAM
BLAM
BLAM

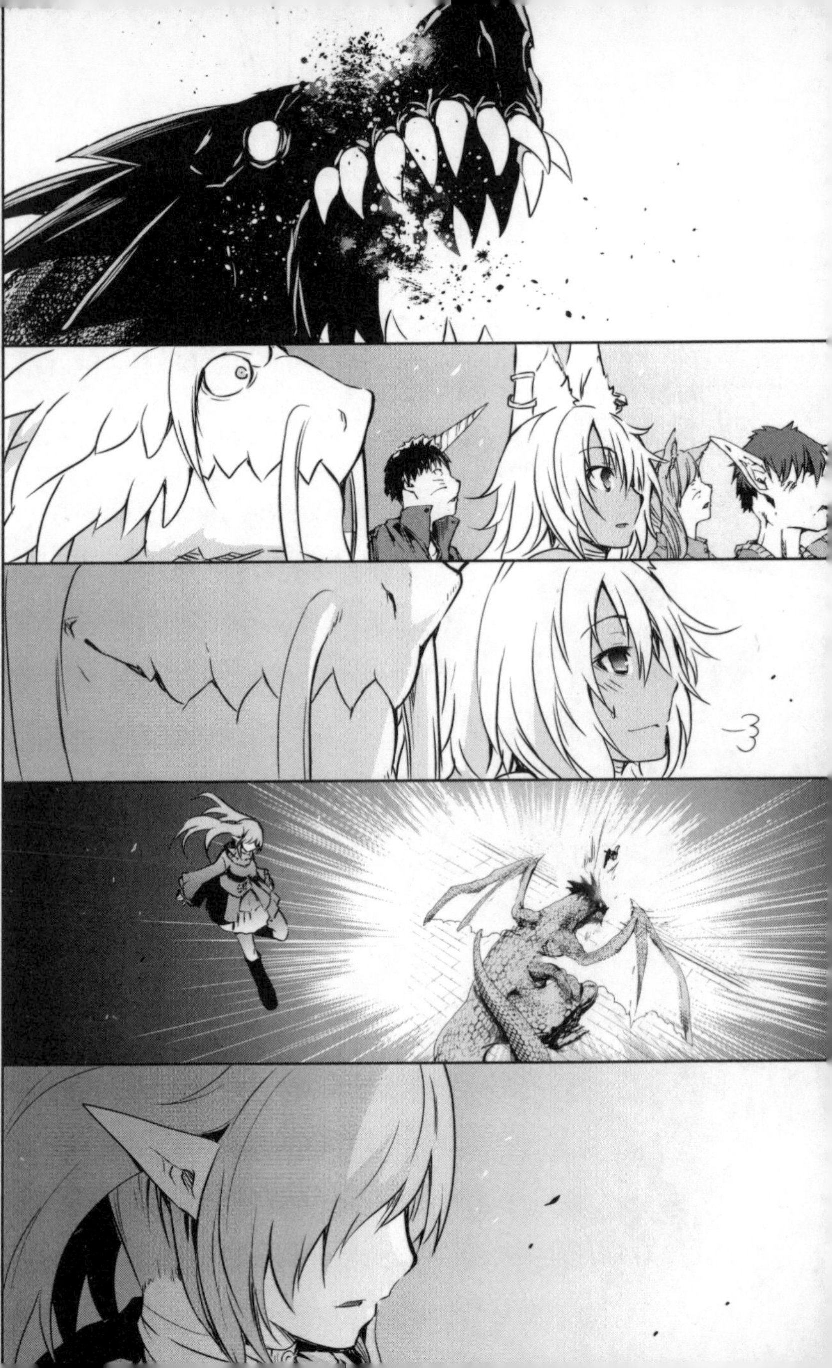

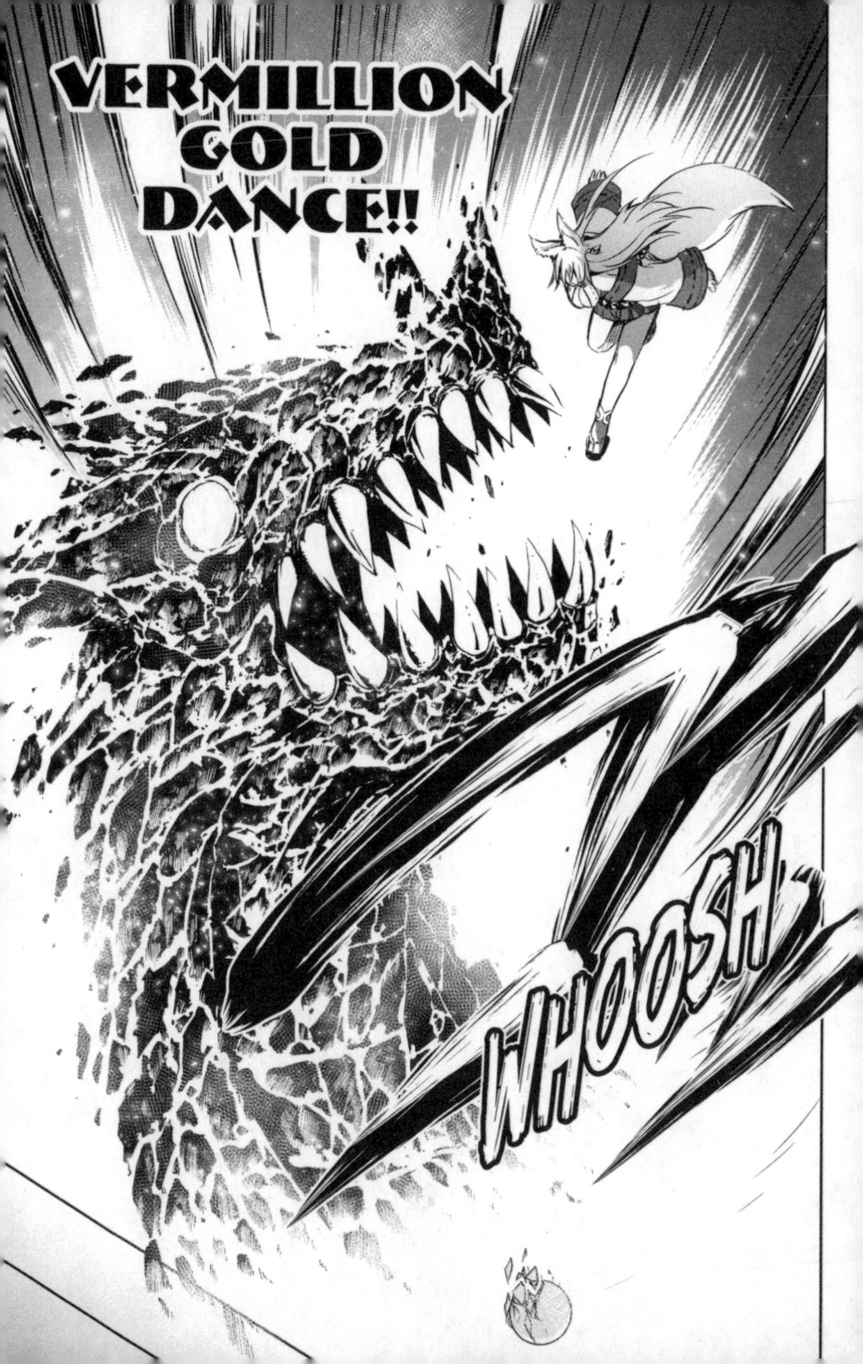
VERMILLION GOLD DANCE!!
WHOOSH

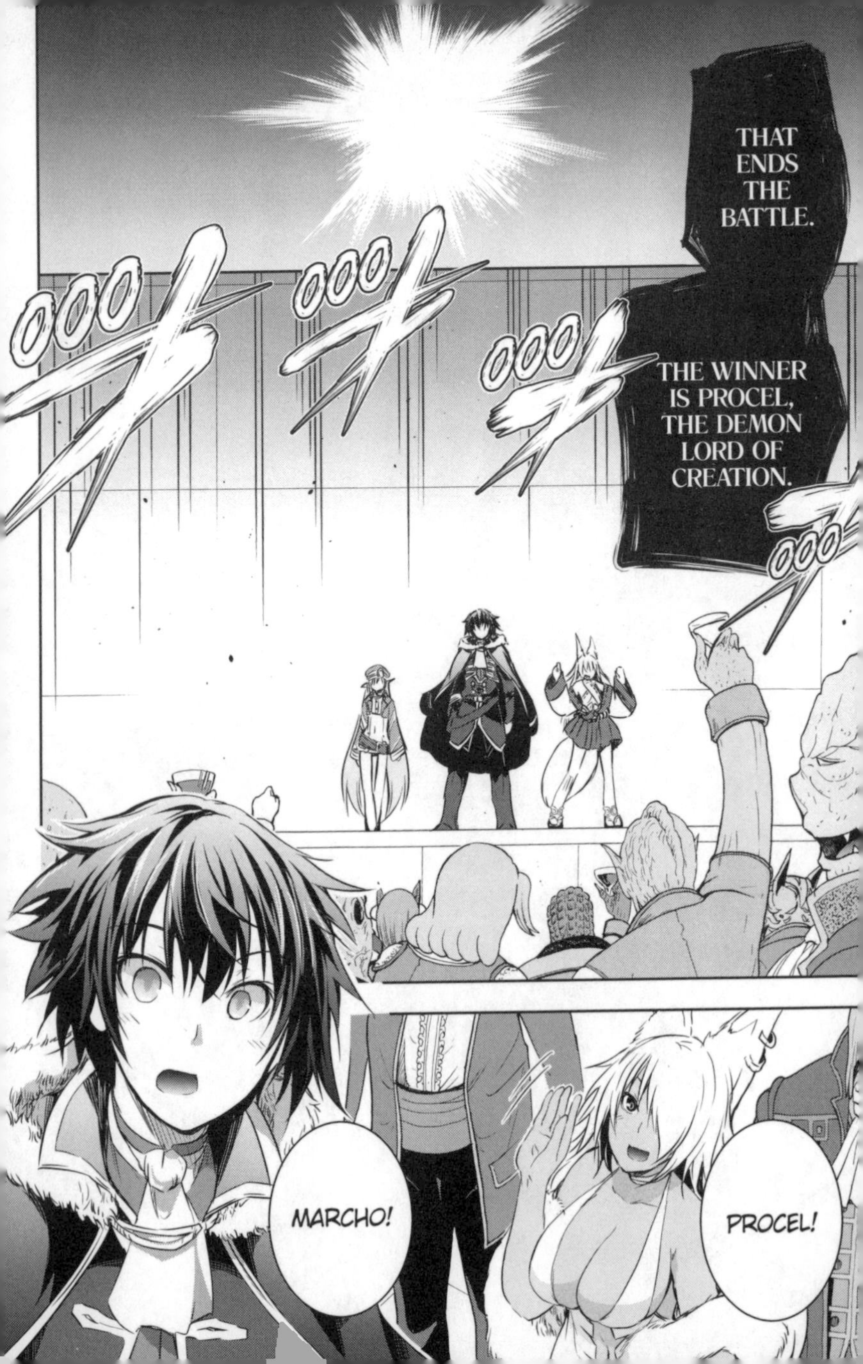
THAT ENDS THE BATTLE.
THE WINNER IS PROCEL, THE DEMON LORD OF CREATION.
OOO
OOO
OOO
OOO
PROCEL!
MARCHO!

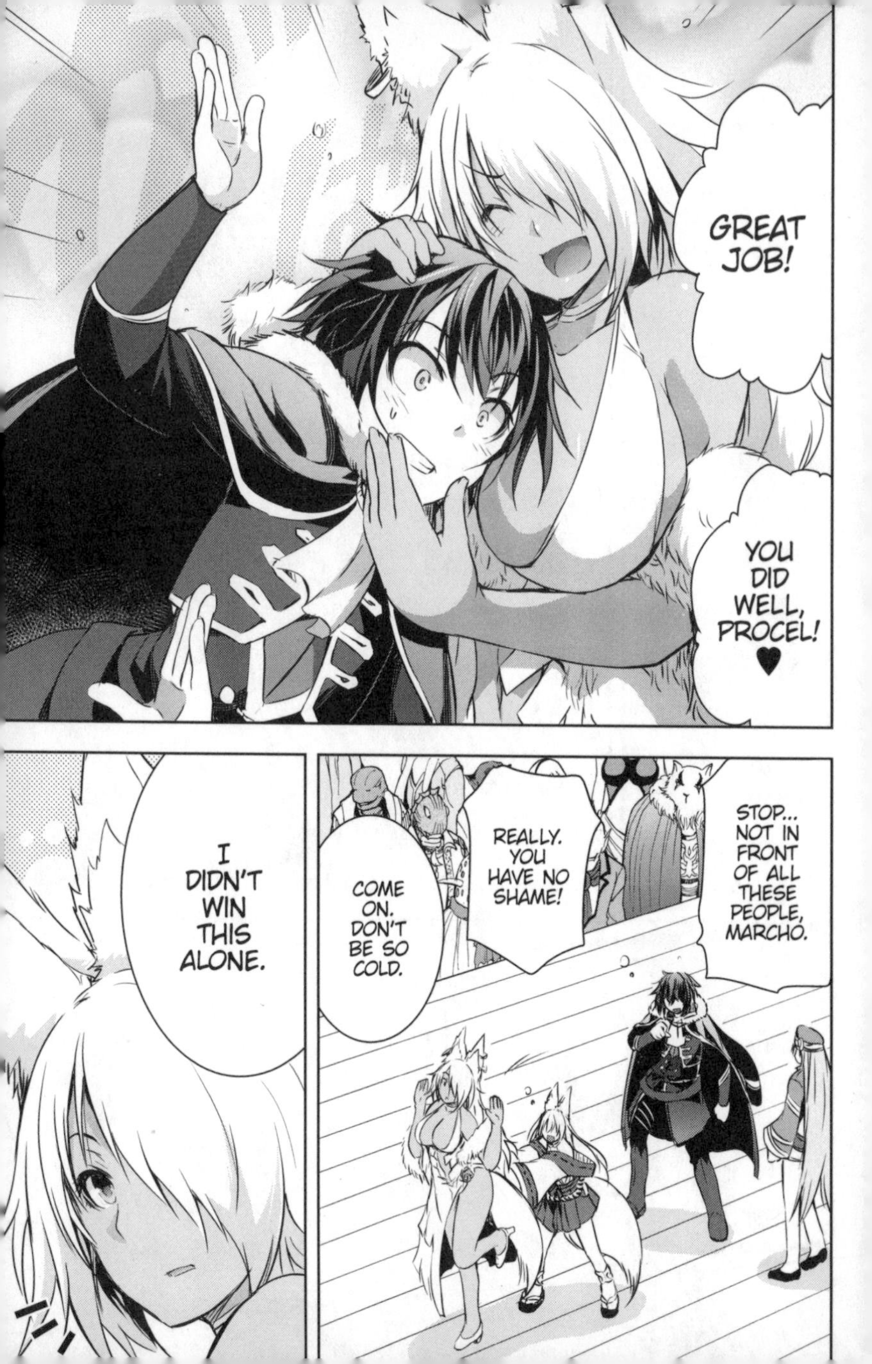
GREAT JOB!
YOU DID WELL, PROCEL! ♥
STOP... NOT IN FRONT OF ALL THESE PEOPLE, MARCHO.
REALLY. YOU HAVE NO SHAME!
COME ON. DON'T BE SO COLD.
I DIDN'T WIN THIS ALONE.

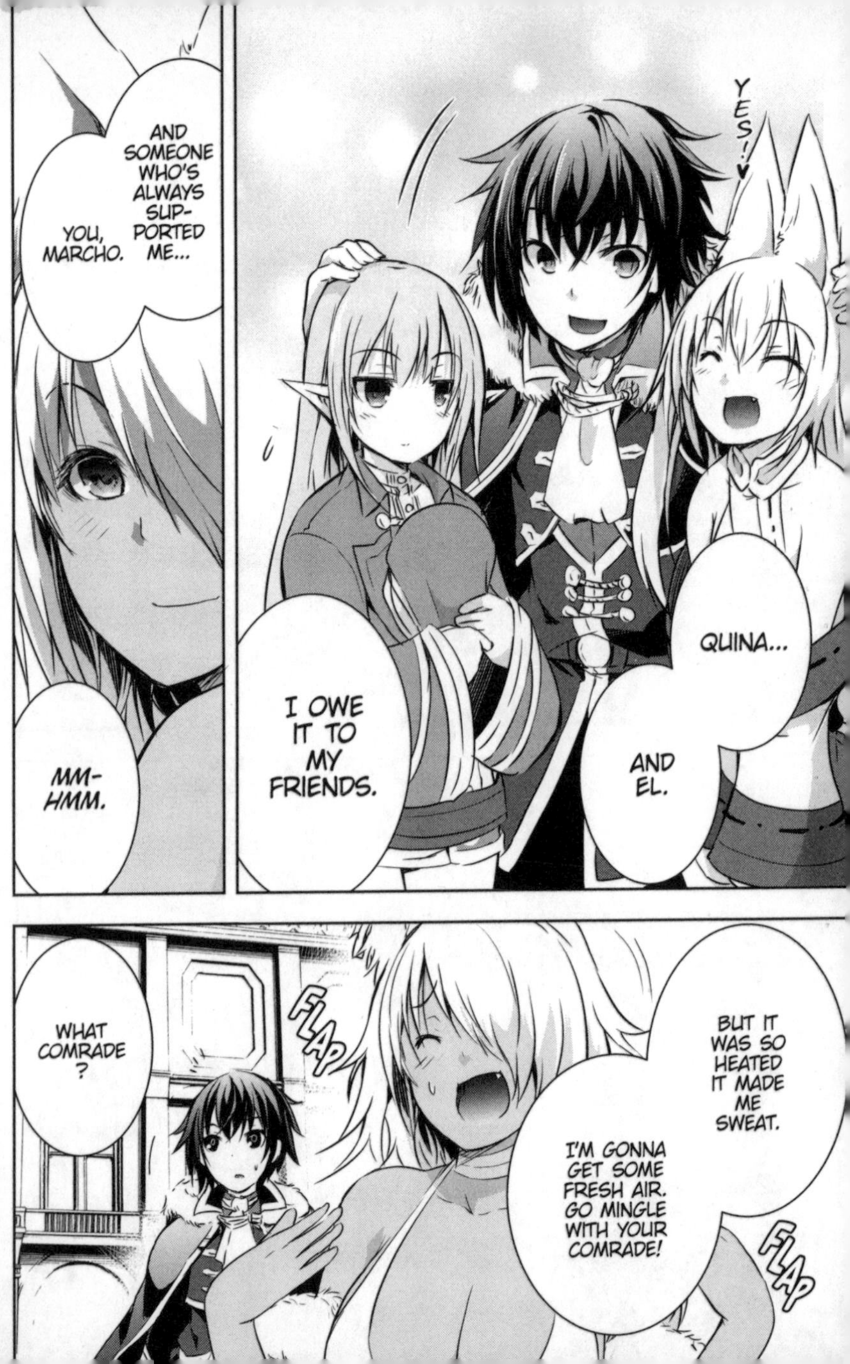
YES!
QUINA...
AND EL.
I OWE IT TO MY FRIENDS.
AND SOMEONE WHO'S ALWAYS SUP-PORTED ME...
YOU, MARCHO.
MM-HMM.
BUT IT WAS SO HEATED IT MADE ME SWEAT.
FLAP
I'M GONNA GET SOME FRESH AIR. GO MINGLE WITH YOUR COMRADE!
FLAP
WHAT COMRADE?

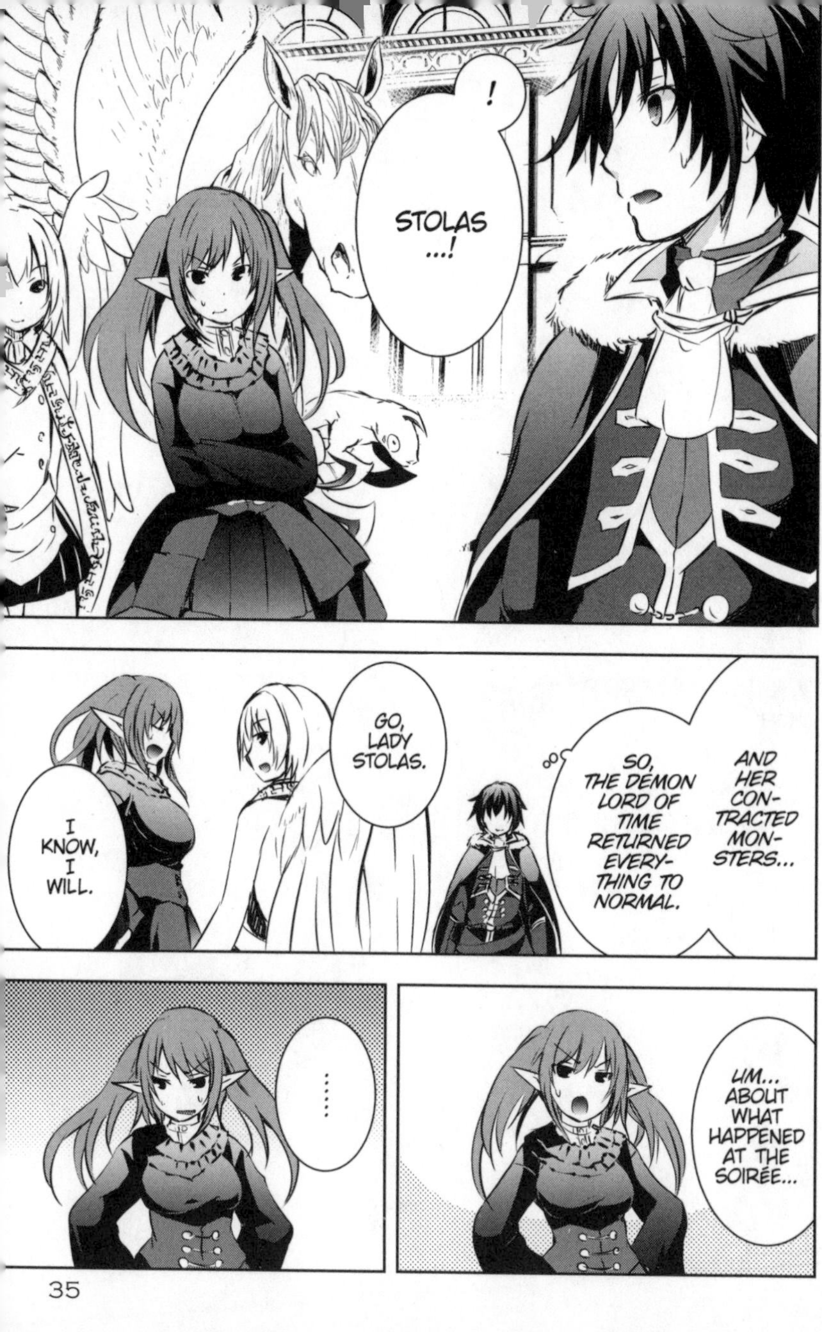
!
STOLAS ...!
SO, THE DEMON LORD OF TIME RETURNED EVERYTHING TO NORMAL.
AND HER CONTRACTED MONSTERS...
GO, LADY STOLAS.
I KNOW, I WILL.
UM... ABOUT WHAT HAPPENED AT THE SOIRÉE...
......

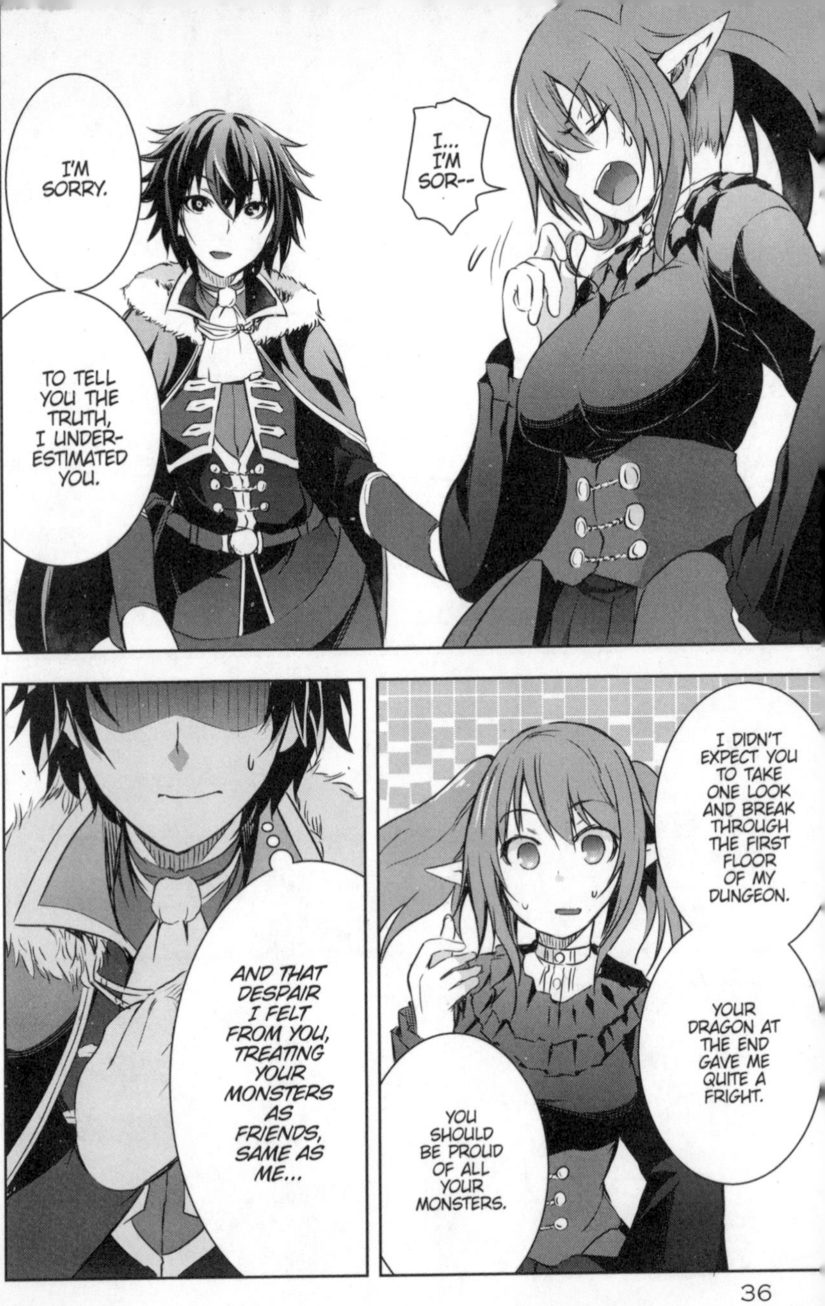
I... I'M SOR--
I'M SORRY.
TO TELL YOU THE TRUTH, I UNDER-ESTIMATED YOU.
I DIDN'T EXPECT YOU TO TAKE ONE LOOK AND BREAK THROUGH THE FIRST FLOOR OF MY DUNGEON.
YOUR DRAGON AT THE END GAVE ME QUITE A FRIGHT.
YOU SHOULD BE PROUD OF ALL YOUR MONSTERS.
AND THAT DESPAIR I FELT FROM YOU, TREATING YOUR MONSTERS AS FRIENDS, SAME AS ME...

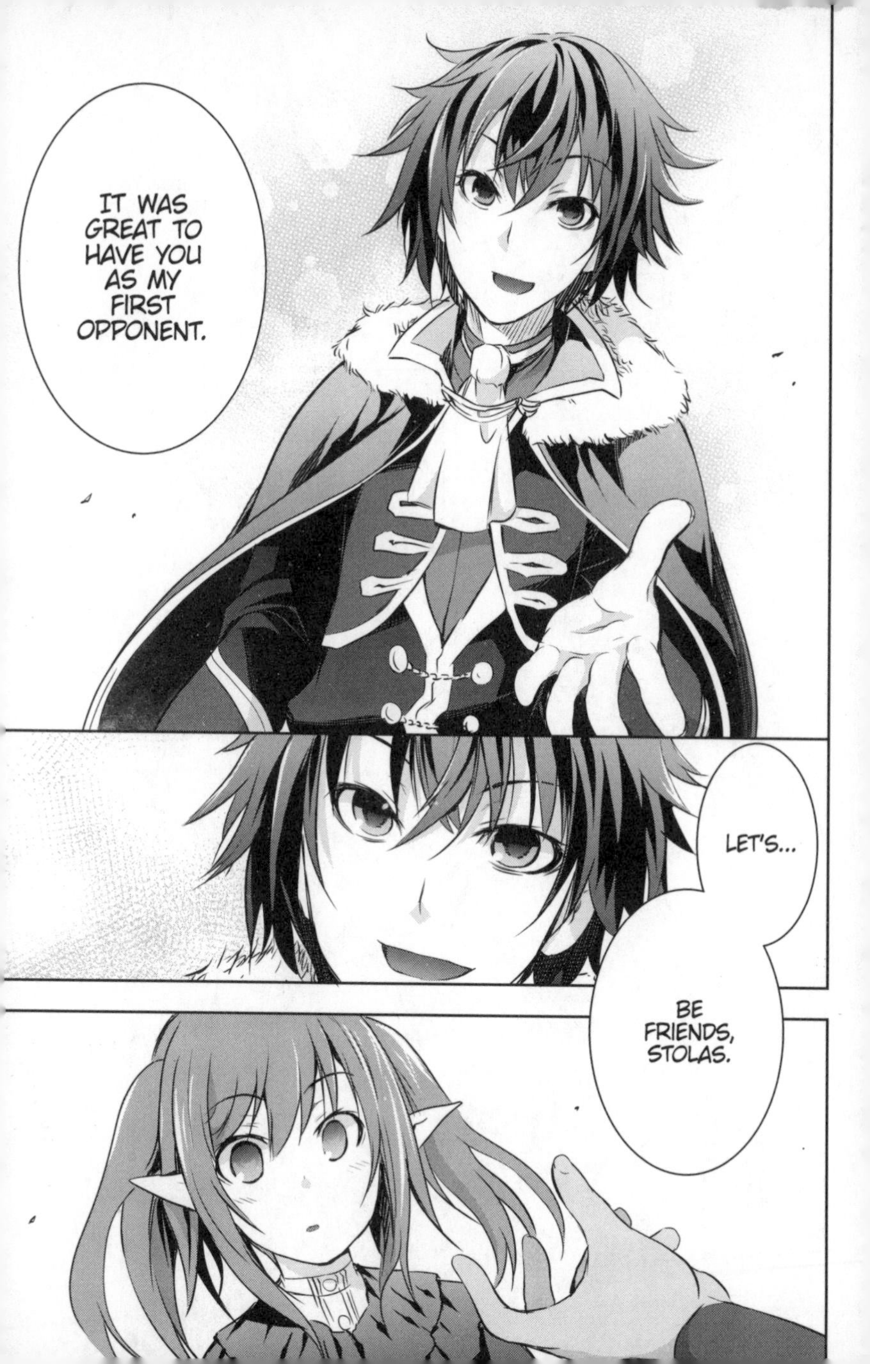
IT WAS GREAT TO HAVE YOU AS MY FIRST OPPONENT.
LET'S...
BE FRIENDS, STOLAS.

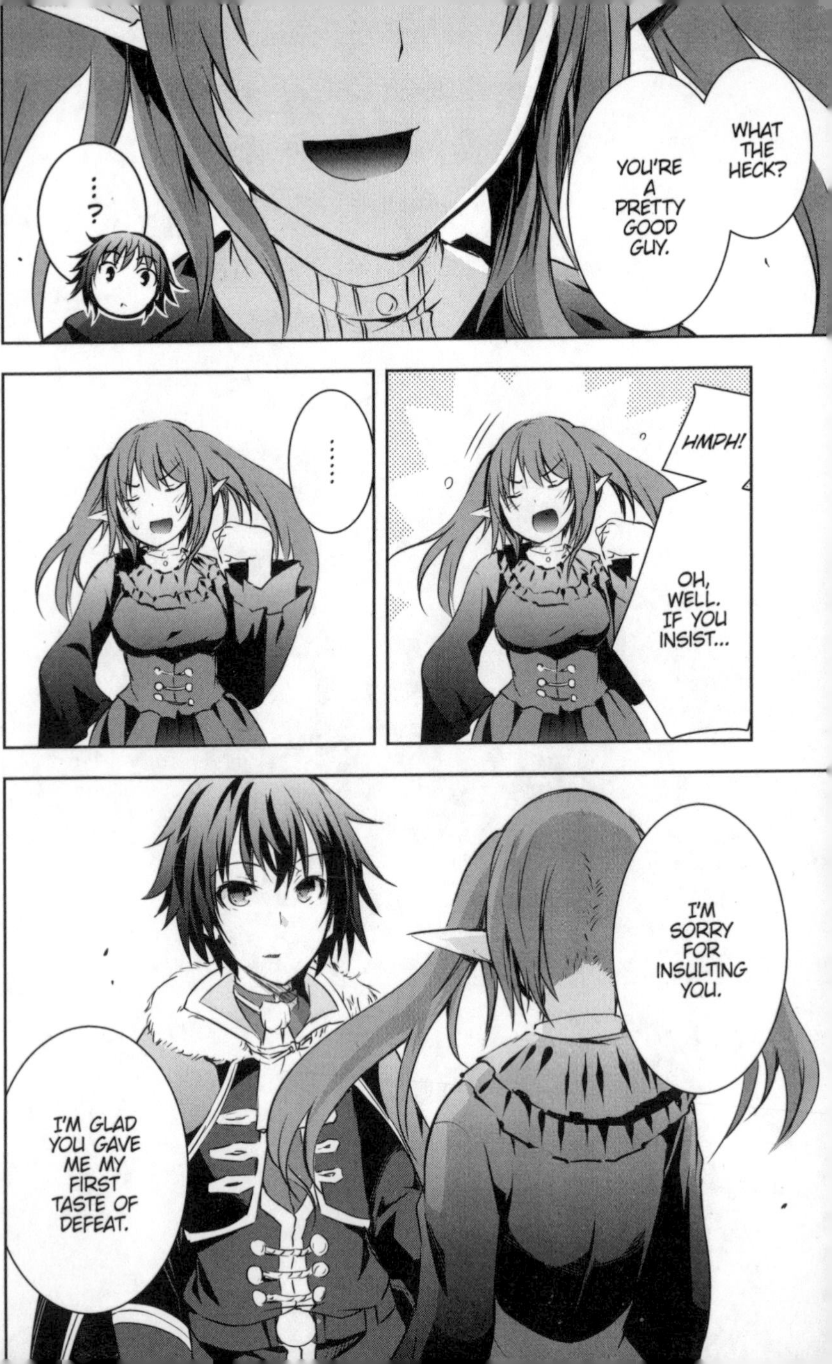
WHAT THE HECK?
YOU'RE A PRETTY GOOD GUY.
...?
HMPH!
OH, WELL. IF YOU INSIST...
......
I'M SORRY FOR INSULTING YOU.
I'M GLAD YOU GAVE ME MY FIRST TASTE OF DEFEAT.

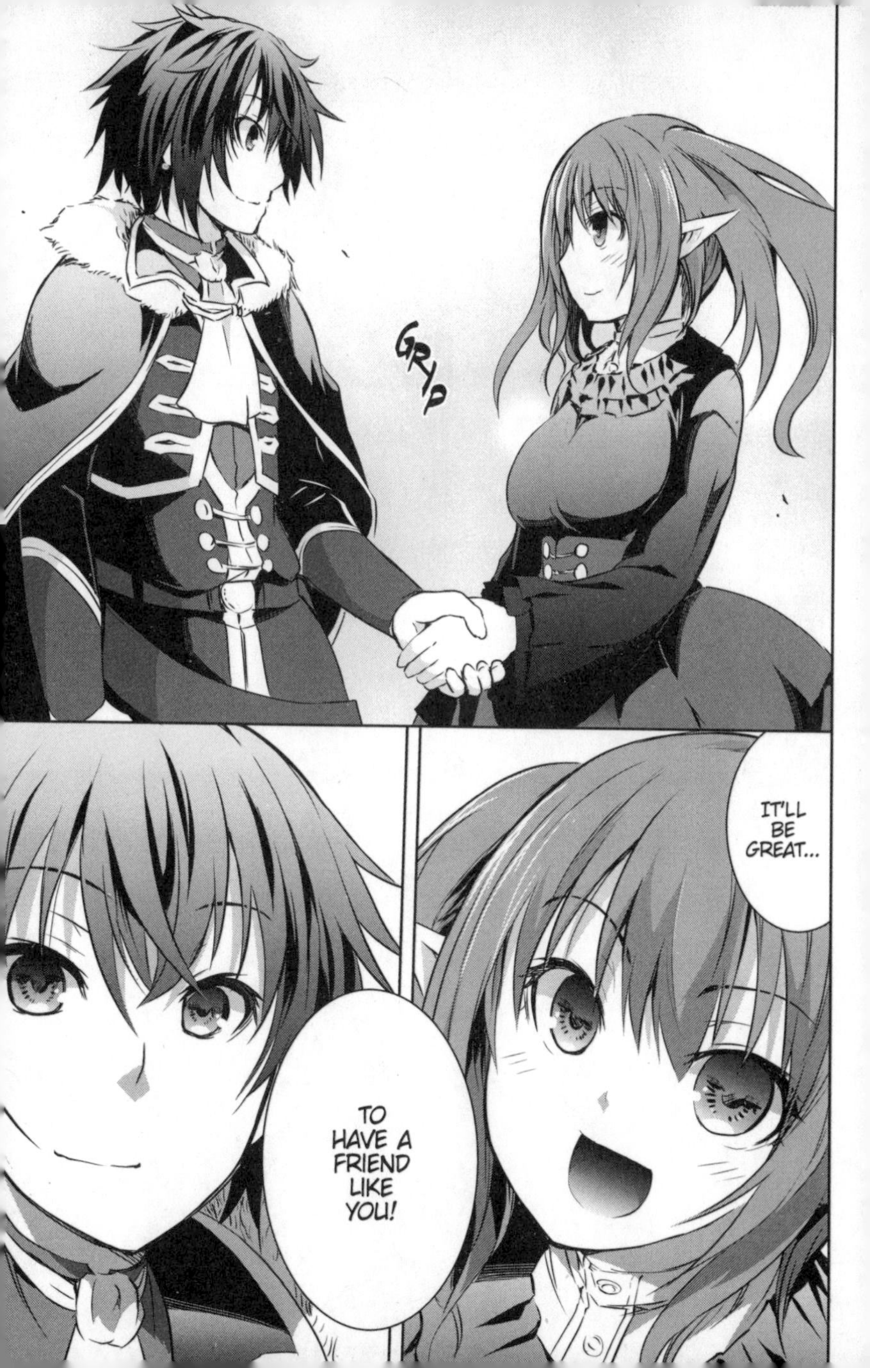
GRIP
IT'LL BE GREAT...
TO HAVE A FRIEND LIKE YOU!

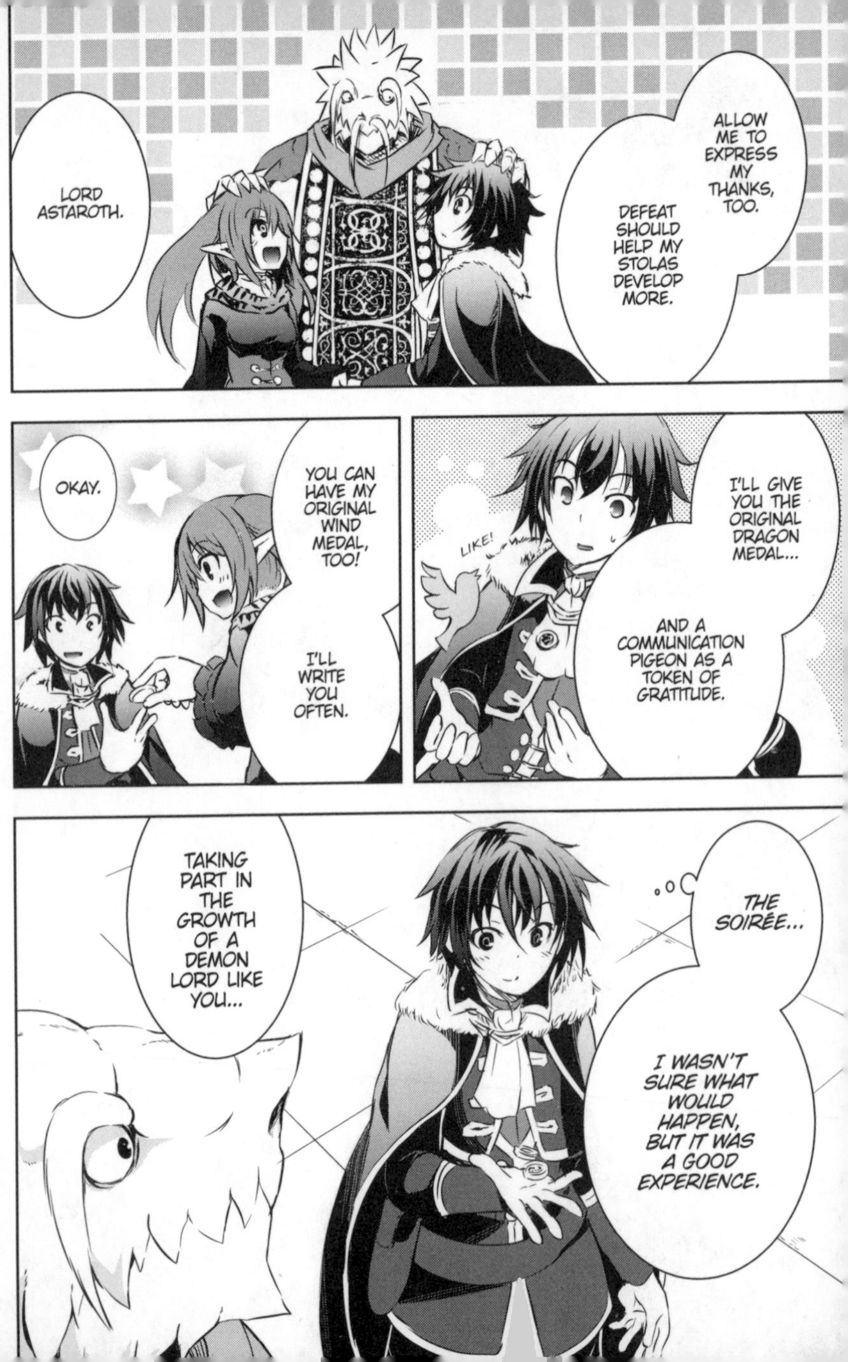
ALLOW ME TO EXPRESS MY THANKS, TOO.
DEFEAT SHOULD HELP MY STOLAS DEVELOP MORE.
LORD ASTAROTH.
I'LL GIVE YOU THE ORIGINAL DRAGON MEDAL...
AND A COMMUNICATION PIGEON AS A TOKEN OF GRATITUDE.
LIKE!
YOU CAN HAVE MY ORIGINAL WIND MEDAL, TOO!
I'LL WRITE YOU OFTEN.
OKAY.
THE SOIRÉE...
I WASN'T SURE WHAT WOULD HAPPEN, BUT IT WAS A GOOD EXPERIENCE.
TAKING PART IN THE GROWTH OF A DEMON LORD LIKE YOU...

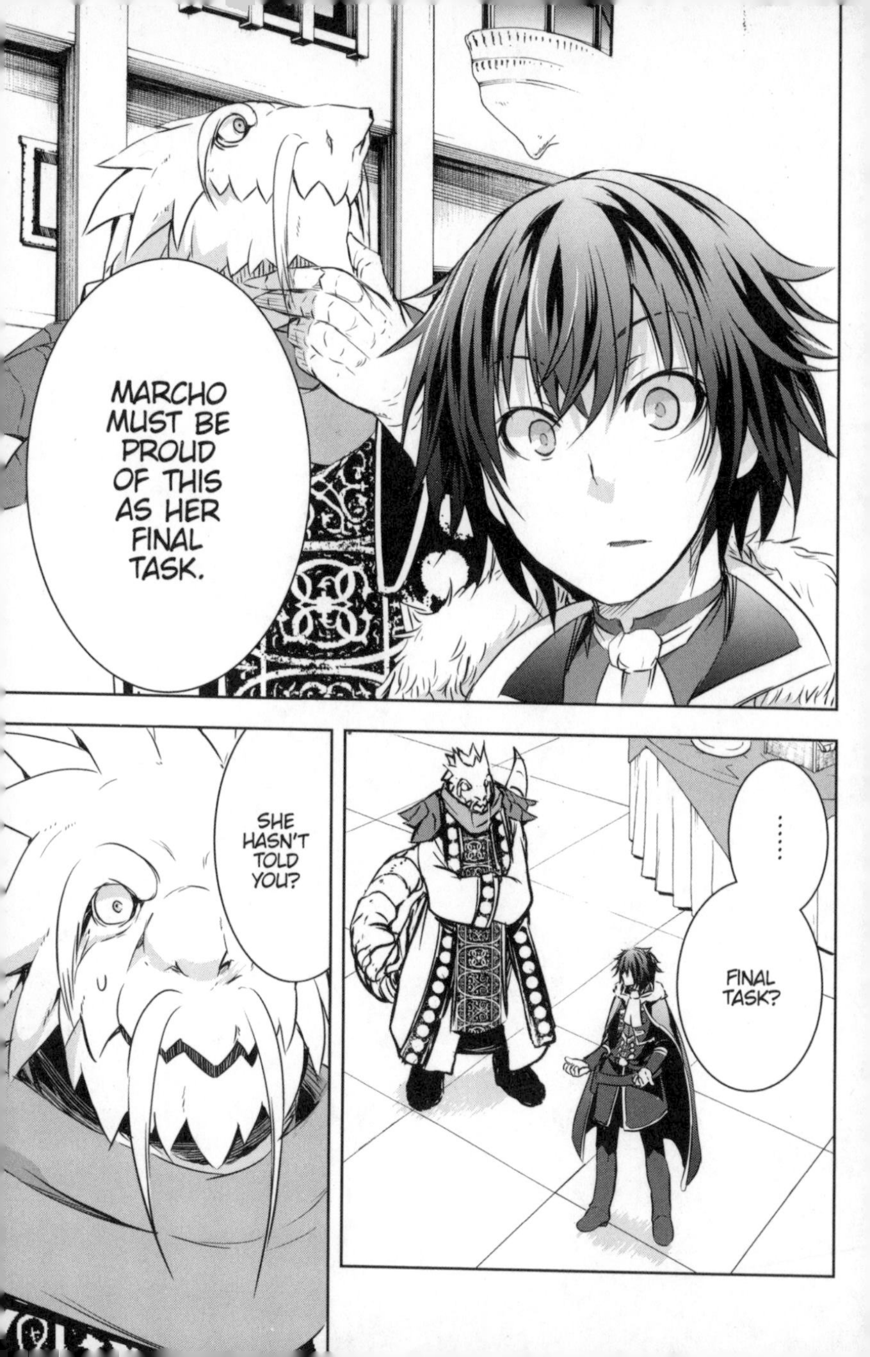
MARCHO MUST BE PROUD OF THIS AS HER FINAL TASK.
......
FINAL TASK?
SHE HASN'T TOLD YOU?

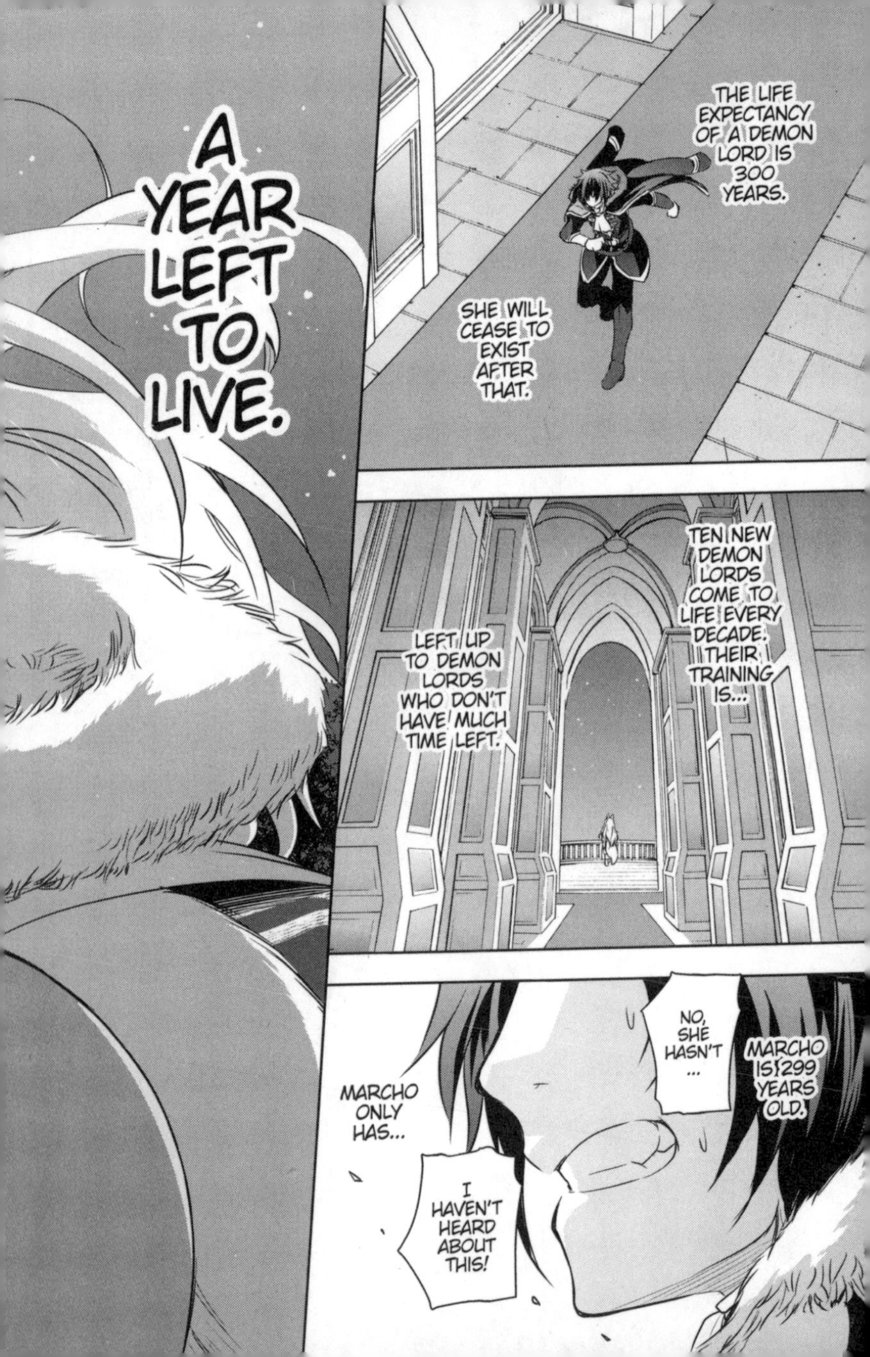
THE LIFE EXPECTANCY OF A DEMON LORD IS 300 YEARS.
SHE WILL CEASE TO EXIST AFTER THAT.
TEN NEW DEMON LORDS COME TO LIFE EVERY DECADE. THEIR TRAINING IS...
LEFT UP TO DEMON LORDS WHO DON'T HAVE MUCH TIME LEFT.
MARCHO IS 299 YEARS OLD.
NO, SHE HASN'T...
MARCHO ONLY HAS...
I HAVEN'T HEARD ABOUT THIS!
A YEAR LEFT TO LIVE.

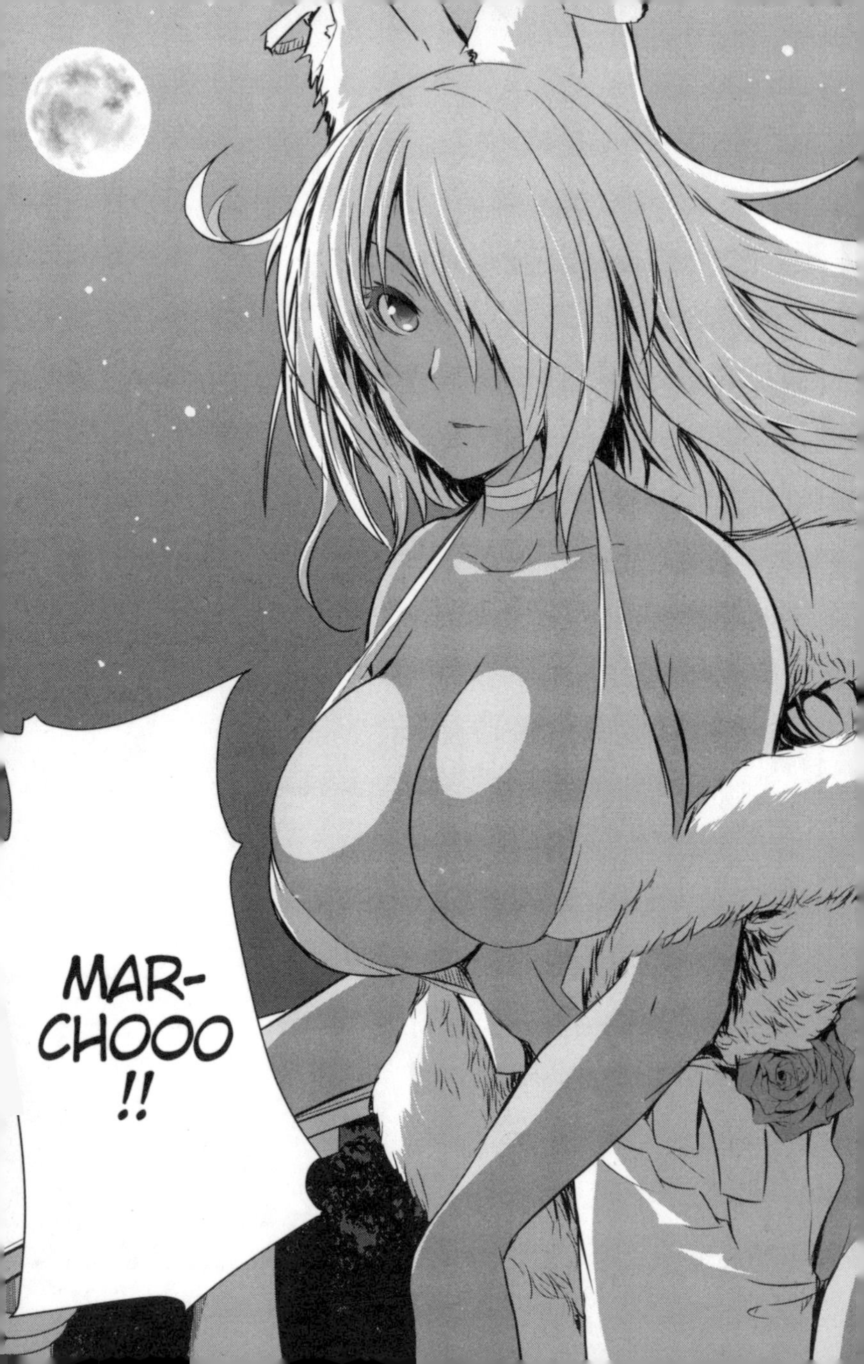
MAR-CHOOO !!

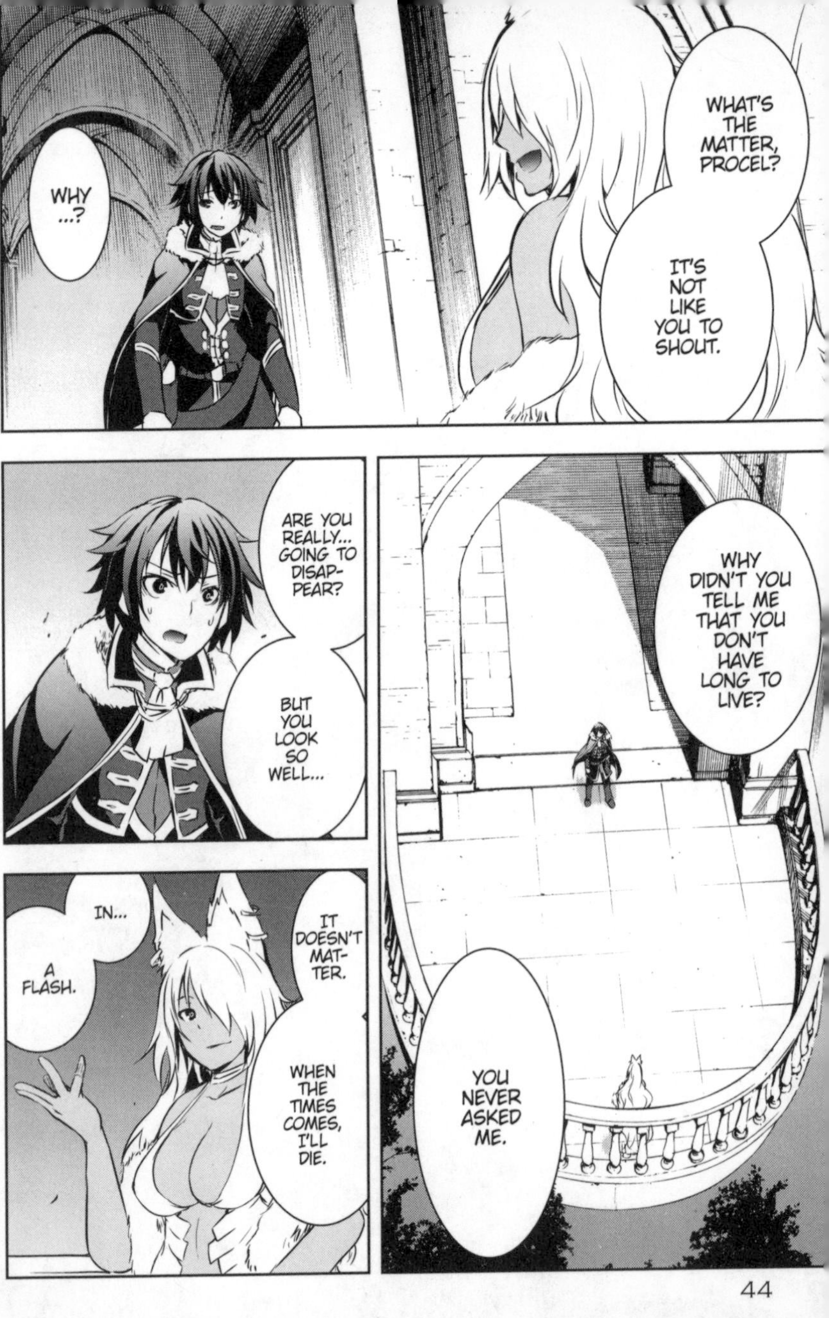
WHAT'S THE MATTER, PROCEL?
IT'S NOT LIKE YOU TO SHOUT.
WHY ...?
WHY DIDN'T YOU TELL ME THAT YOU DON'T HAVE LONG TO LIVE?
YOU NEVER ASKED ME.
ARE YOU REALLY... GOING TO DISAP-PEAR?
BUT YOU LOOK SO WELL...
IT DOESN'T MAT-TER.
WHEN THE TIMES COMES, I'LL DIE.
IN...
A FLASH.

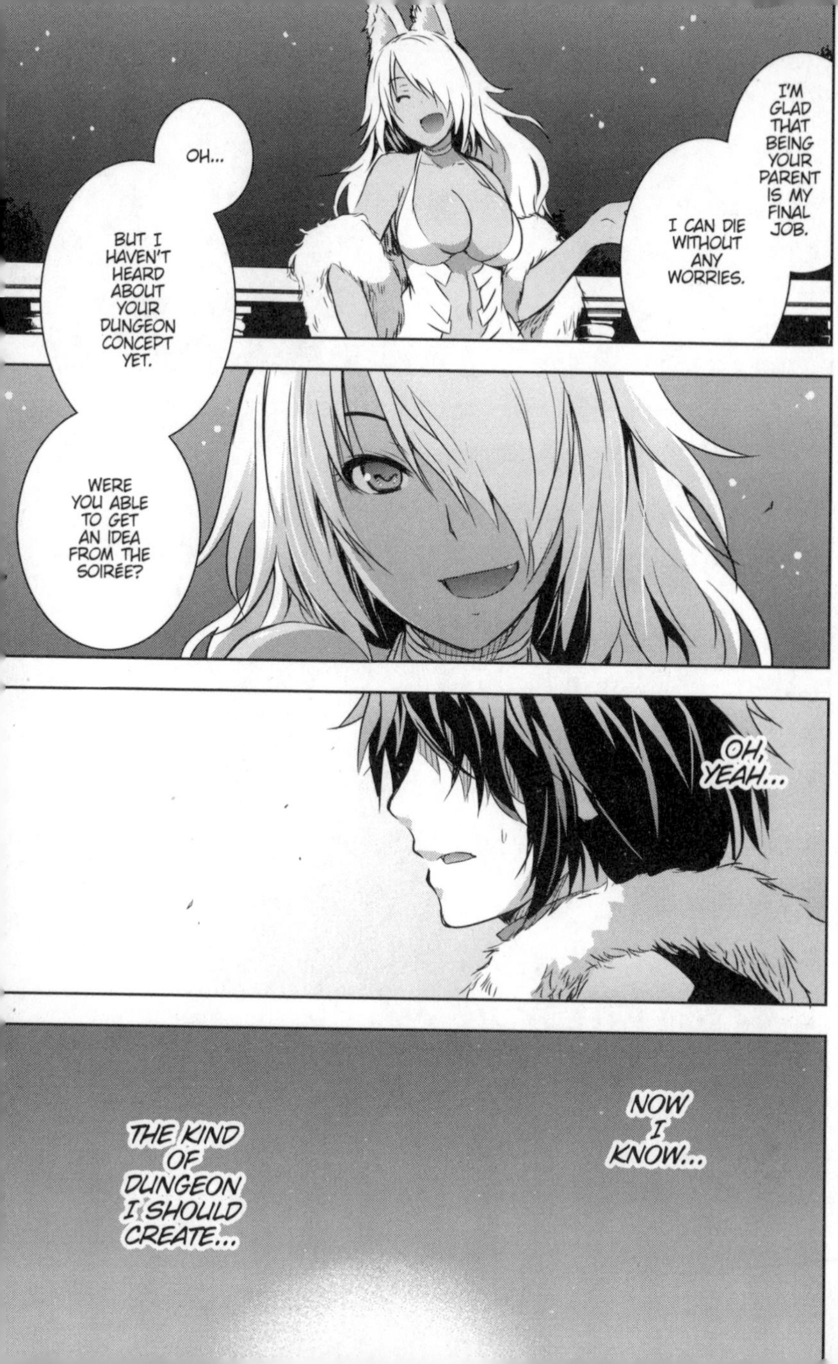
I'M GLAD THAT BEING YOUR PARENT IS MY FINAL JOB.
I CAN DIE WITHOUT ANY WORRIES.
OH...
BUT I HAVEN'T HEARD ABOUT YOUR DUNGEON CONCEPT YET.
WERE YOU ABLE TO GET AN IDEA FROM THE SOIRÉE?
OH, YEAH...
NOW I KNOW...
THE KIND OF DUNGEON I SHOULD CREATE...

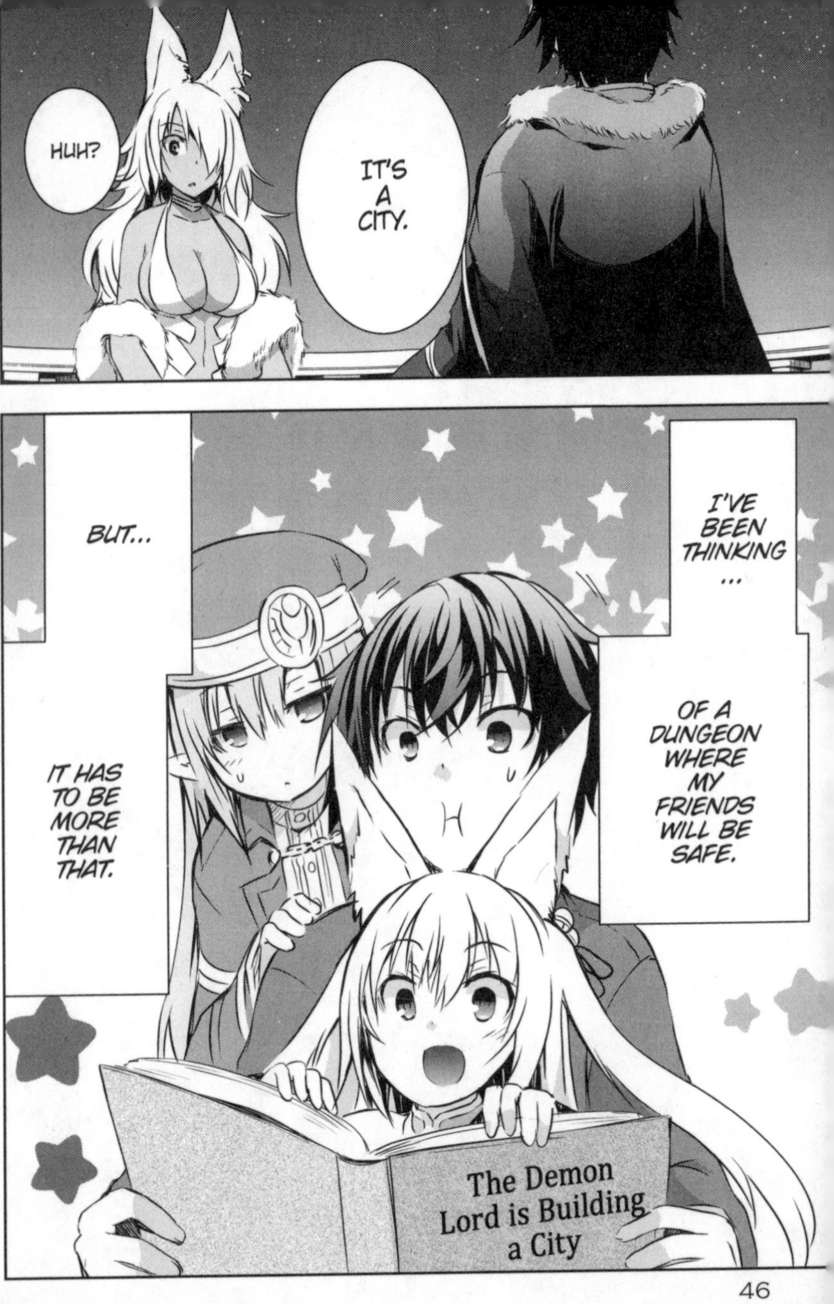
IT'S A CITY.
HUH?
I'VE BEEN THINKING ...
OF A DUNGEON WHERE MY FRIENDS WILL BE SAFE.
BUT...
IT HAS TO BE MORE THAN THAT.
The Demon Lord is Building a City

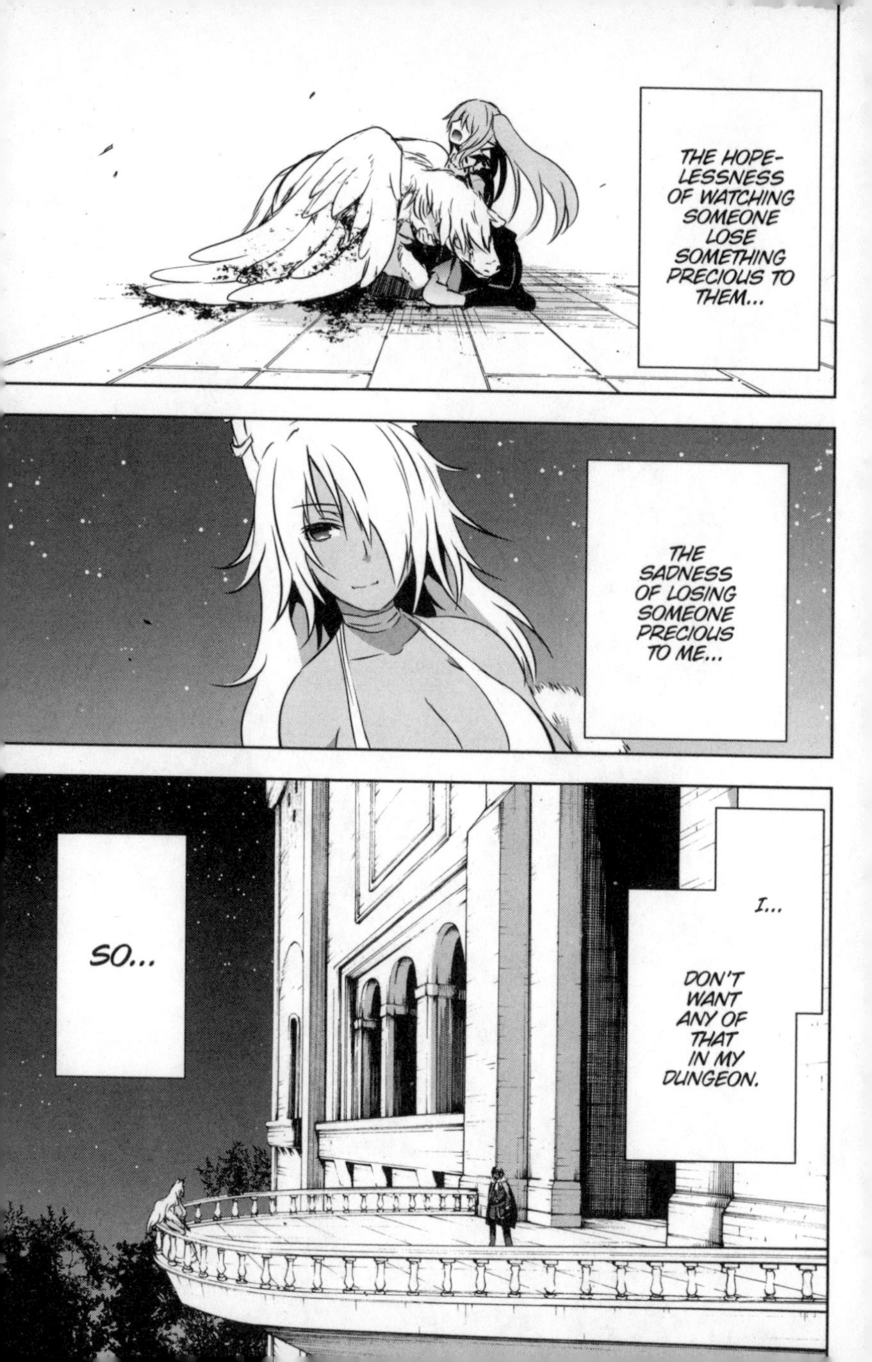
THE HOPE-LESSNESS OF WATCHING SOMEONE LOSE SOMETHING PRECIOUS TO THEM...
THE SADNESS OF LOSING SOMEONE PRECIOUS TO ME...
I...
DON'T WANT ANY OF THAT IN MY DUNGEON.
SO...

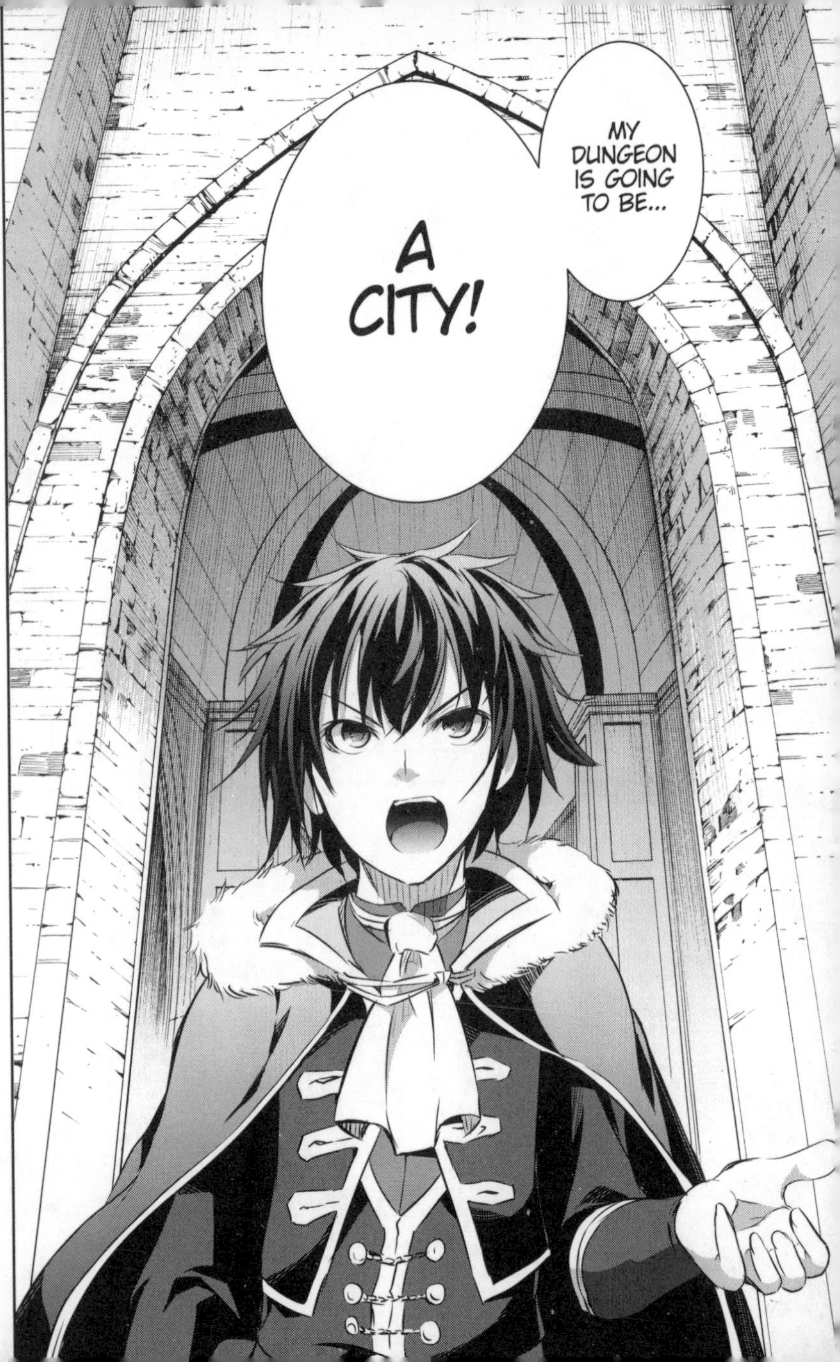
MY DUNGEON IS GOING TO BE...
A CITY!

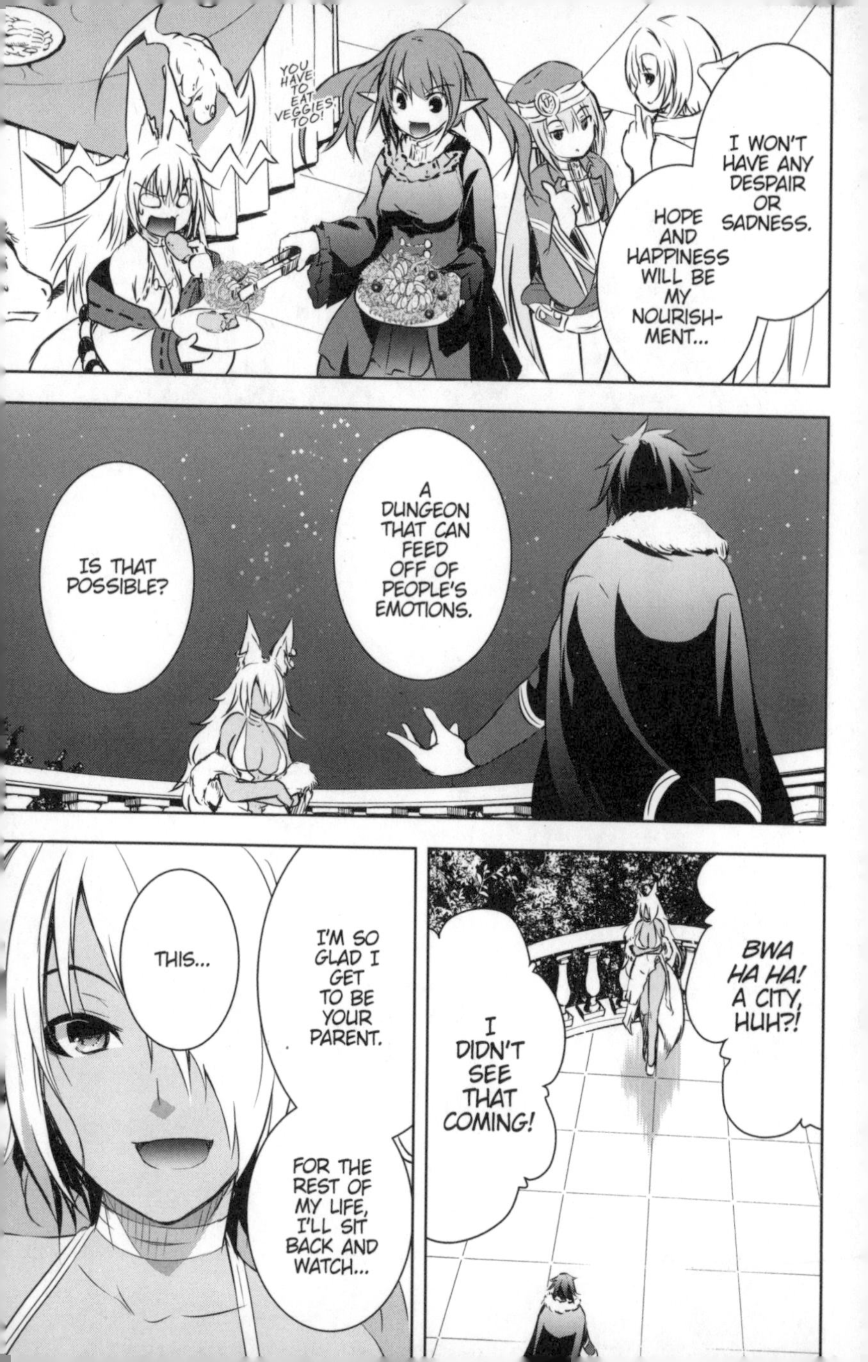
I WON'T HAVE ANY DESPAIR OR SADNESS.
HOPE AND HAPPINESS WILL BE MY NOURISH-MENT...
YOU HAVE TO EAT VEGGIES, TOO!
A DUNGEON THAT CAN FEED OFF OF PEOPLE'S EMOTIONS.
IS THAT POSSIBLE?
BWA HA HA! A CITY, HUH?!
I DIDN'T SEE THAT COMING!
I'M SO GLAD I GET TO BE YOUR PARENT.
THIS...
FOR THE REST OF MY LIFE, I'LL SIT BACK AND WATCH...

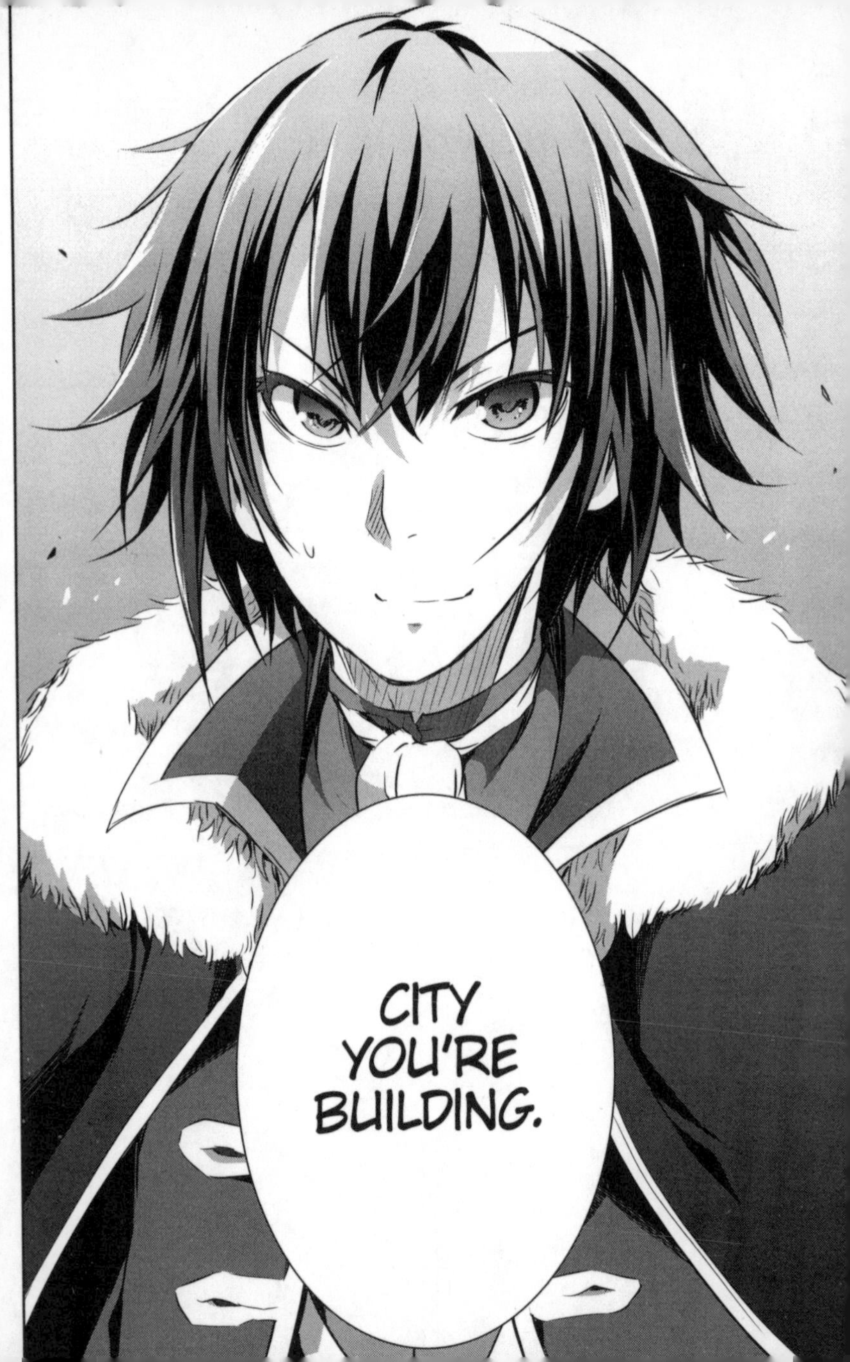
CITY YOU'RE BUILDING.

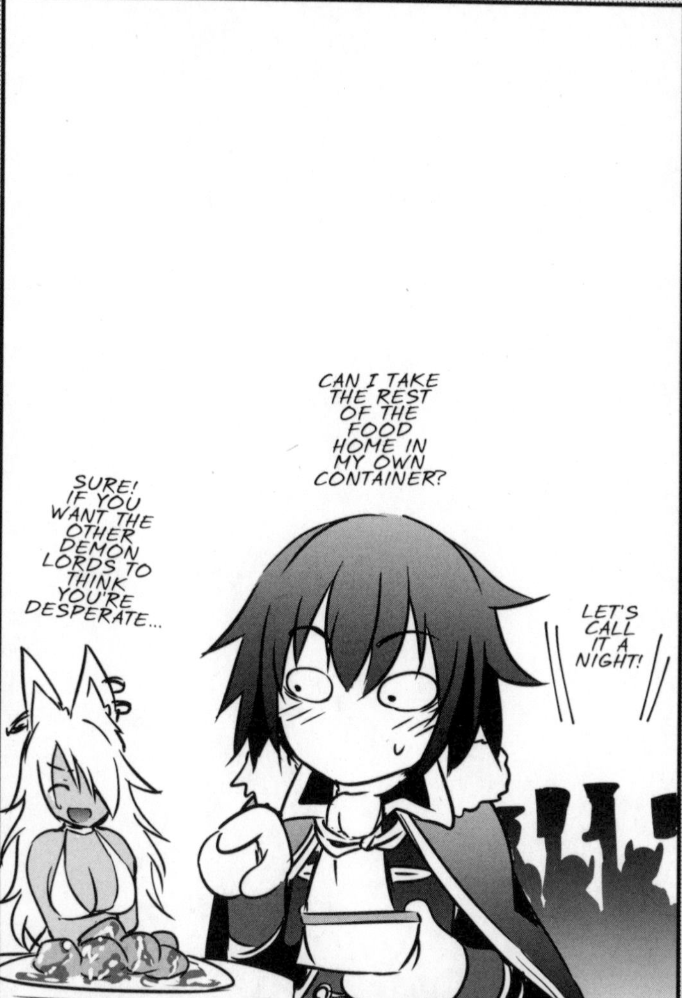
LET'S CALL IT A NIGHT!
CAN I TAKE THE REST OF THE FOOD HOME IN MY OWN CONTAINER?
SURE! IF YOU WANT THE OTHER DEMON LORDS TO THINK YOU'RE DESPERATE...

DUNGEON BUILDER:
THE DEMON KING'S LABYRINTH IS A MODERN CITY!

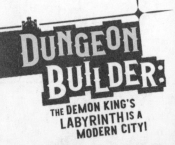

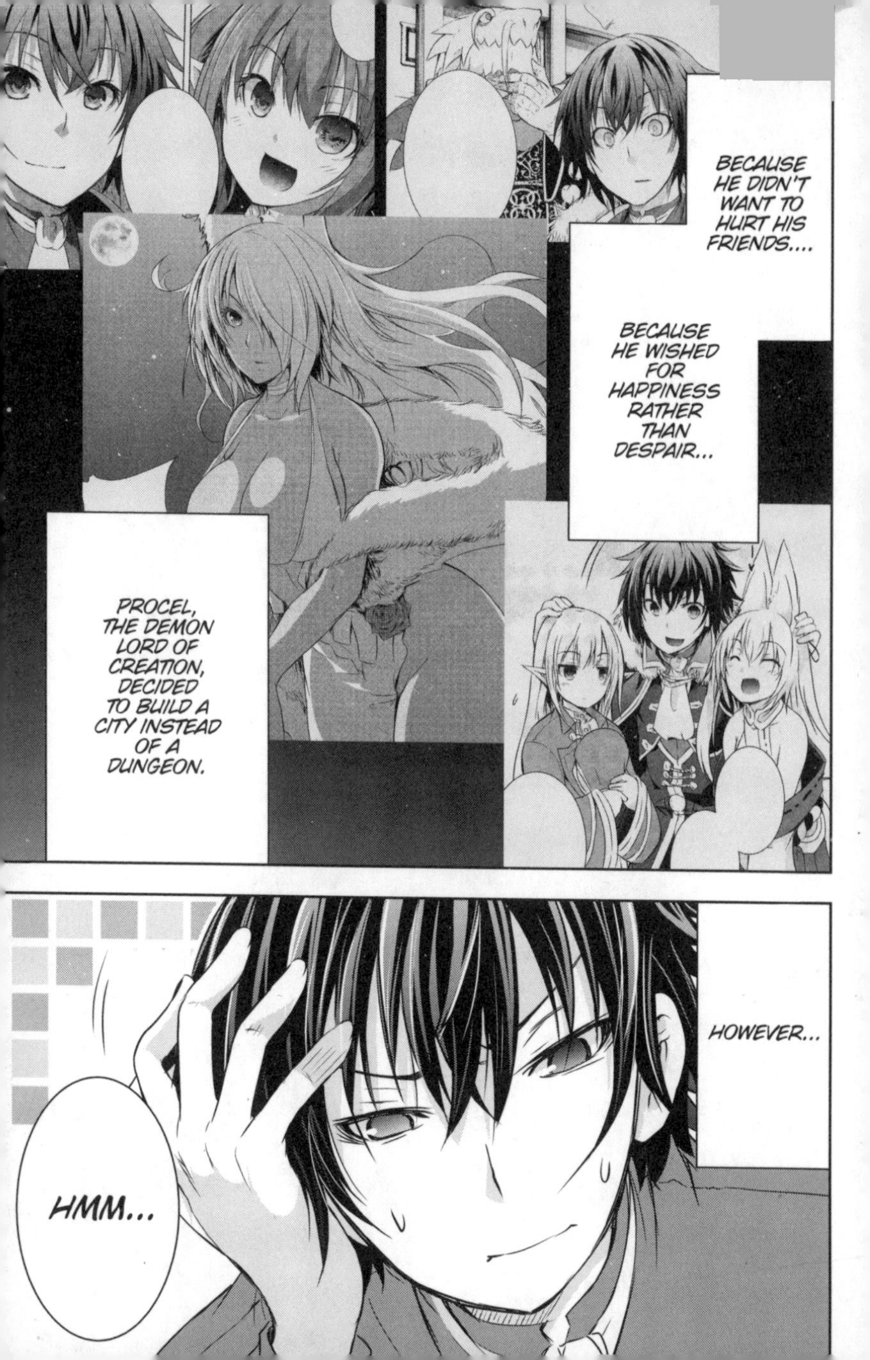
BECAUSE HE DIDN'T WANT TO HURT HIS FRIENDS....
BECAUSE HE WISHED FOR HAPPINESS RATHER THAN DESPAIR...
PROCEL, THE DEMON LORD OF CREATION, DECIDED TO BUILD A CITY INSTEAD OF A DUNGEON.
HOWEVER...
HMM...

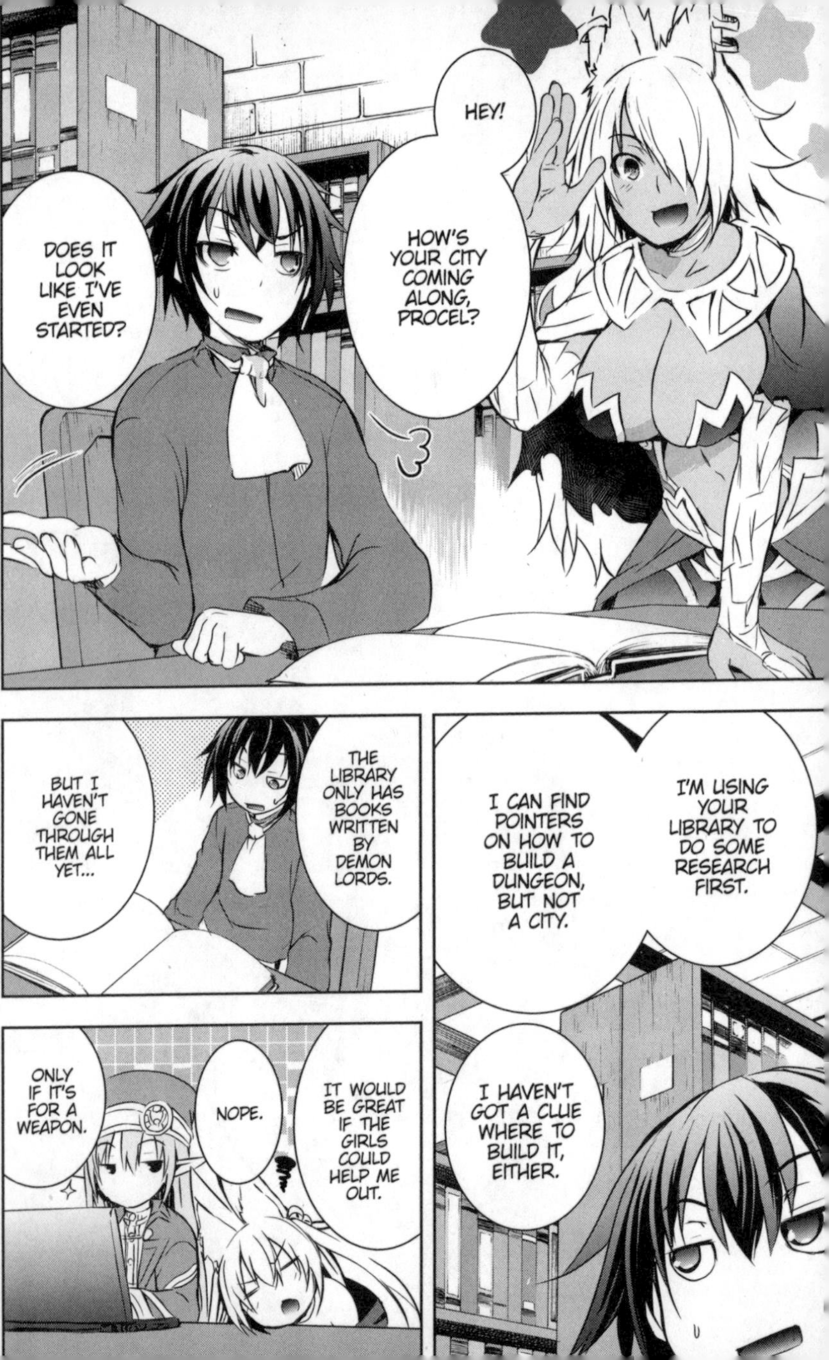
HEY!
HOW'S YOUR CITY COMING ALONG, PROCEL?
DOES IT LOOK LIKE I'VE EVEN STARTED?
I'M USING YOUR LIBRARY TO DO SOME RESEARCH FIRST.
I CAN FIND POINTERS ON HOW TO BUILD A DUNGEON, BUT NOT A CITY.
THE LIBRARY ONLY HAS BOOKS WRITTEN BY DEMON LORDS.
BUT I HAVEN'T GONE THROUGH THEM ALL YET...
I HAVEN'T GOT A CLUE WHERE TO BUILD IT, EITHER.
IT WOULD BE GREAT IF THE GIRLS COULD HELP ME OUT.
NOPE.
ONLY IF IT'S FOR A WEAPON.

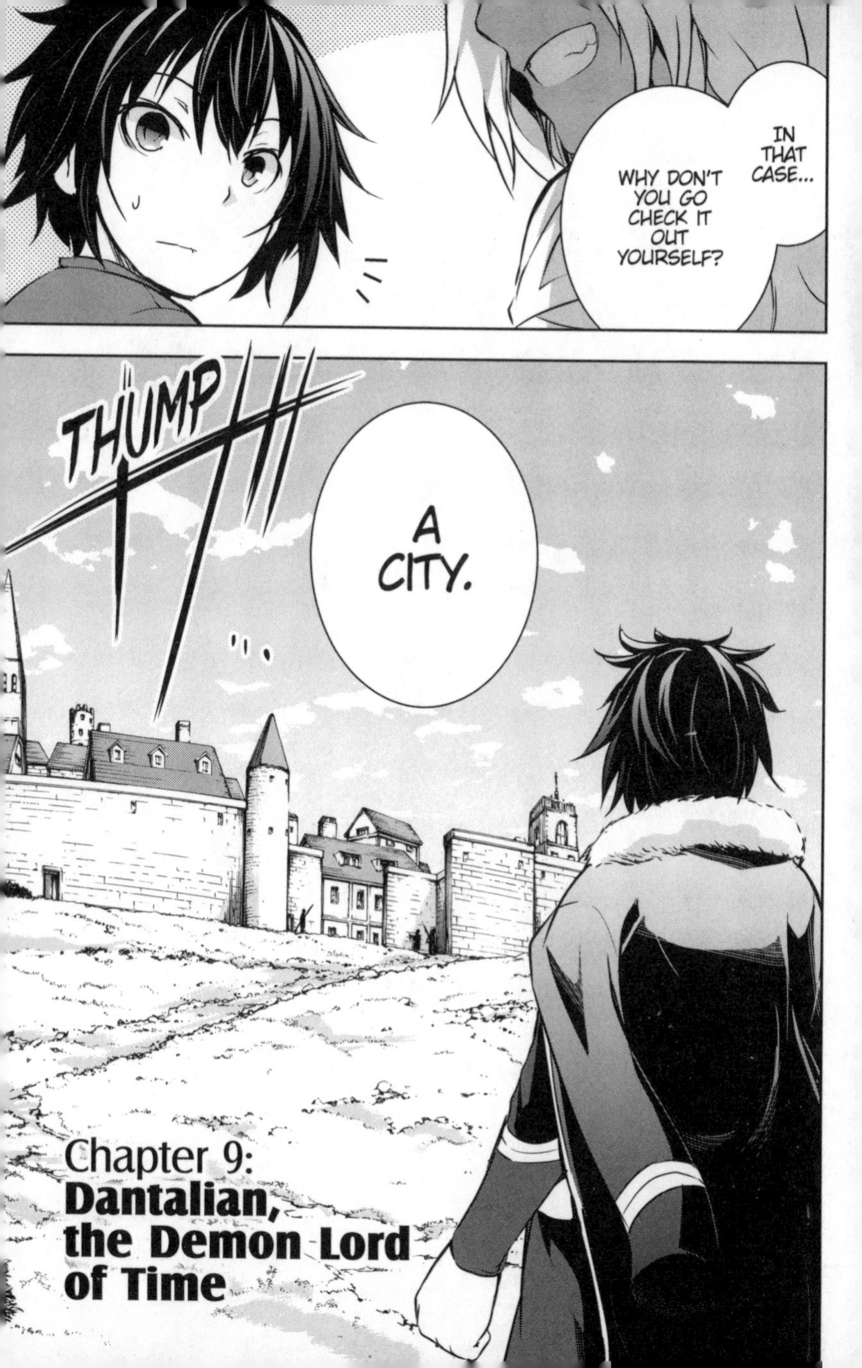
IN THAT CASE...
WHY DON'T YOU GO CHECK IT OUT YOURSELF?
A CITY.
THUMP
Chapter 9:
Dantalian, the Demon Lord of Time

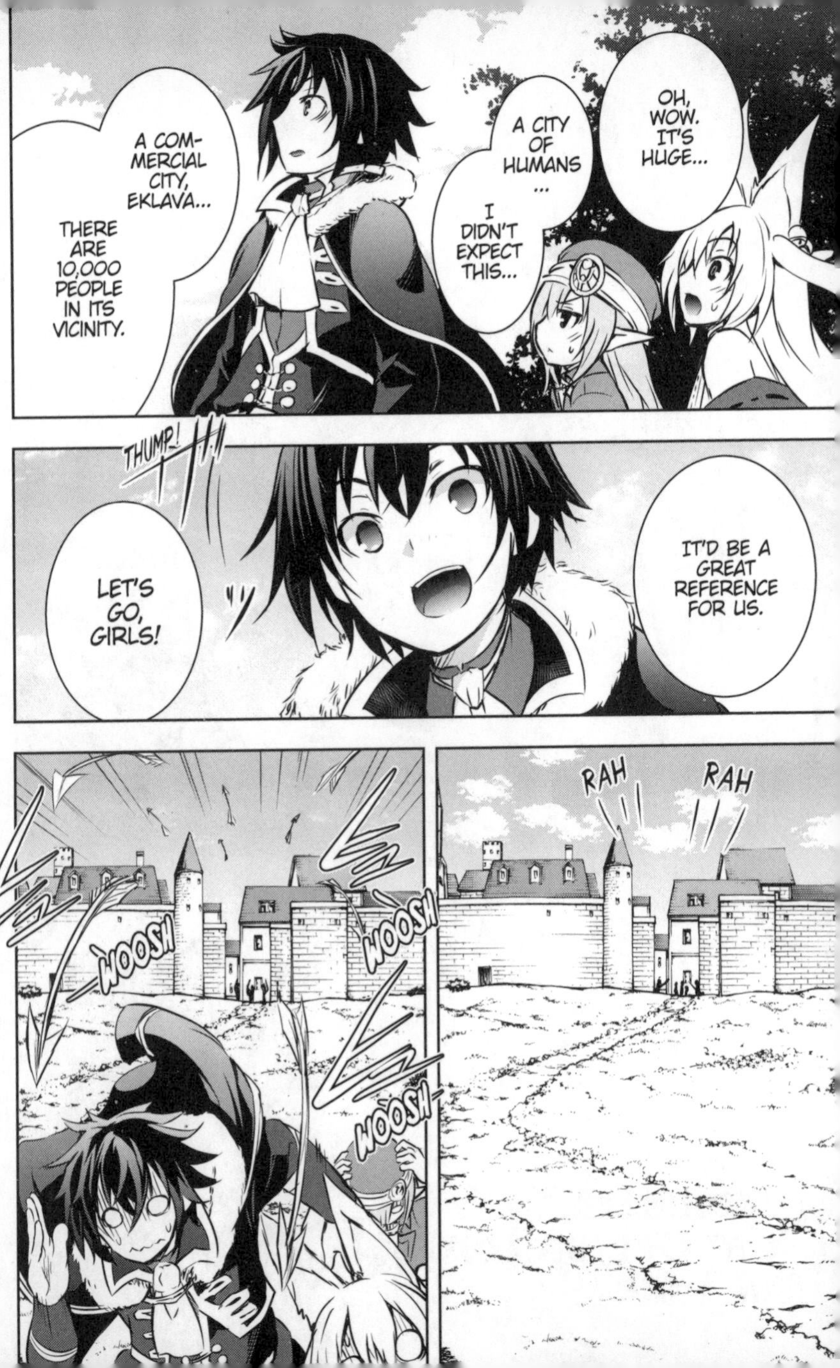
OH, WOW. IT'S HUGE...
A CITY OF HUMANS ...
I DIDN'T EXPECT THIS...
A COM-MERCIAL CITY, EKLAVA...
THERE ARE 10,000 PEOPLE IN ITS VICINITY.
IT'D BE A GREAT REFERENCE FOR US.
THUMP!
LET'S GO, GIRLS!
RAH
RAH
WOOSH
WOOSH
WOOSH

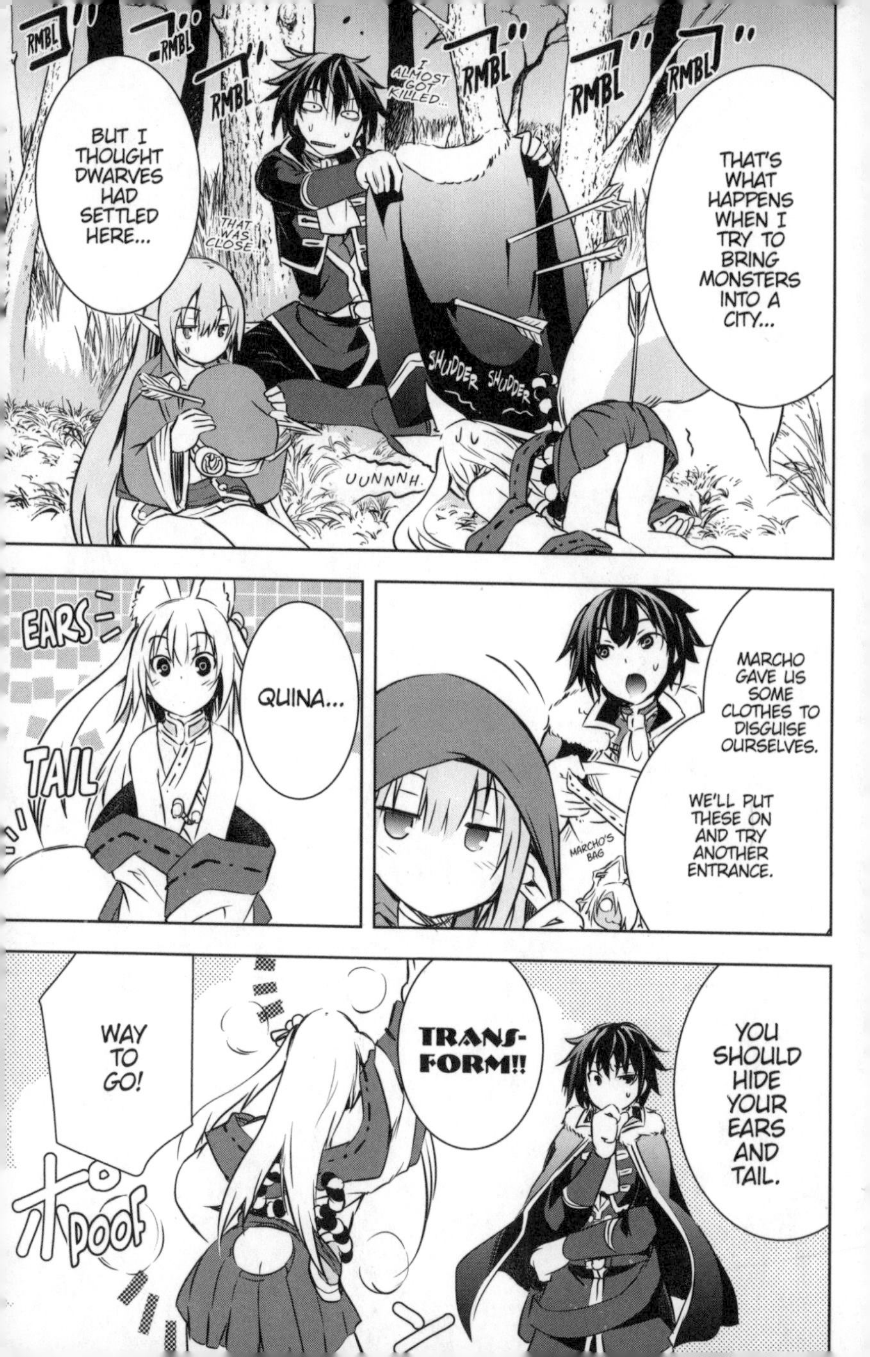
RMBL RMBL RMBL RMBL RMBL RMBL
THAT'S WHAT HAPPENS WHEN I TRY TO BRING MONSTERS INTO A CITY...
I ALMOST GOT KILLED...
BUT I THOUGHT DWARVES HAD SETTLED HERE...
THAT WAS CLOSE...
SHUDDER SHUDDER
UUNNNH.
MARCHO GAVE US SOME CLOTHES TO DISGUISE OURSELVES.
WE'LL PUT THESE ON AND TRY ANOTHER ENTRANCE.
MARCHO'S BAG
QUINA...
EARS
TAIL
YOU SHOULD HIDE YOUR EARS AND TAIL.
TRANS-FORM!!
WAY TO GO!
POOF

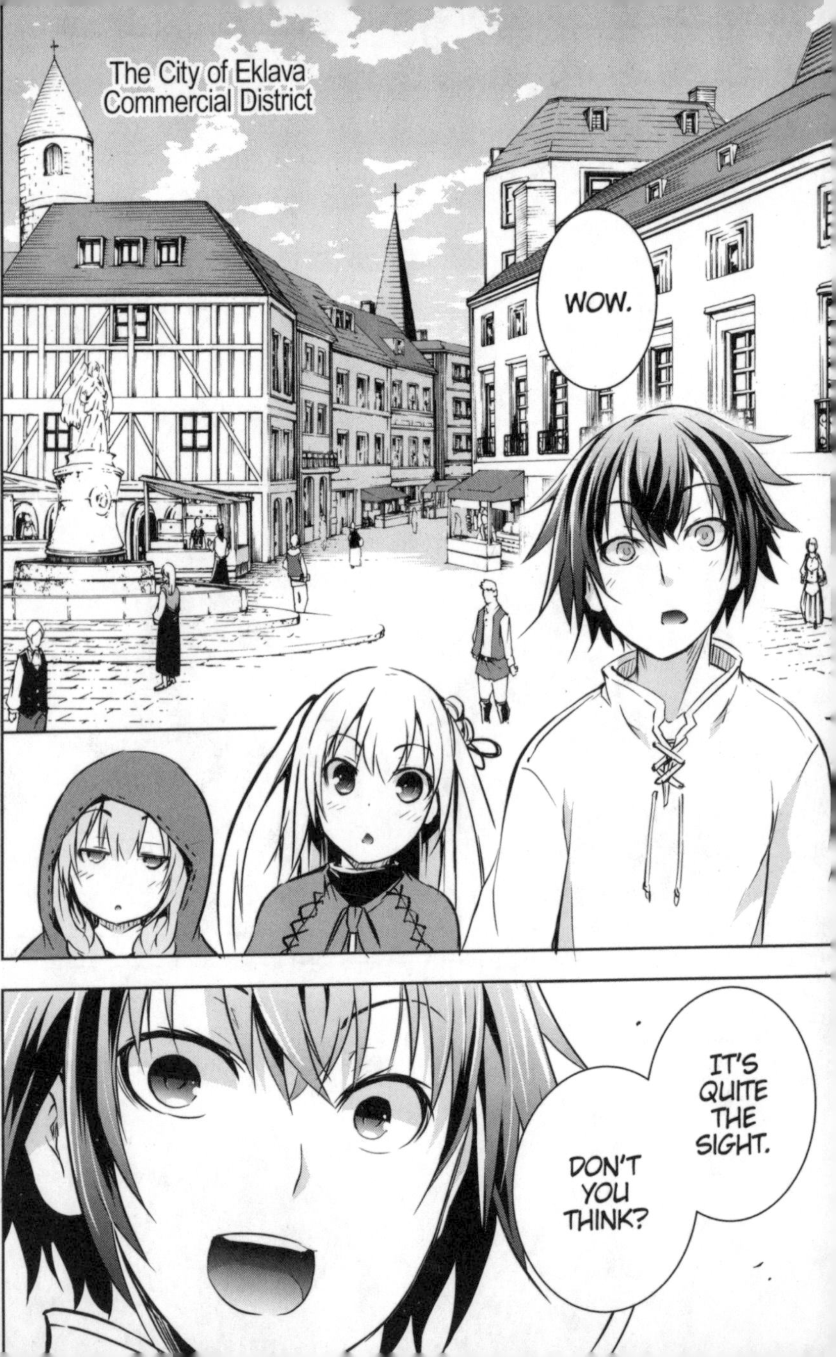
The City of Eklava Commercial District
WOW.
IT'S QUITE THE SIGHT.
DON'T YOU THINK?

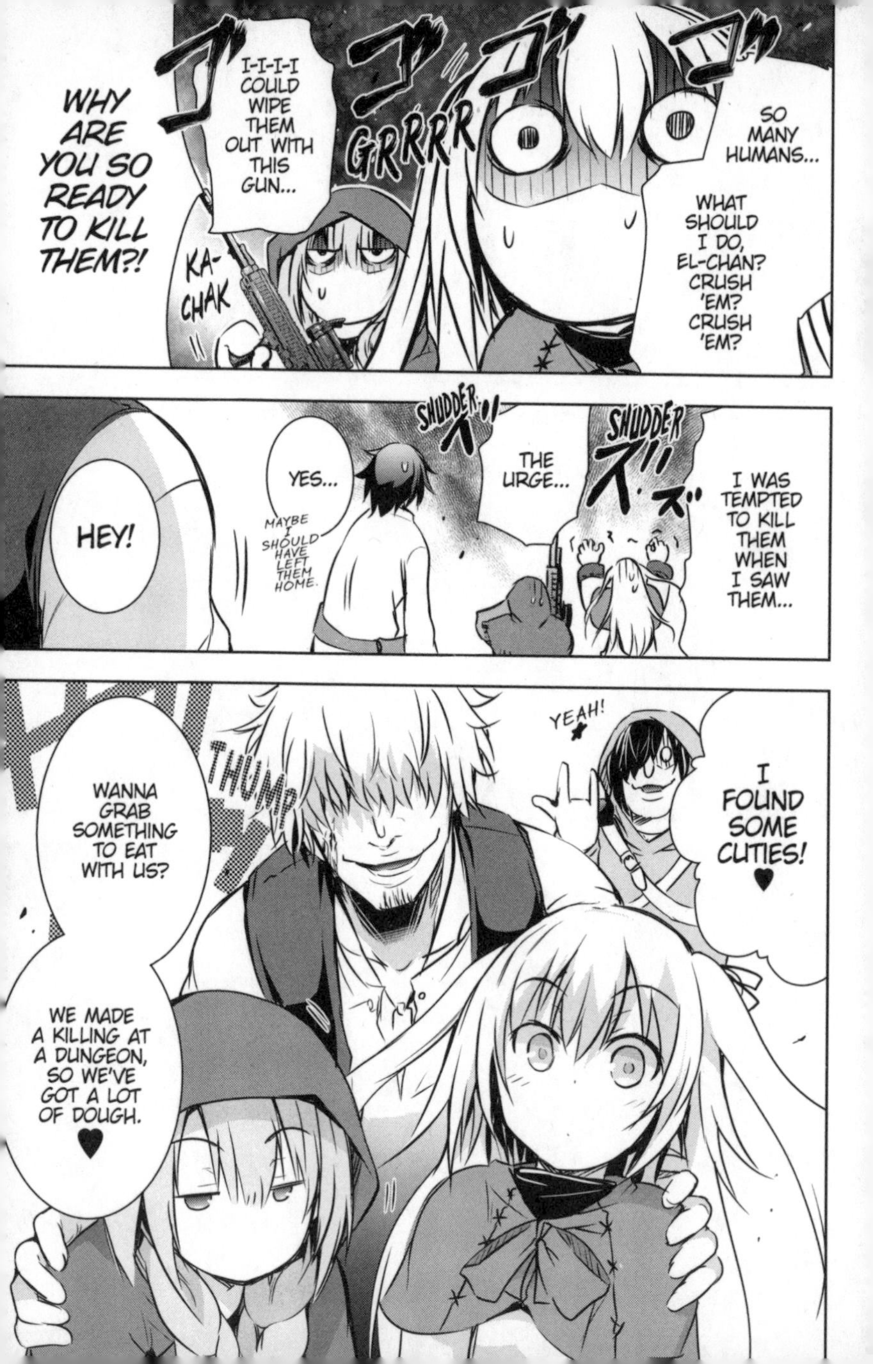
SO MANY HUMANS...
WHAT SHOULD I DO, EL-CHAN? CRUSH 'EM? CRUSH 'EM?
GRRRR
I-I-I-I COULD WIPE THEM OUT WITH THIS GUN...
KA-CHAK
WHY ARE YOU SO READY TO KILL THEM?!
I WAS TEMPTED TO KILL THEM WHEN I SAW THEM...
SHUDDER
THE URGE...
SHUDDER
YES...
MAYBE I SHOULD HAVE LEFT THEM HOME.
HEY!
I FOUND SOME CUTIES! ♥
YEAH!
THUMP
WANNA GRAB SOMETHING TO EAT WITH US?
WE MADE A KILLING AT A DUNGEON, SO WE'VE GOT A LOT OF DOUGH. ♥

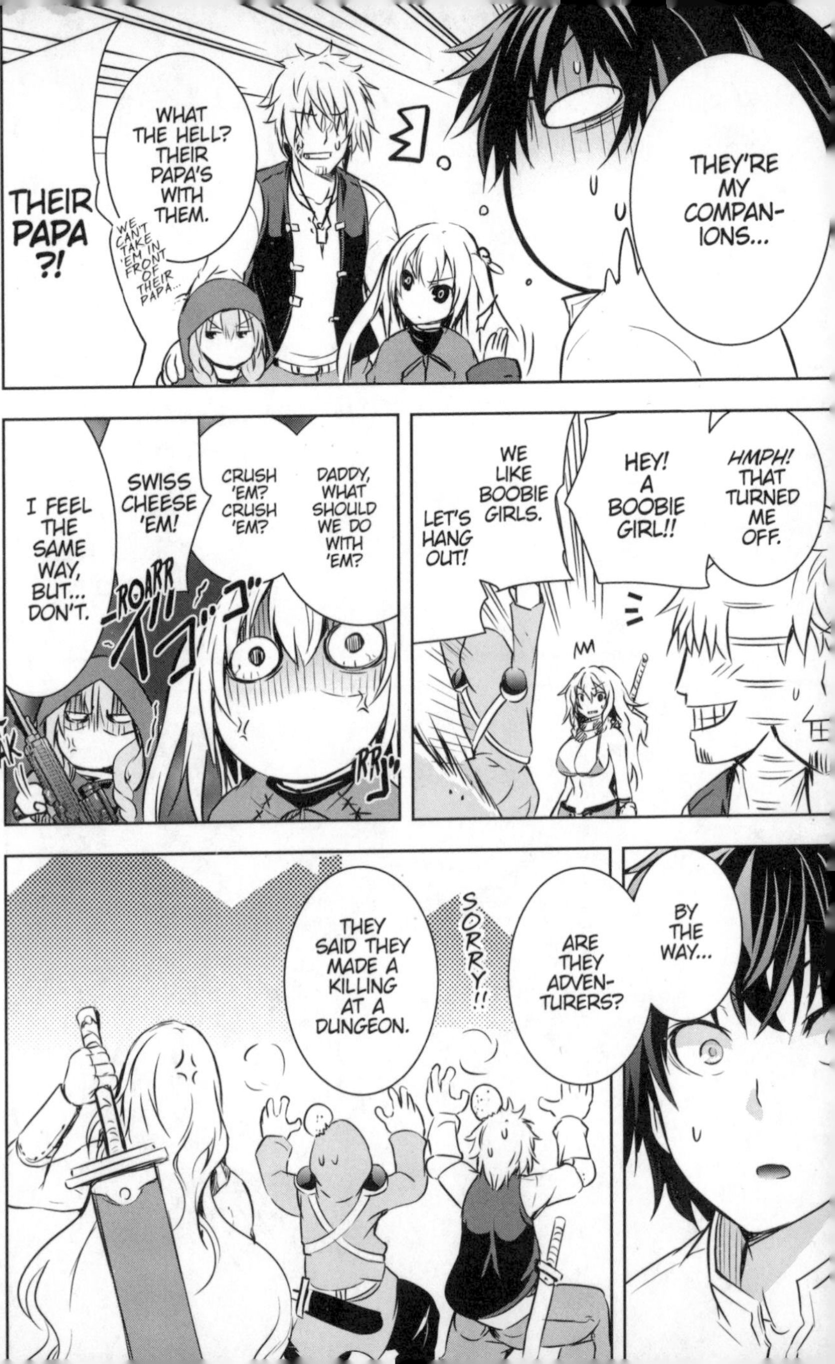
THEY'RE MY COMPANIONS...
WHAT THE HELL? THEIR PAPA'S WITH THEM.
WE CAN'T TAKE 'EM IN FRONT OF THEIR PAPA...
THEIR PAPA ?!
HMPH! THAT TURNED ME OFF.
HEY! A BOOBIE GIRL!!
WE LIKE BOOBIE GIRLS.
LET'S HANG OUT!
DADDY, WHAT SHOULD WE DO WITH 'EM?
CRUSH 'EM? CRUSH 'EM?
SWISS CHEESE 'EM!
I FEEL THE SAME WAY, BUT... DON'T.
ROARR
KA-CHAK
RR...
BY THE WAY...
ARE THEY ADVENTURERS?
SORRY!!
THEY SAID THEY MADE A KILLING AT A DUNGEON.

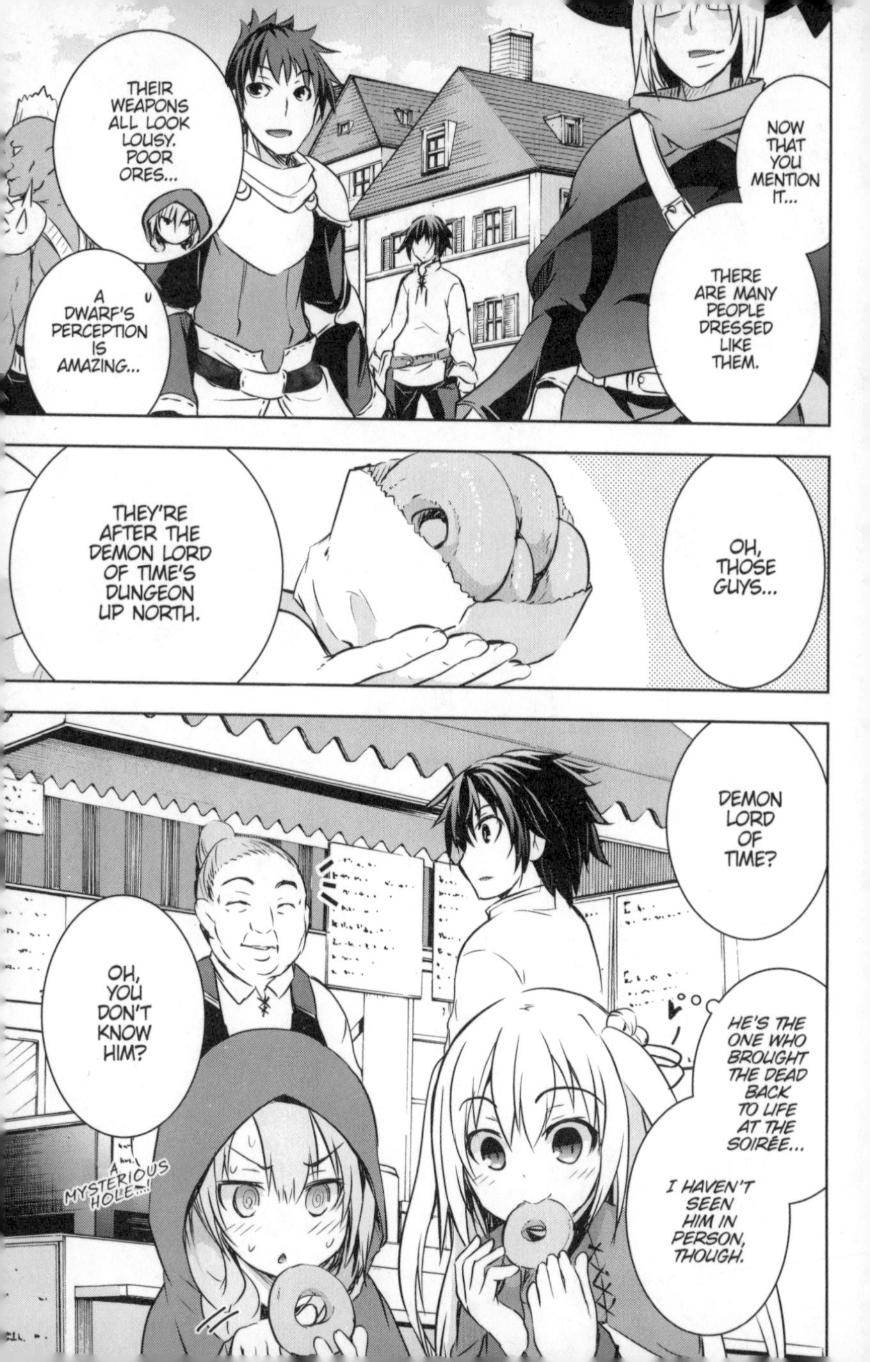
NOW THAT YOU MENTION IT...
THERE ARE MANY PEOPLE DRESSED LIKE THEM.
THEIR WEAPONS ALL LOOK LOUSY. POOR ORES...
A DWARF'S PERCEPTION IS AMAZING...
OH, THOSE GUYS...
THEY'RE AFTER THE DEMON LORD OF TIME'S DUNGEON UP NORTH.
DEMON LORD OF TIME?
HE'S THE ONE WHO BROUGHT THE DEAD BACK TO LIFE AT THE SOIRÉE...
I HAVEN'T SEEN HIM IN PERSON, THOUGH.
OH, YOU DON'T KNOW HIM?
A MYSTERIOUS HOLE...!

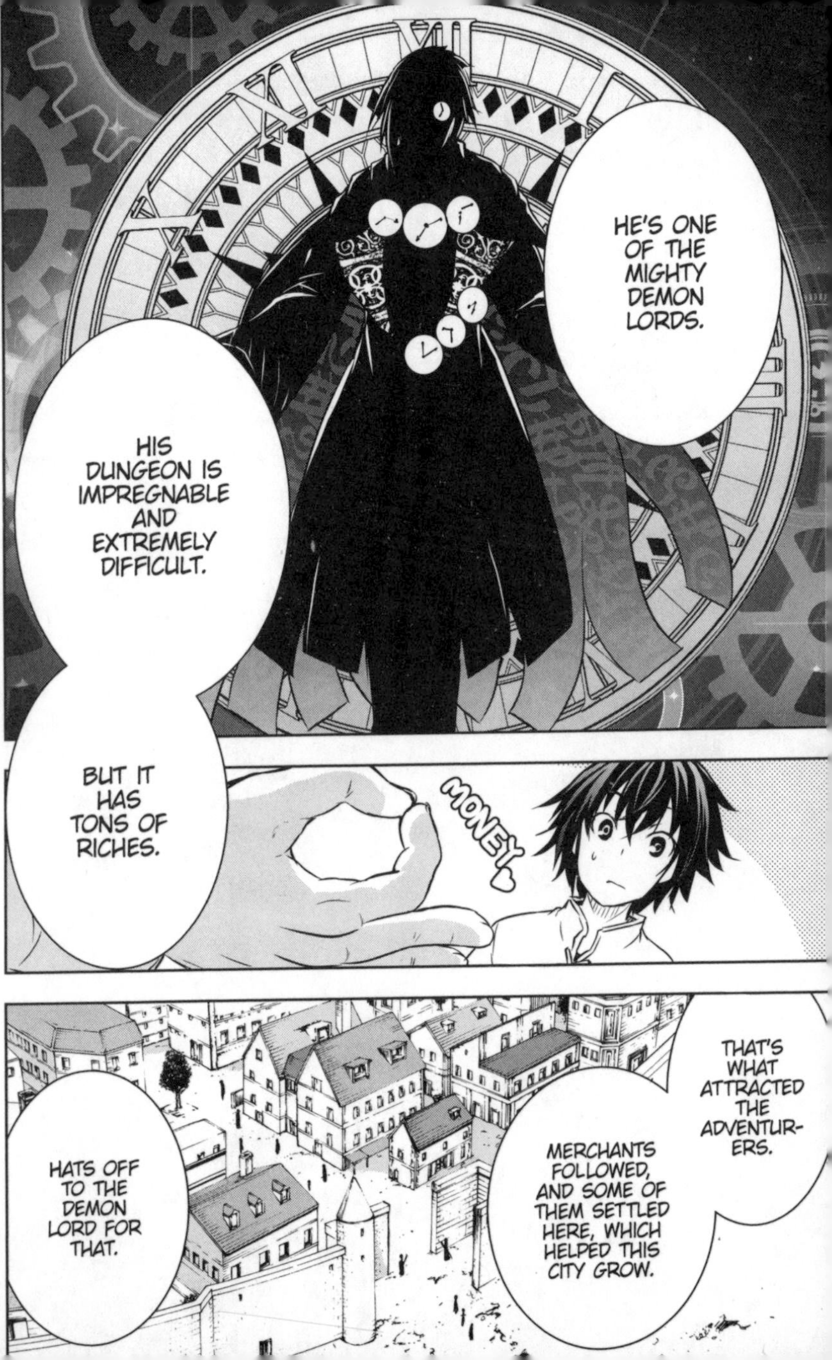
HE'S ONE OF THE MIGHTY DEMON LORDS.
HIS DUNGEON IS IMPREGNABLE AND EXTREMELY DIFFICULT.
MONEY
BUT IT HAS TONS OF RICHES.
THAT'S WHAT ATTRACTED THE ADVENTURERS.
MERCHANTS FOLLOWED, AND SOME OF THEM SETTLED HERE, WHICH HELPED THIS CITY GROW.
HATS OFF TO THE DEMON LORD FOR THAT.

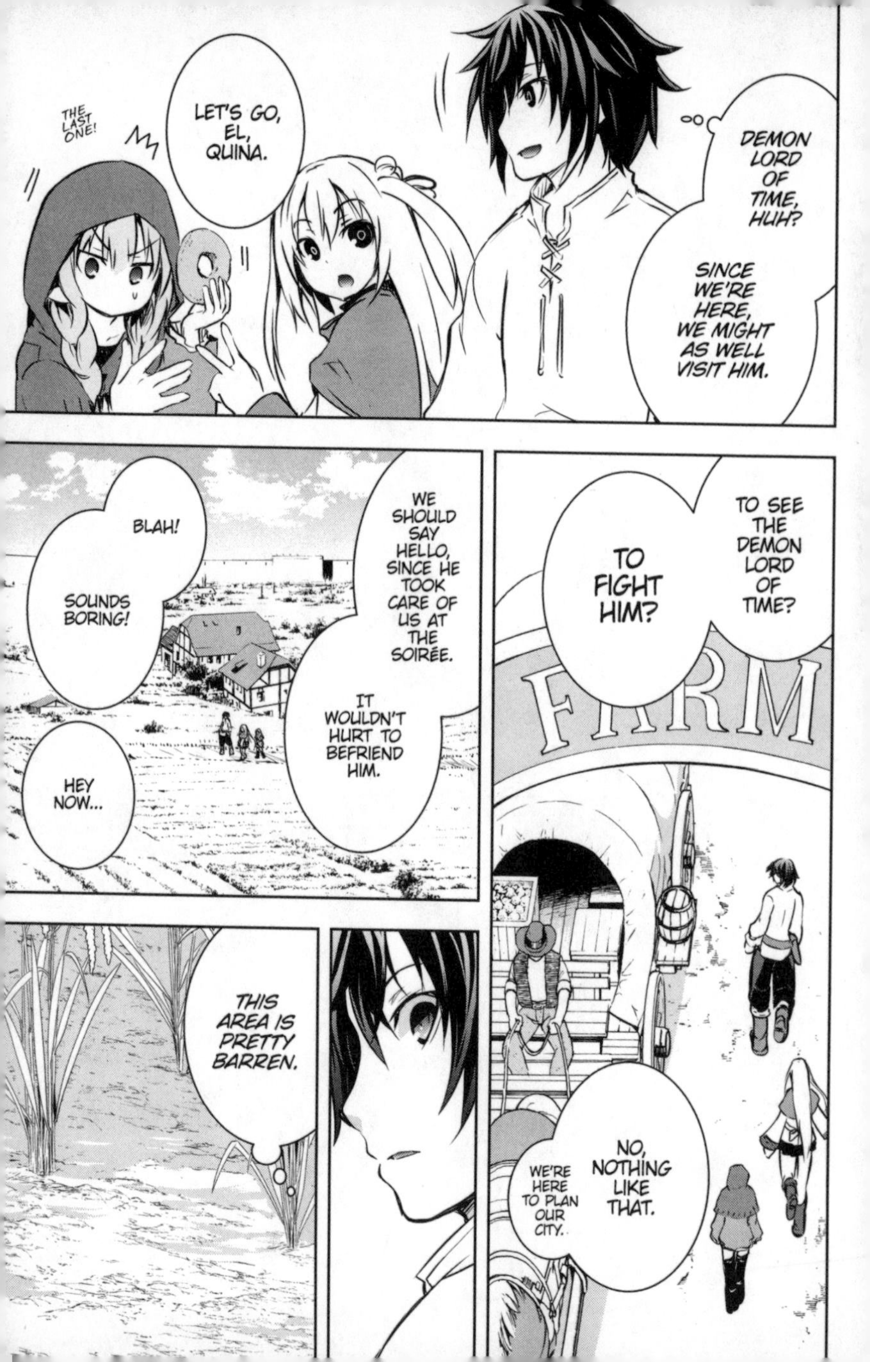
DEMON LORD OF TIME, HUH?
SINCE WE'RE HERE, WE MIGHT AS WELL VISIT HIM.
LET'S GO, EL, QUINA.
THE LAST ONE!
TO SEE THE DEMON LORD OF TIME?
TO FIGHT HIM?
FARM
NO, NOTHING LIKE THAT.
WE'RE HERE TO PLAN OUR CITY.
WE SHOULD SAY HELLO, SINCE HE TOOK CARE OF US AT THE SOIRÉE.
IT WOULDN'T HURT TO BEFRIEND HIM.
BLAH!
SOUNDS BORING!
HEY NOW...
THIS AREA IS PRETTY BARREN.

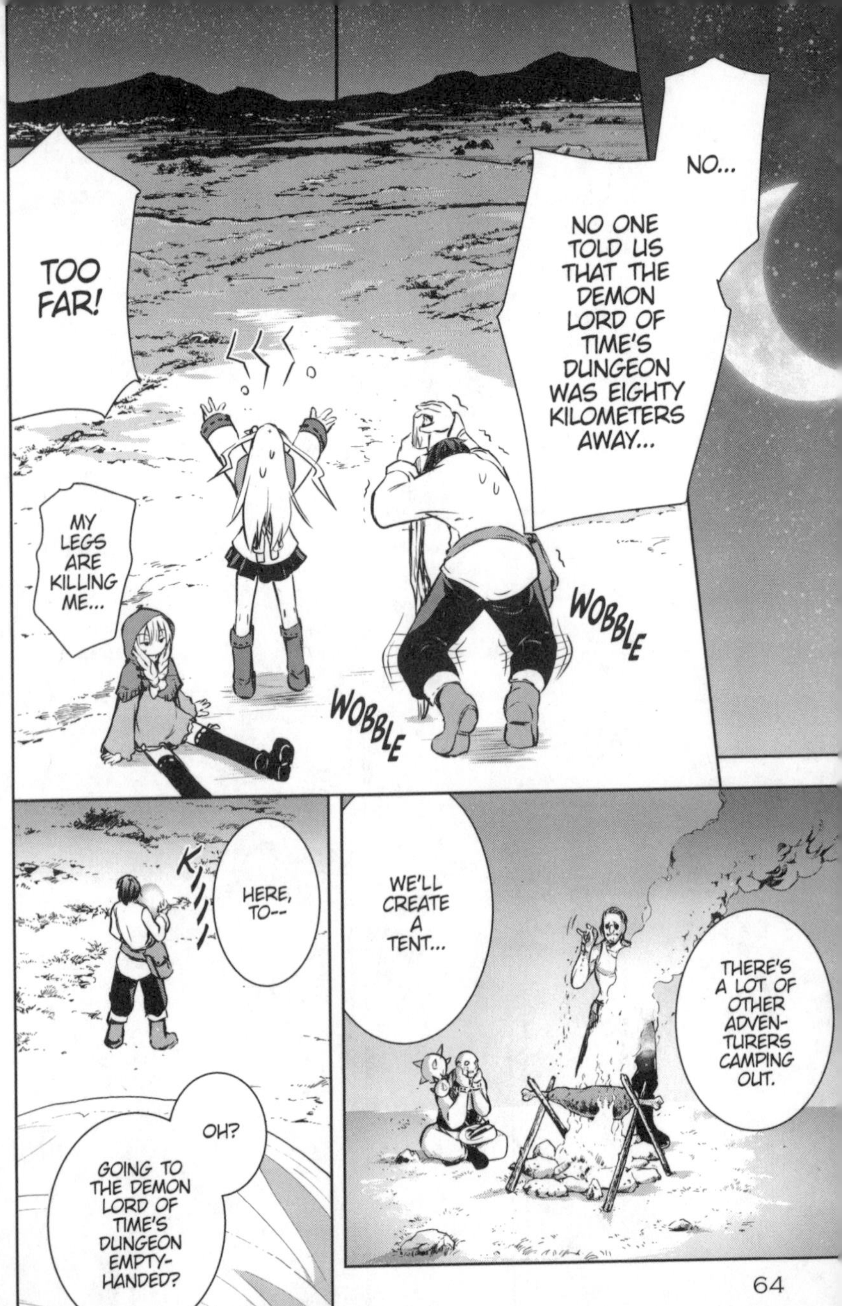
NO...
NO ONE TOLD US THAT THE DEMON LORD OF TIME'S DUNGEON WAS EIGHTY KILOMETERS AWAY...
TOO FAR!
WOBBLE
WOBBLE
MY LEGS ARE KILLING ME...
WE'LL CREATE A TENT...
THERE'S A LOT OF OTHER ADVEN-TURERS CAMPING OUT.
HERE, TO--
OH?
GOING TO THE DEMON LORD OF TIME'S DUNGEON EMPTY-HANDED?

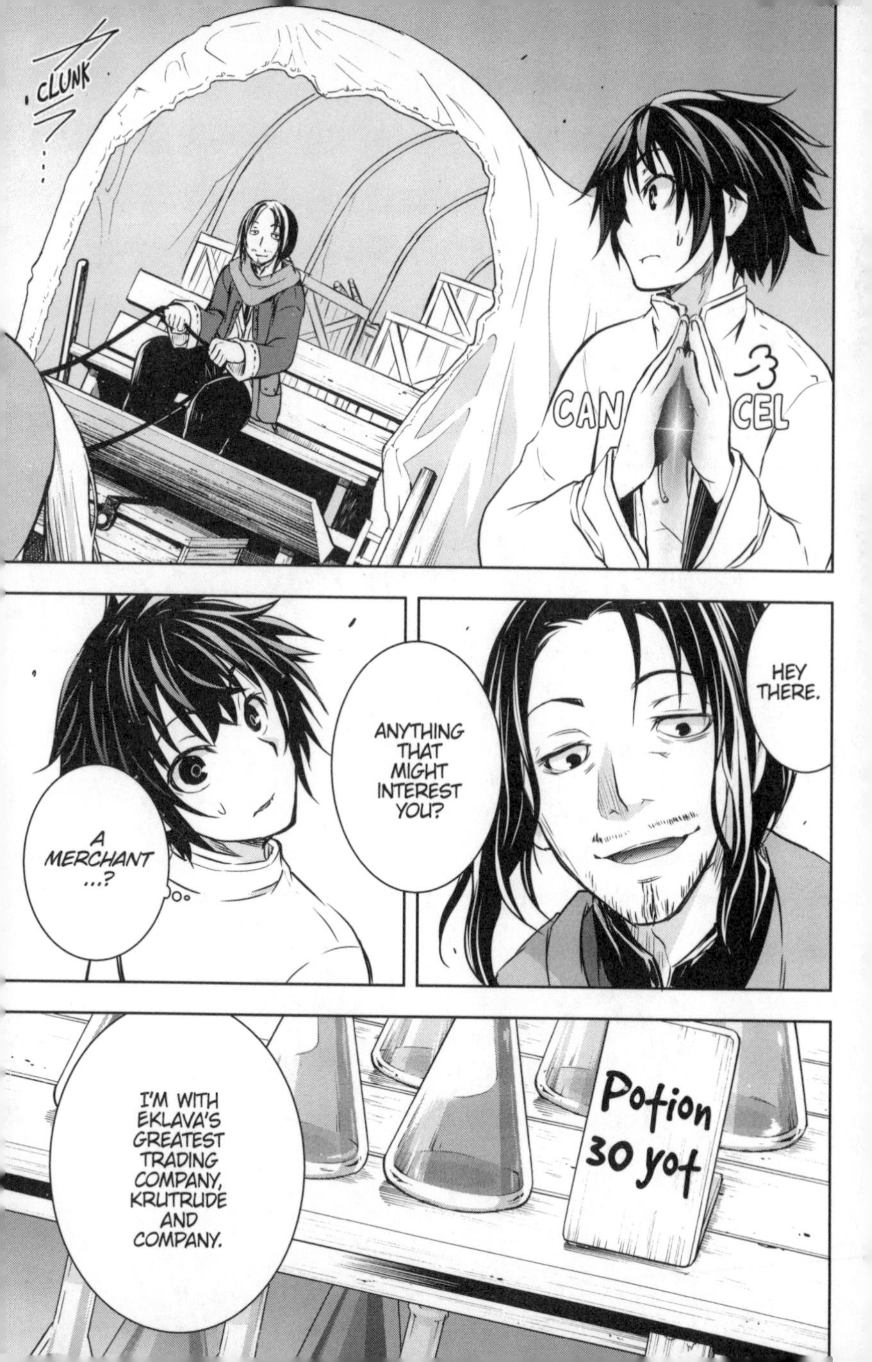
CLUNK
CAN CEL
HEY THERE.
ANYTHING THAT MIGHT INTEREST YOU?
A MERCHANT ...?
I'M WITH EKLAVA'S GREATEST TRADING COMPANY, KRUTRUDE AND COMPANY.
Potion 30 yot

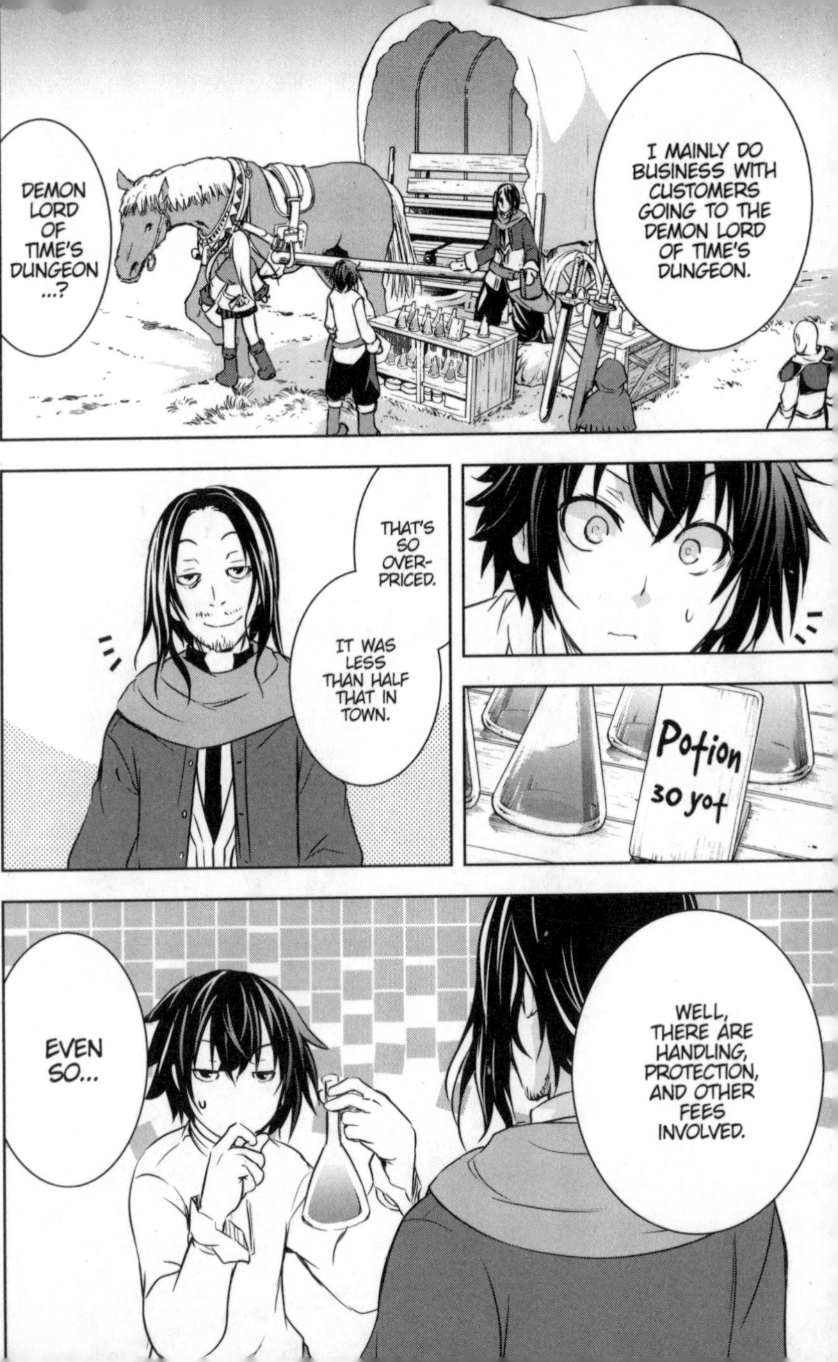
I MAINLY DO BUSINESS WITH CUSTOMERS GOING TO THE DEMON LORD OF TIME'S DUNGEON.
DEMON LORD OF TIME'S DUNGEON ...?
Potion 30 yot
THAT'S SO OVER-PRICED.
IT WAS LESS THAN HALF THAT IN TOWN.
WELL, THERE ARE HANDLING, PROTECTION, AND OTHER FEES INVOLVED.
EVEN SO...

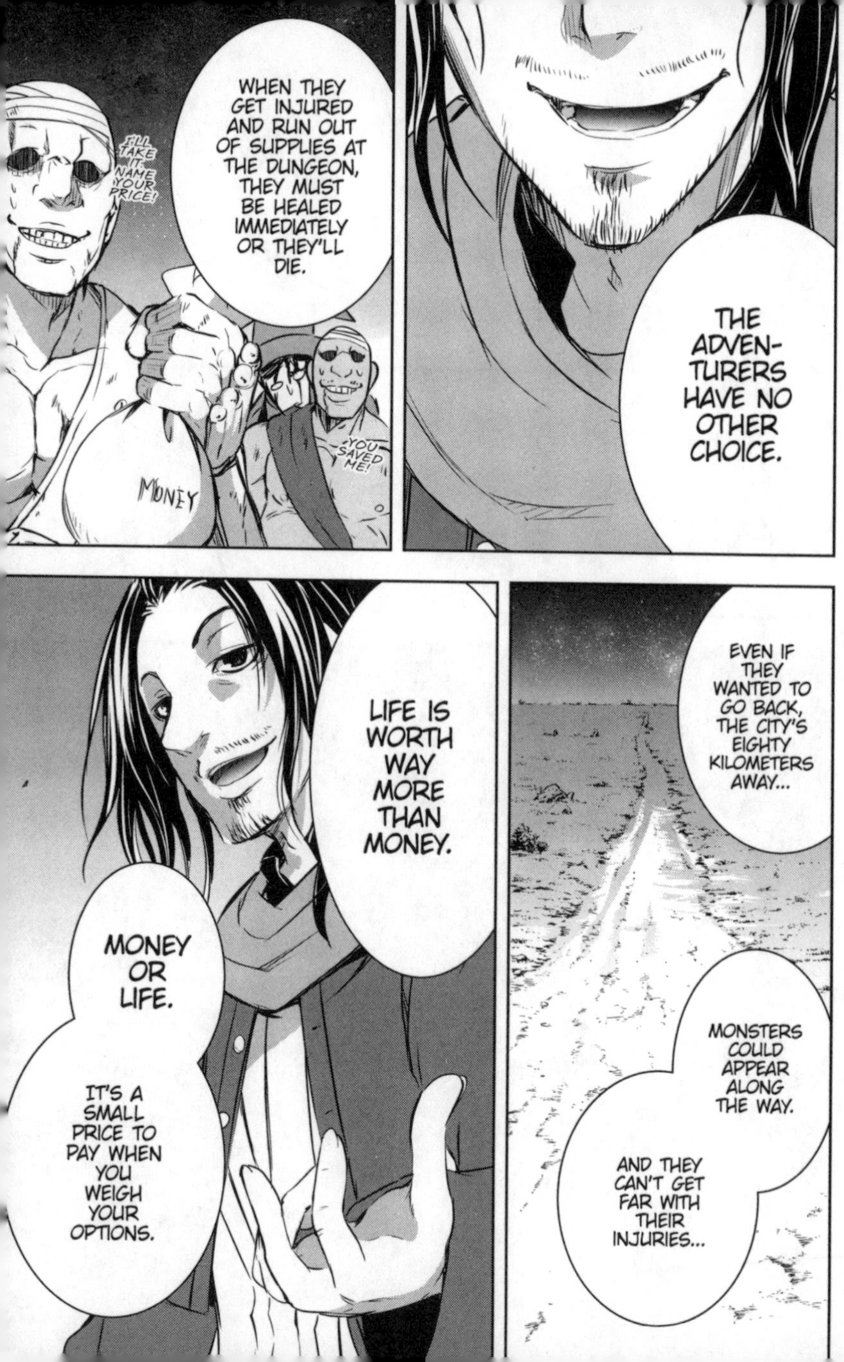
THE ADVEN-TURERS HAVE NO OTHER CHOICE.
WHEN THEY GET INJURED AND RUN OUT OF SUPPLIES AT THE DUNGEON, THEY MUST BE HEALED IMMEDIATELY OR THEY'LL DIE.
I'LL TAKE IT. NAME YOUR PRICE!
YOU SAVED ME!
MONEY
EVEN IF THEY WANTED TO GO BACK, THE CITY'S EIGHTY KILOMETERS AWAY...
MONSTERS COULD APPEAR ALONG THE WAY.
AND THEY CAN'T GET FAR WITH THEIR INJURIES...
LIFE IS WORTH WAY MORE THAN MONEY.
MONEY OR LIFE.
IT'S A SMALL PRICE TO PAY WHEN YOU WEIGH YOUR OPTIONS.

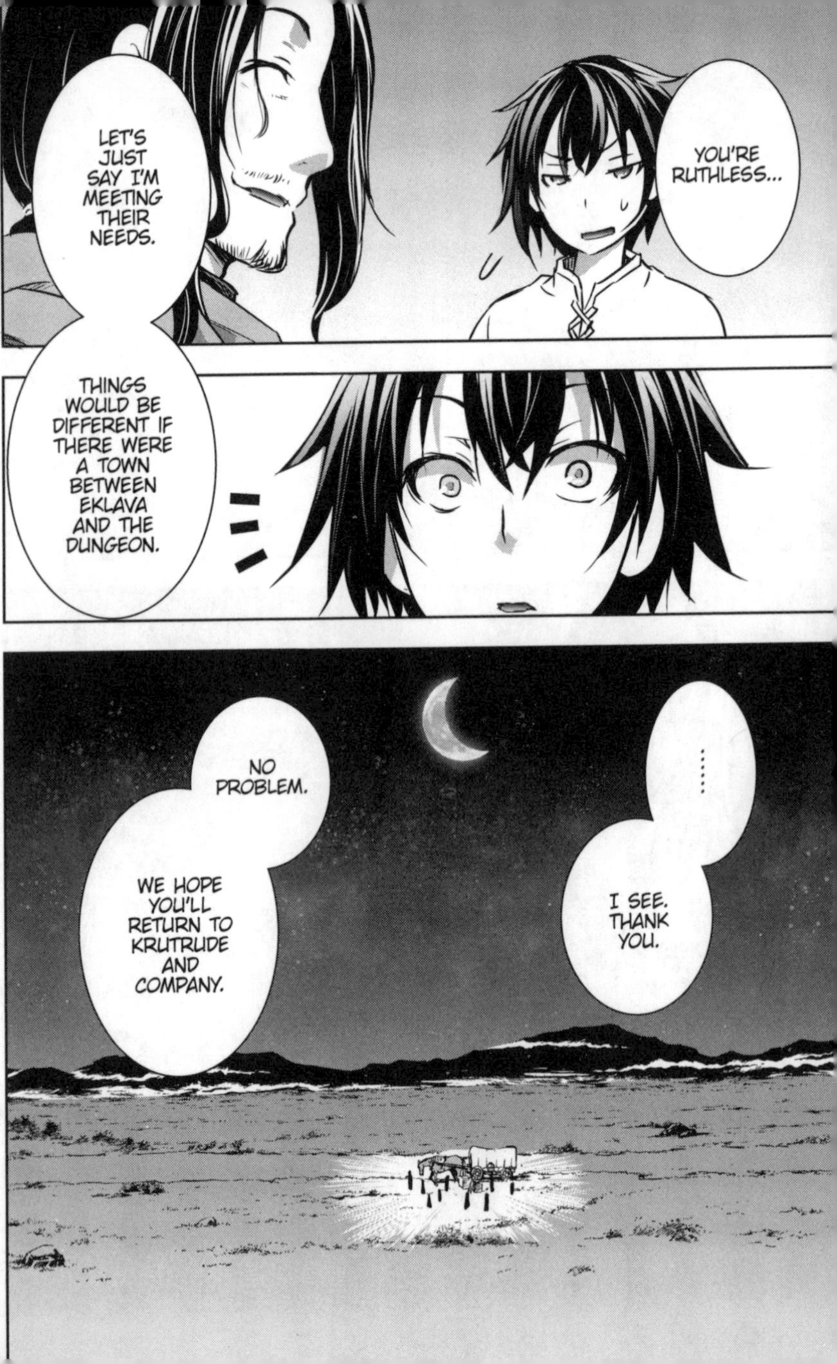
YOU'RE RUTHLESS...
LET'S JUST SAY I'M MEETING THEIR NEEDS.
THINGS WOULD BE DIFFERENT IF THERE WERE A TOWN BETWEEN EKLAVA AND THE DUNGEON.
......
I SEE. THANK YOU.
NO PROBLEM.
WE HOPE YOU'LL RETURN TO KRUTRUDE AND COMPANY.

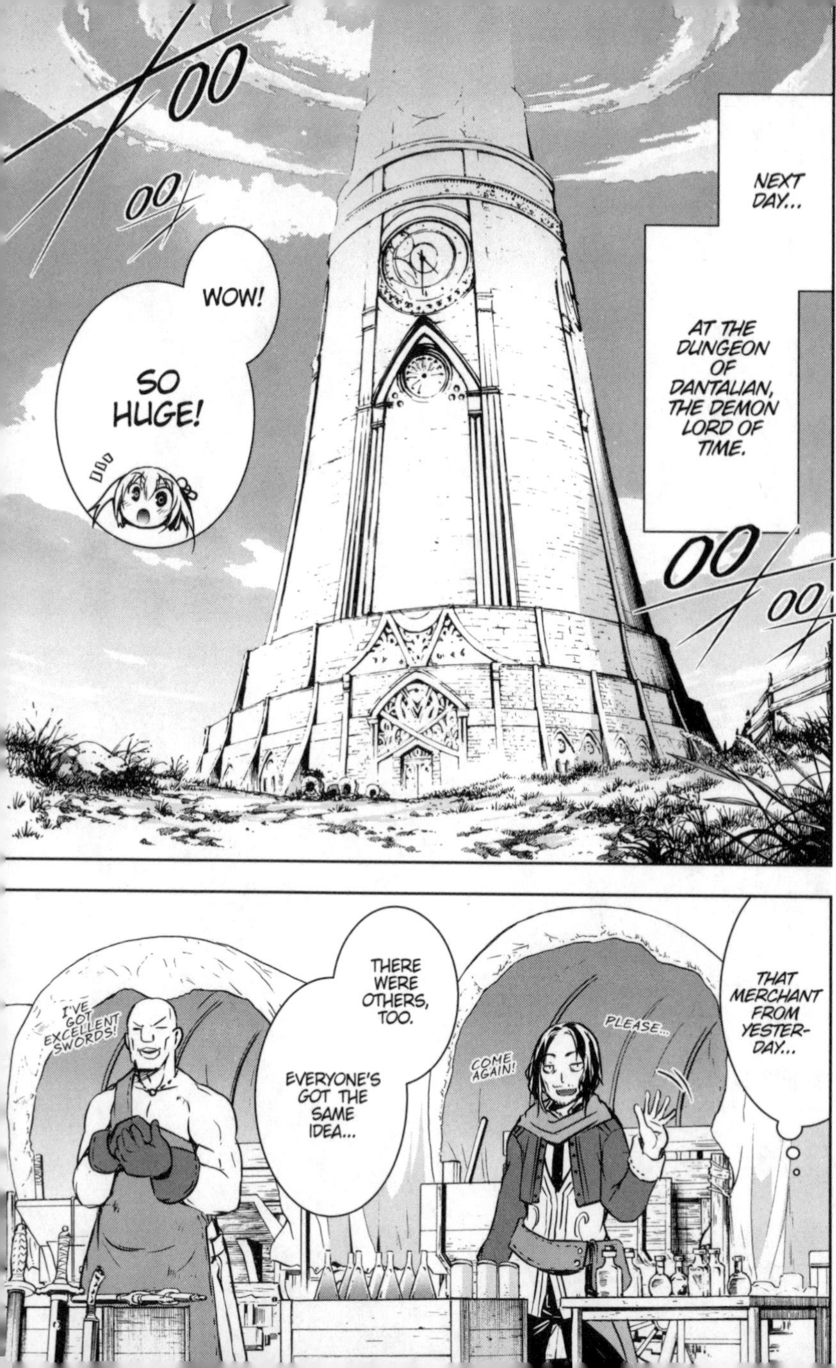
NEXT DAY...
AT THE DUNGEON OF DANTALIAN, THE DEMON LORD OF TIME.
OOOO
WOW!
SO HUGE!
OOOO
THAT MERCHANT FROM YESTER-DAY...
PLEASE...
COME AGAIN!
THERE WERE OTHERS, TOO.
EVERYONE'S GOT THE SAME IDEA...
I'VE GOT EXCELLENT SWORDS!

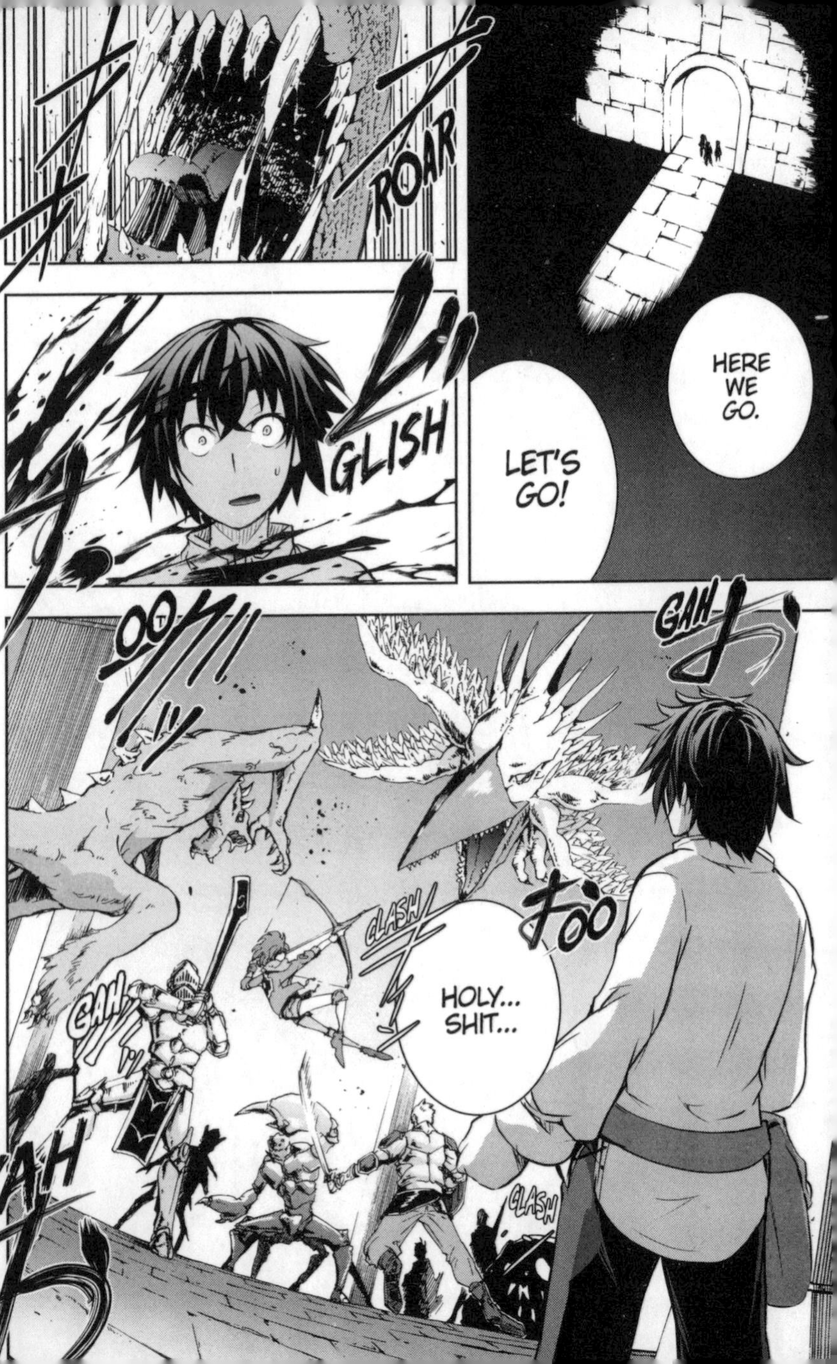
HERE WE GO.
LET'S GO!
ROAR
GLISH
GAH
FOO
HOLY... SHIT...
CLASH
GAH
CLASH
YAH

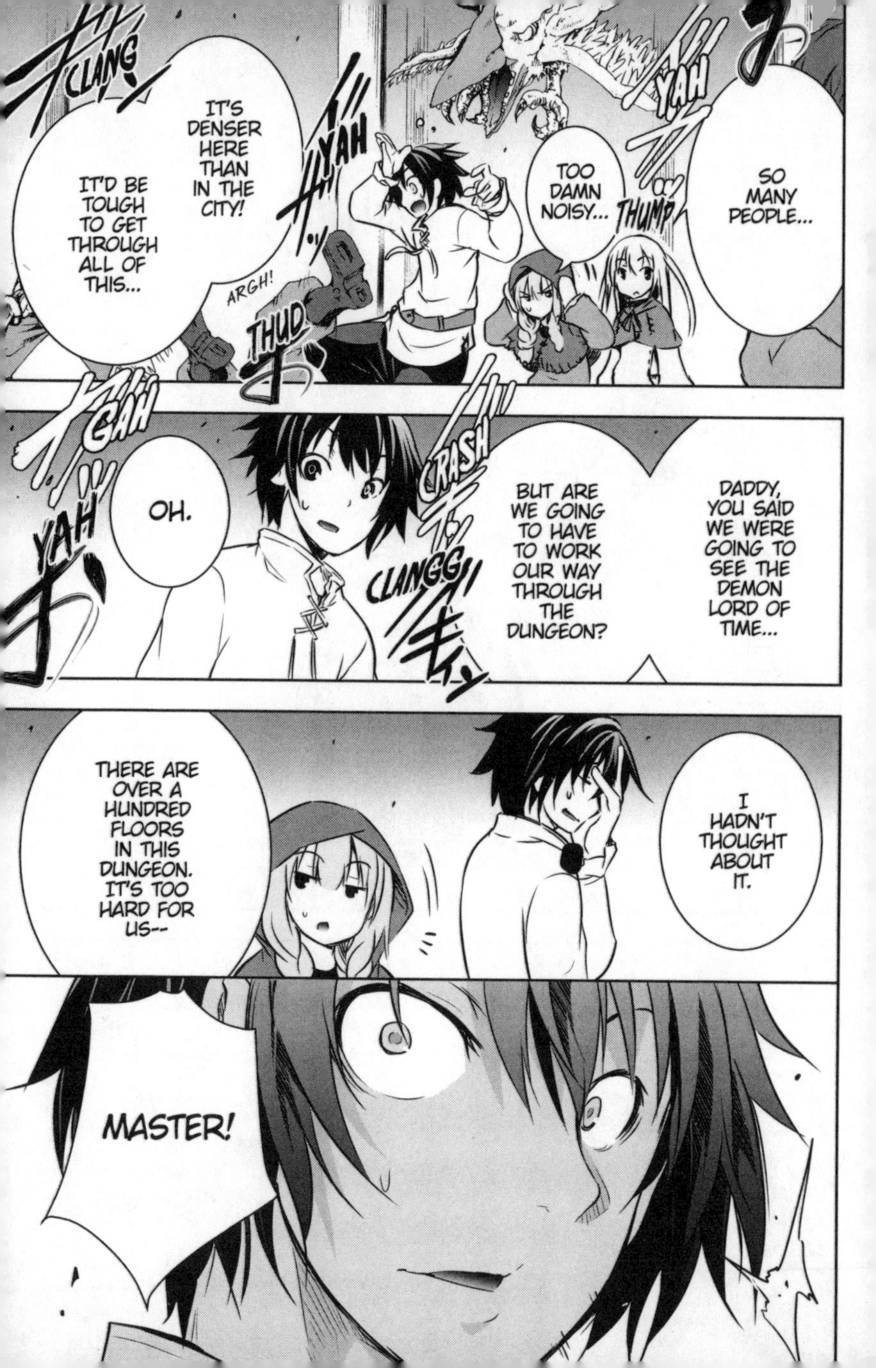
SO MANY PEOPLE...
TOO DAMN NOISY...
THUMP
YAH
IT'S DENSER HERE THAN IN THE CITY!
YAH
IT'D BE TOUGH TO GET THROUGH ALL OF THIS...
ARGH!
THUD
CLANG
DADDY, YOU SAID WE WERE GOING TO SEE THE DEMON LORD OF TIME...
BUT ARE WE GOING TO HAVE TO WORK OUR WAY THROUGH THE DUNGEON?
CRASH
CLANGG
OH.
GAH
YAH
I HADN'T THOUGHT ABOUT IT.
THERE ARE OVER A HUNDRED FLOORS IN THIS DUNGEON. IT'S TOO HARD FOR US--
MASTER!

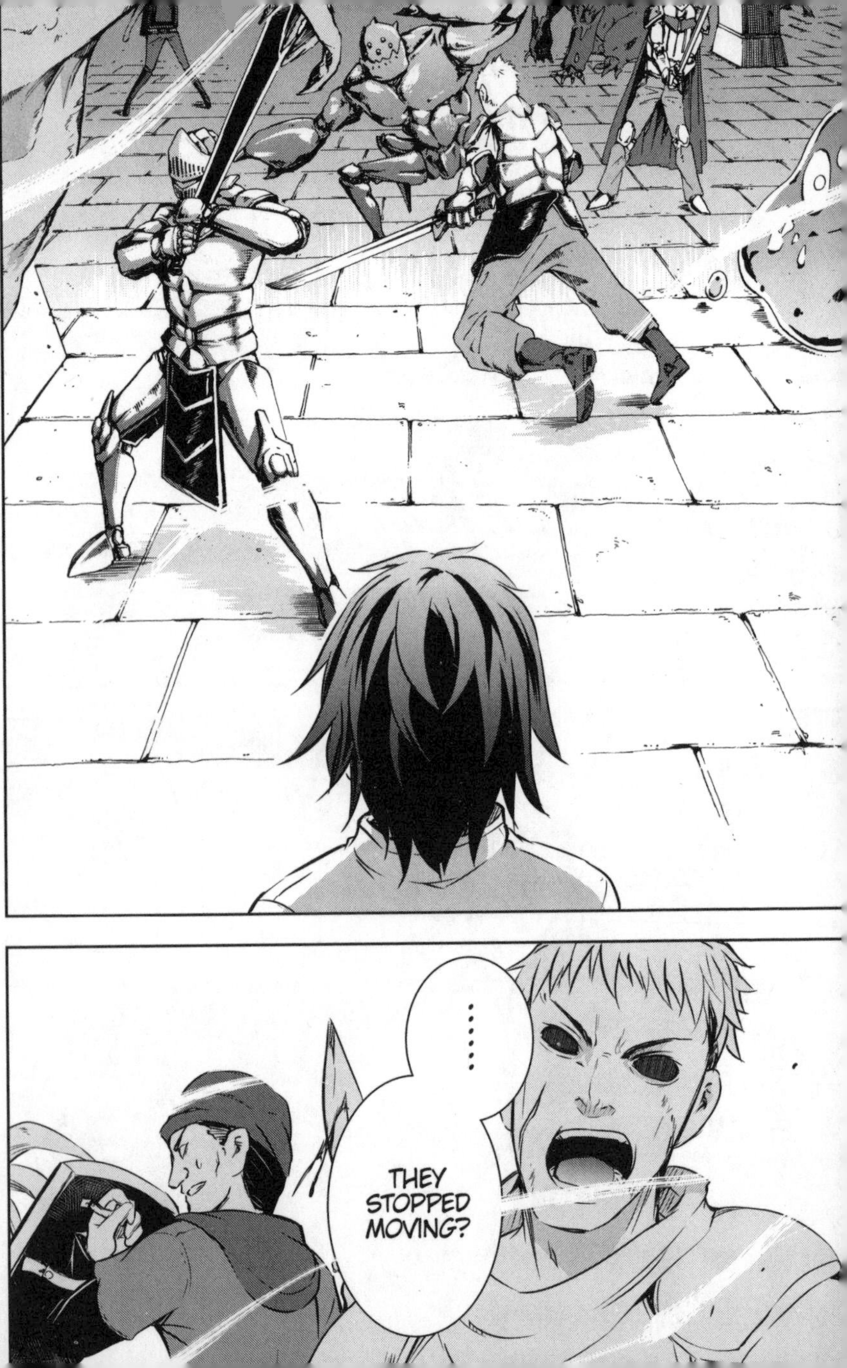
......
THEY STOPPED MOVING?

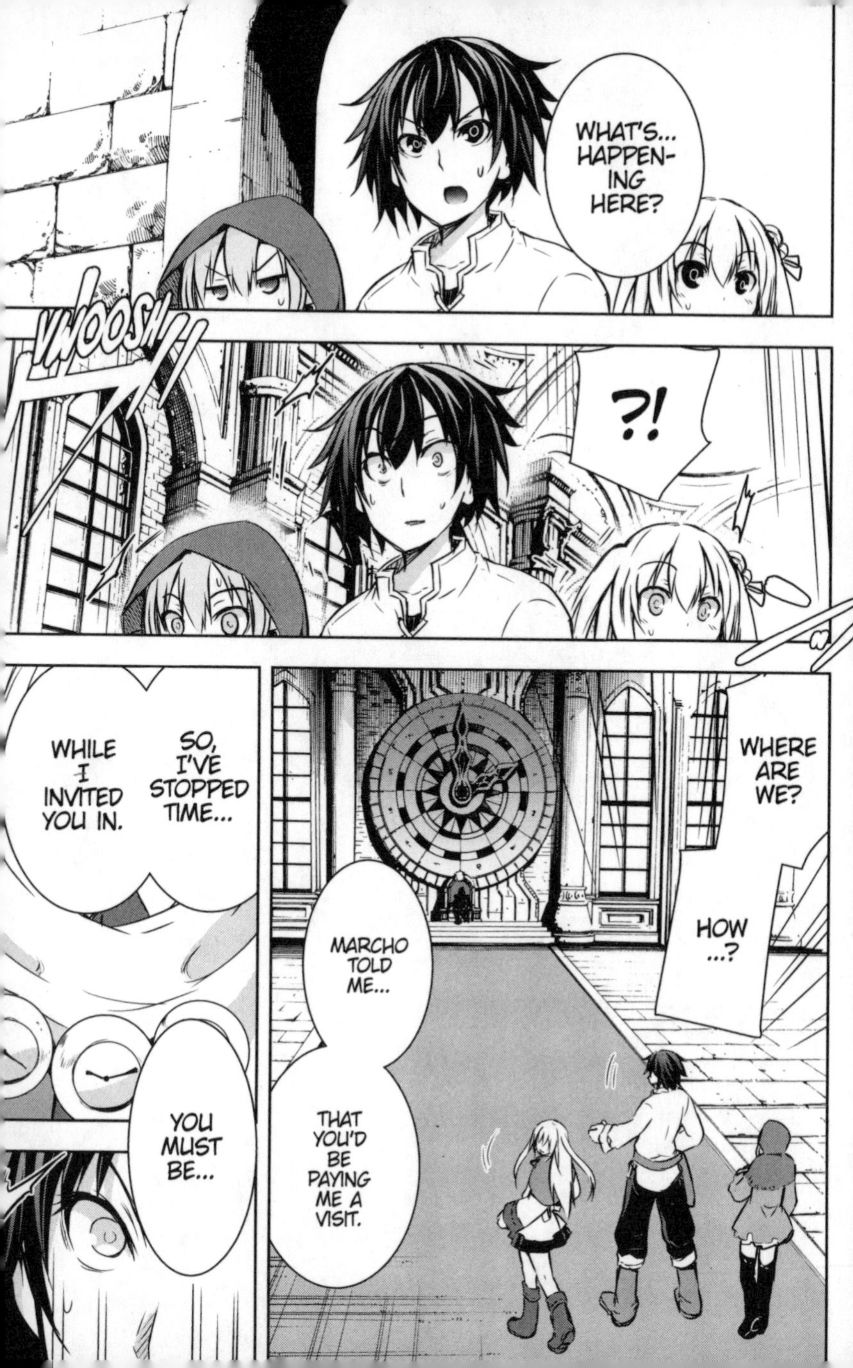
WHAT'S... HAPPEN-ING HERE?
VWOOSH
?!
WHERE ARE WE?
HOW ...?
MARCHO TOLD ME...
THAT YOU'D BE PAYING ME A VISIT.
SO, I'VE STOPPED TIME...
WHILE I INVITED YOU IN.
YOU MUST BE...

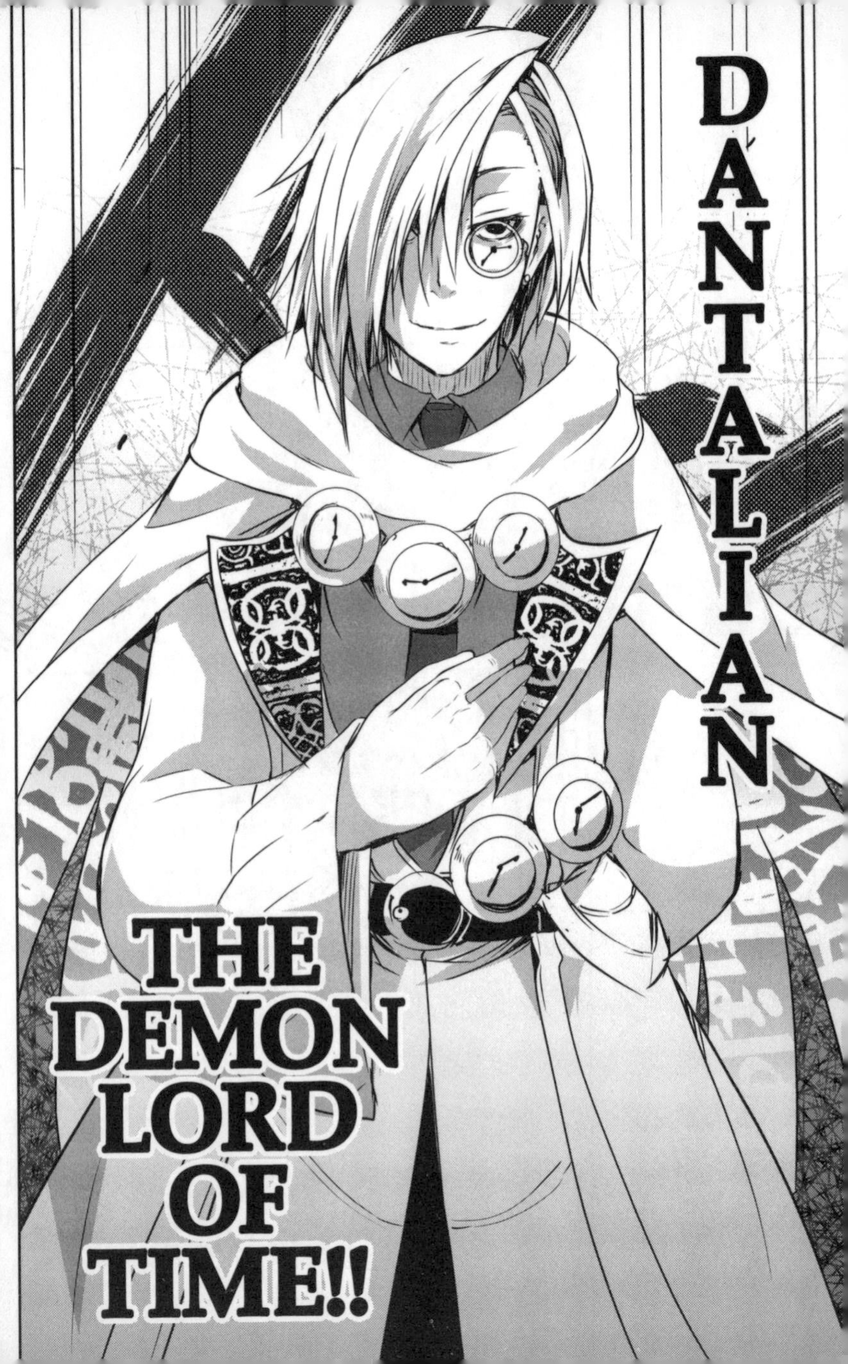
DANTALIAN
THE DEMON LORD OF TIME!!

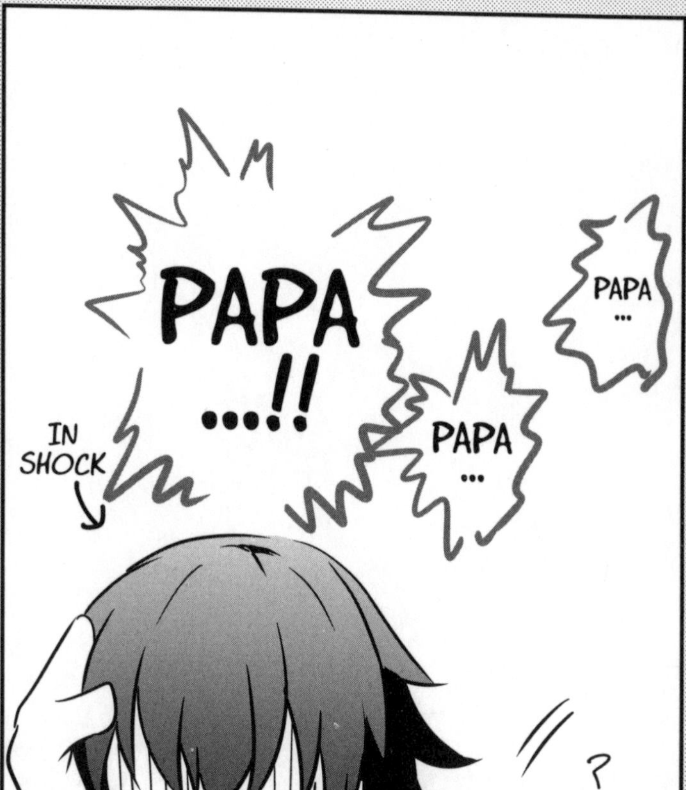
PAPA ...
PAPA ....!!
PAPA ...
IN SHOCK
?
DO I LOOK THAT OLD? OR DO THEY LOOK THAT YOUNG?

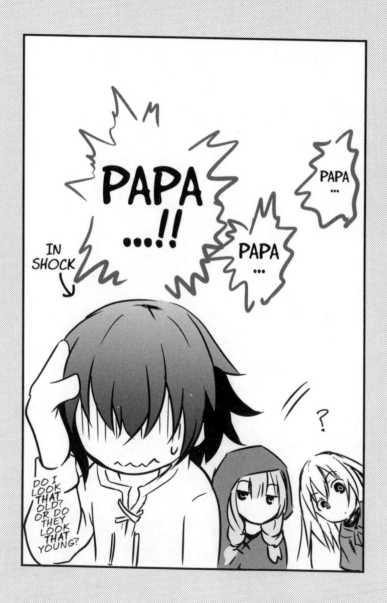

DUNGEON BUILDER:
THE DEMON KING'S LABYRINTH IS A MODERN CITY!

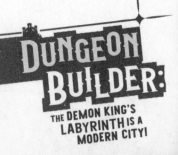

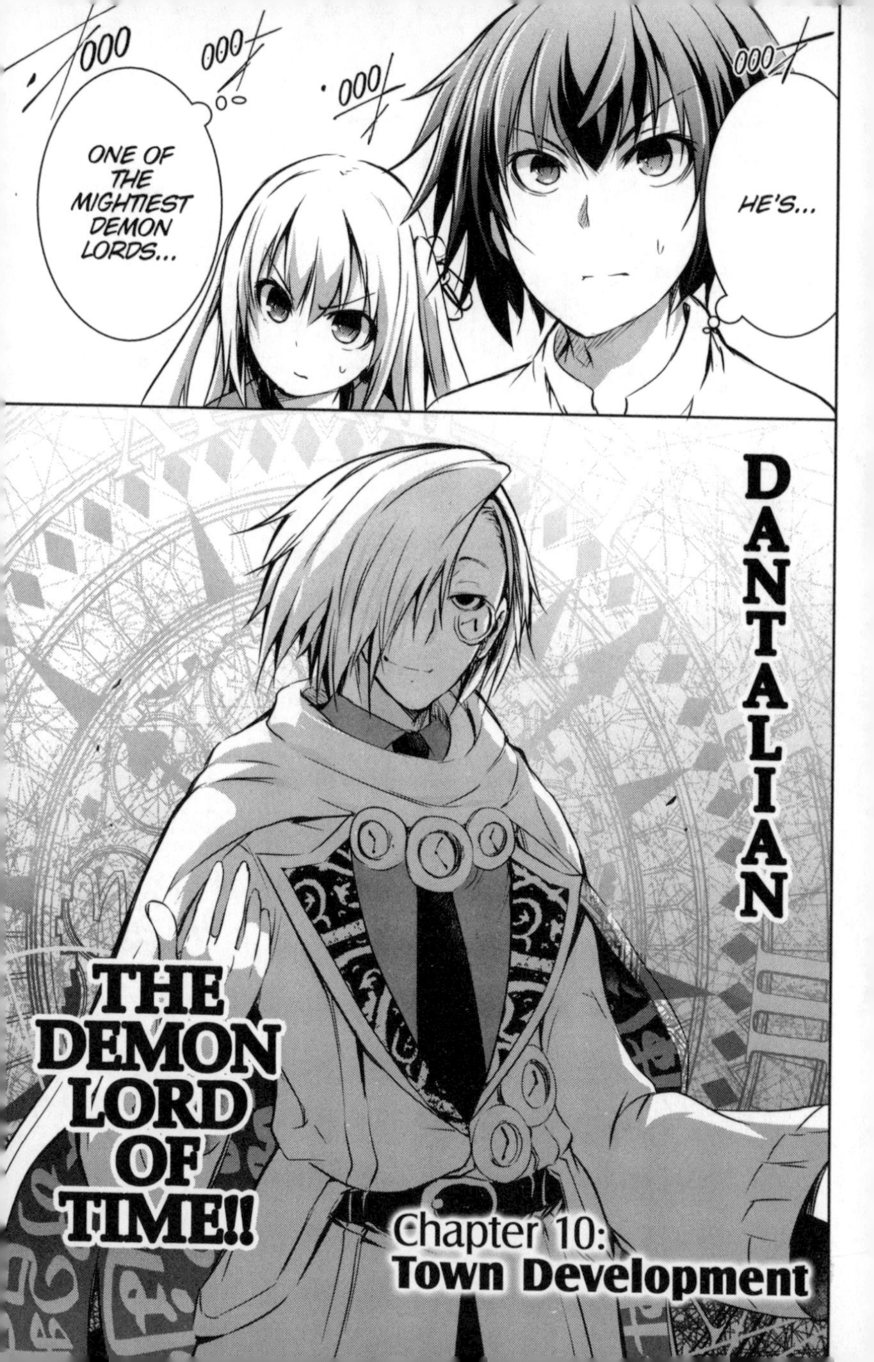
HE'S...
ONE OF THE MIGHTIEST DEMON LORDS...
DANTALIAN
THE DEMON LORD OF TIME!!
Chapter 10:
Town Development

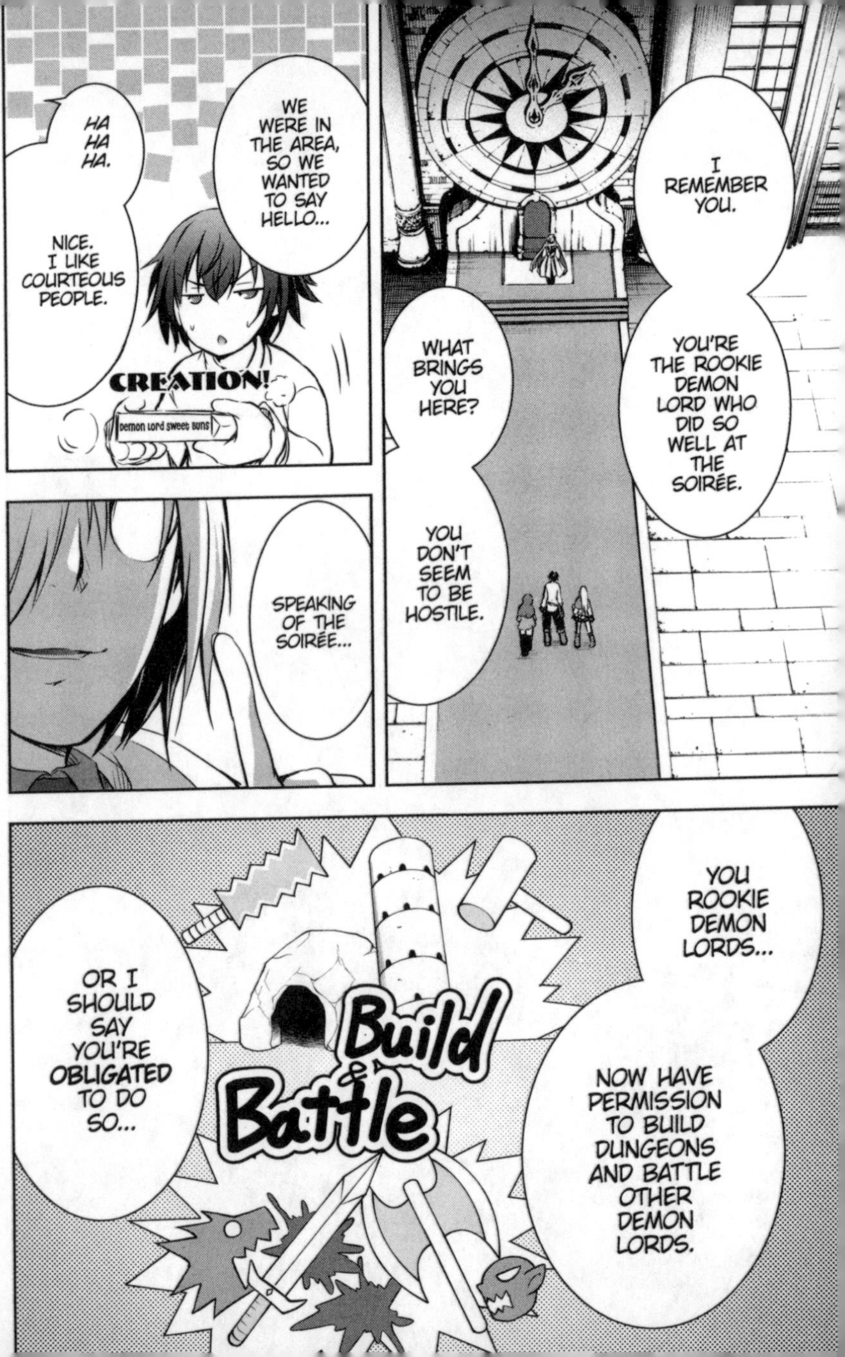
I REMEMBER YOU.
YOU'RE THE ROOKIE DEMON LORD WHO DID SO WELL AT THE SOIRÉE.
WHAT BRINGS YOU HERE?
YOU DON'T SEEM TO BE HOSTILE.
WE WERE IN THE AREA, SO WE WANTED TO SAY HELLO...
HA HA HA.
NICE. I LIKE COURTEOUS PEOPLE.
CREATION!
Demon Lord Sweet Buns
SPEAKING OF THE SOIRÉE...
YOU ROOKIE DEMON LORDS...
NOW HAVE PERMISSION TO BUILD DUNGEONS AND BATTLE OTHER DEMON LORDS.
Build & Battle
OR I SHOULD SAY YOU'RE OBLIGATED TO DO SO...

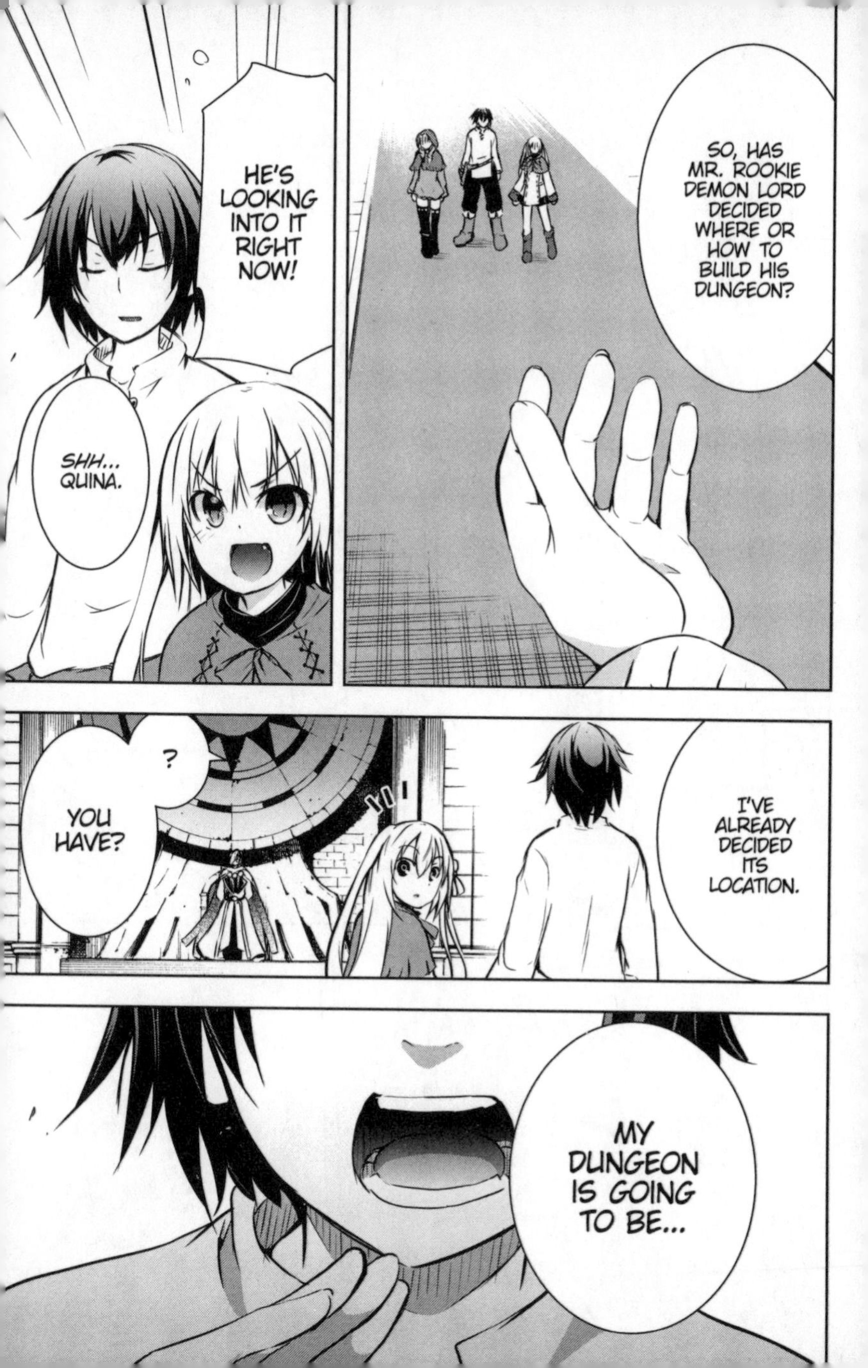
SO, HAS MR. ROOKIE DEMON LORD DECIDED WHERE OR HOW TO BUILD HIS DUNGEON?
HE'S LOOKING INTO IT RIGHT NOW!
SHH... QUINA.
I'VE ALREADY DECIDED ITS LOCATION.
?
YOU HAVE?
MY DUNGEON IS GOING TO BE...

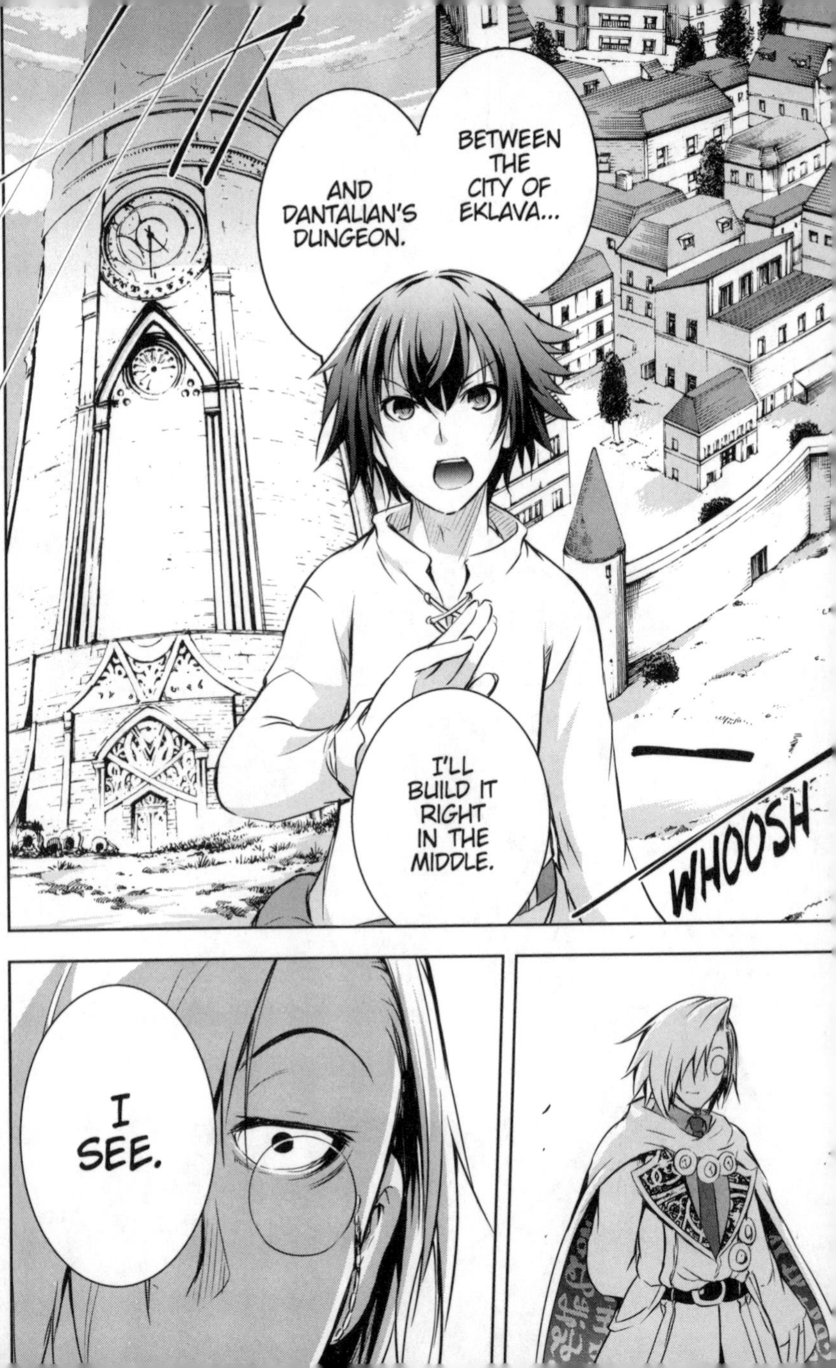
BETWEEN THE CITY OF EKLAVA...
AND DANTALIAN'S DUNGEON.
I'LL BUILD IT RIGHT IN THE MIDDLE.
WHOOSH
I SEE.

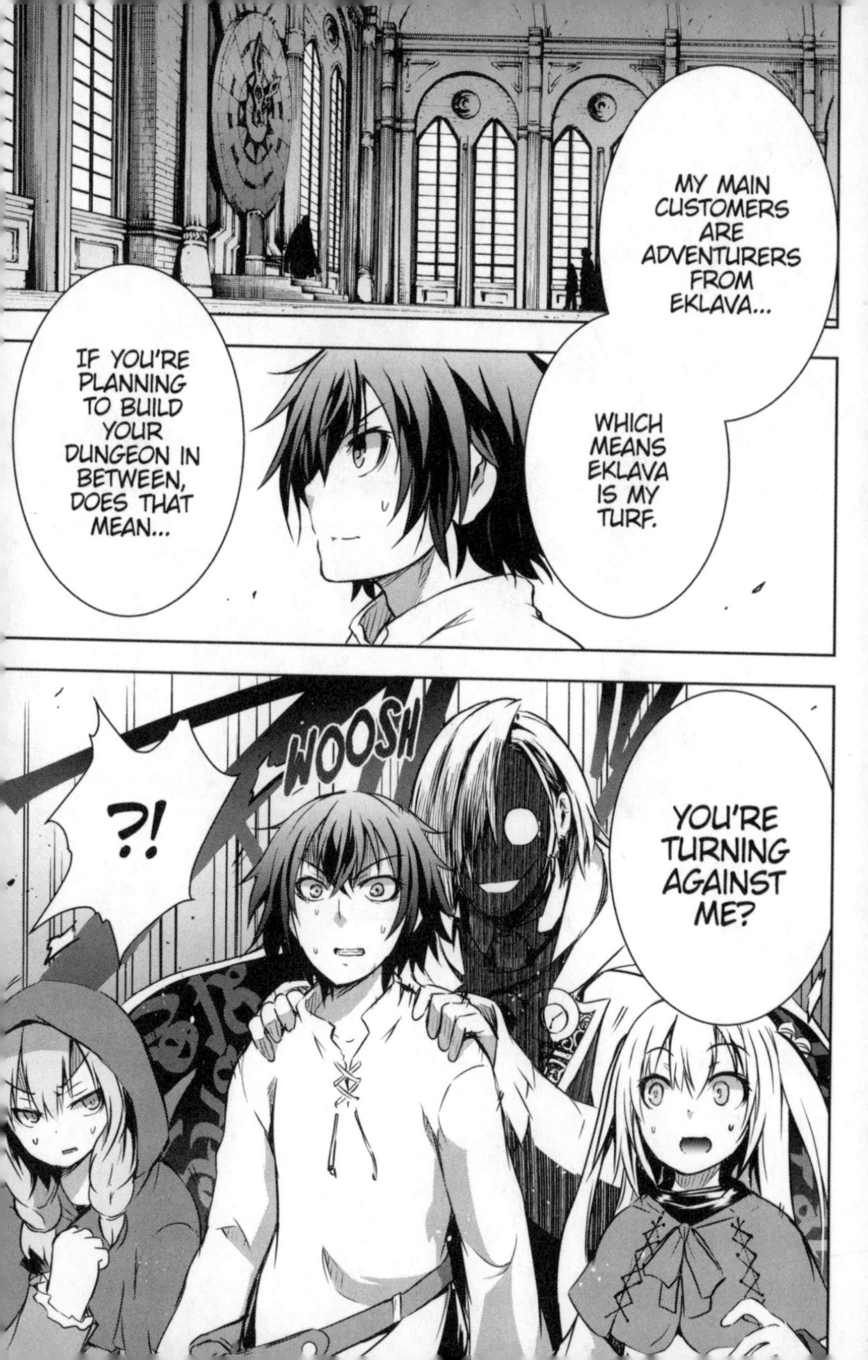
MY MAIN CUSTOMERS ARE ADVENTURERS FROM EKLAVA...
WHICH MEANS EKLAVA IS MY TURF.
IF YOU'RE PLANNING TO BUILD YOUR DUNGEON IN BETWEEN, DOES THAT MEAN...
YOU'RE TURNING AGAINST ME?
WOOSH
?!

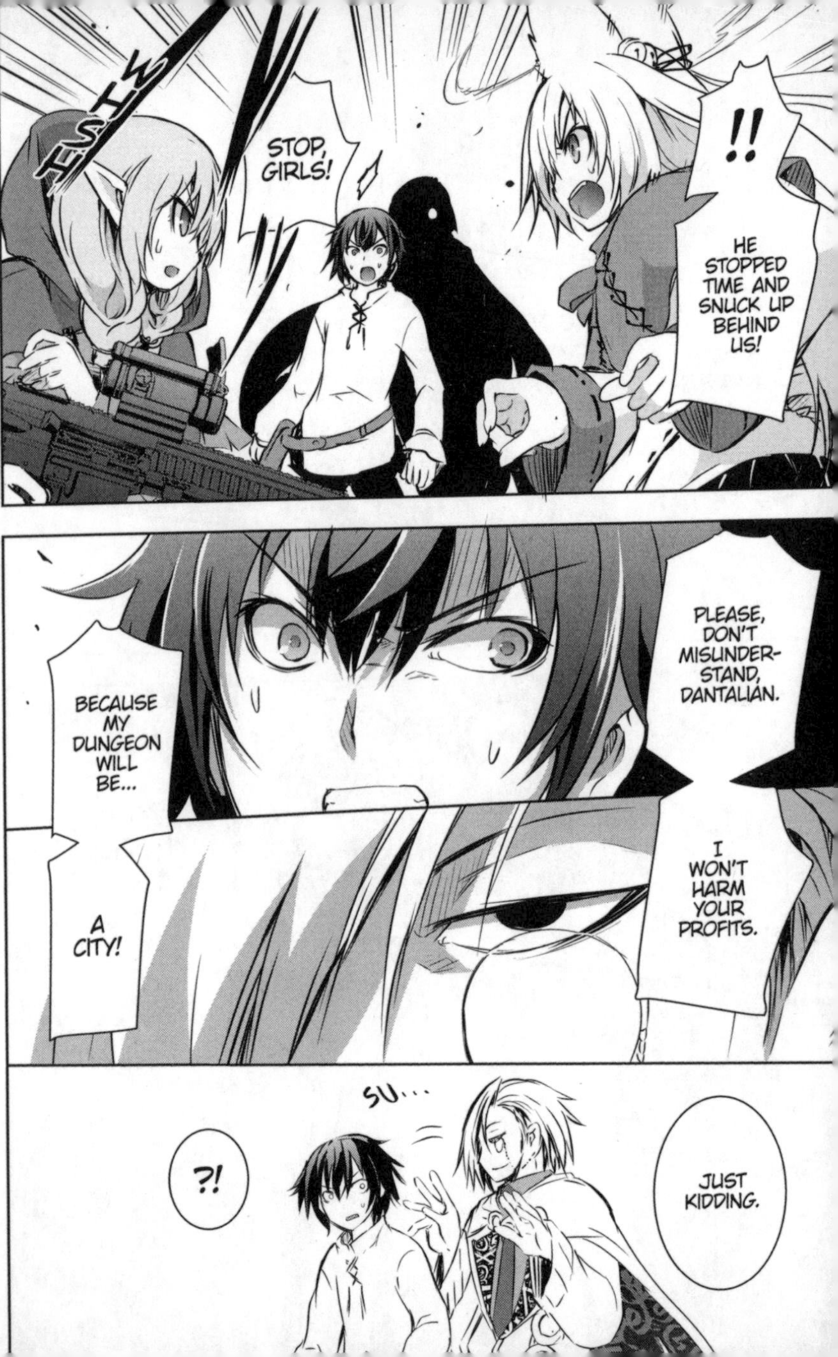
!!
HE STOPPED TIME AND SNUCK UP BEHIND US!
STOP, GIRLS!
WHSH
PLEASE, DON'T MISUNDER-STAND, DANTALIAN.
BECAUSE MY DUNGEON WILL BE...
I WON'T HARM YOUR PROFITS.
A CITY!
JUST KIDDING.
SU...
?!

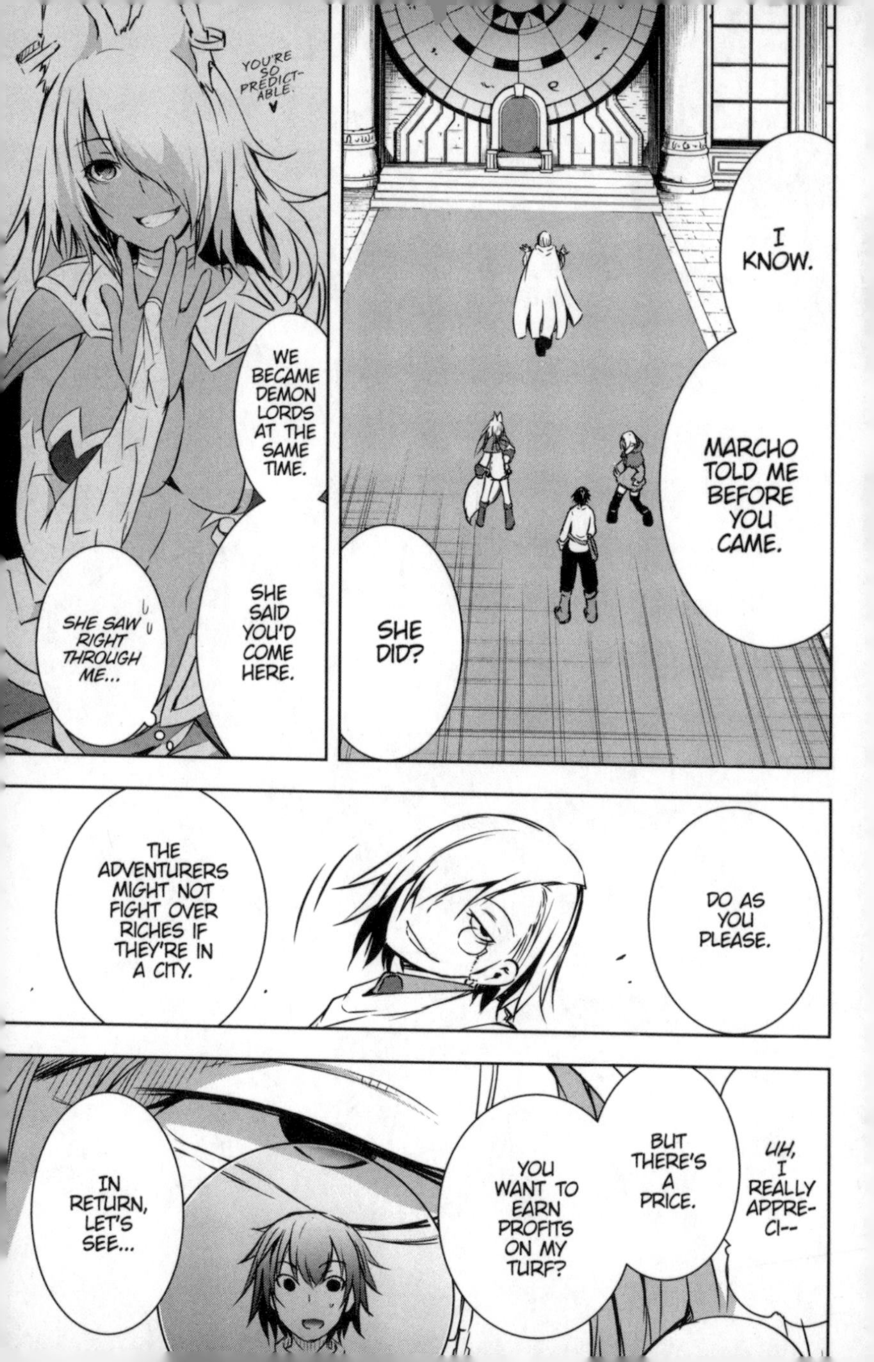
I KNOW.
MARCHO TOLD ME BEFORE YOU CAME.
SHE DID?
YOU'RE SO PREDICT-ABLE.
WE BECAME DEMON LORDS AT THE SAME TIME.
SHE SAID YOU'D COME HERE.
SHE SAW RIGHT THROUGH ME...
DO AS YOU PLEASE.
THE ADVENTURERS MIGHT NOT FIGHT OVER RICHES IF THEY'RE IN A CITY.
UH, I REALLY APPRE-CI--
BUT THERE'S A PRICE.
YOU WANT TO EARN PROFITS ON MY TURF?
IN RETURN, LET'S SEE...

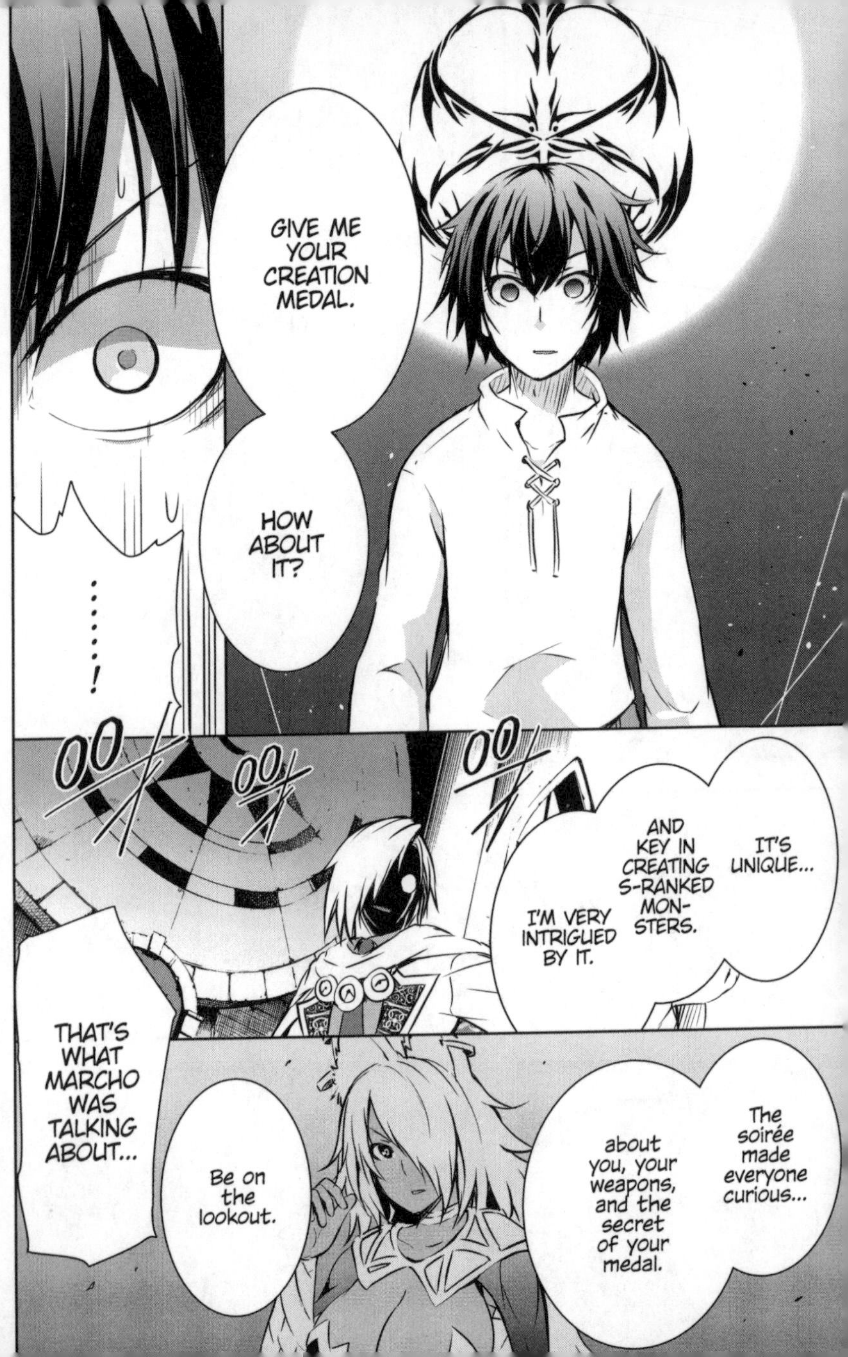
GIVE ME YOUR CREATION MEDAL.
HOW ABOUT IT?
......!
IT'S UNIQUE...
AND KEY IN CREATING S-RANKED MONSTERS.
I'M VERY INTRIGUED BY IT.
The soirée made everyone curious...
about you, your weapons, and the secret of your medal.
Be on the lookout.
THAT'S WHAT MARCHO WAS TALKING ABOUT...

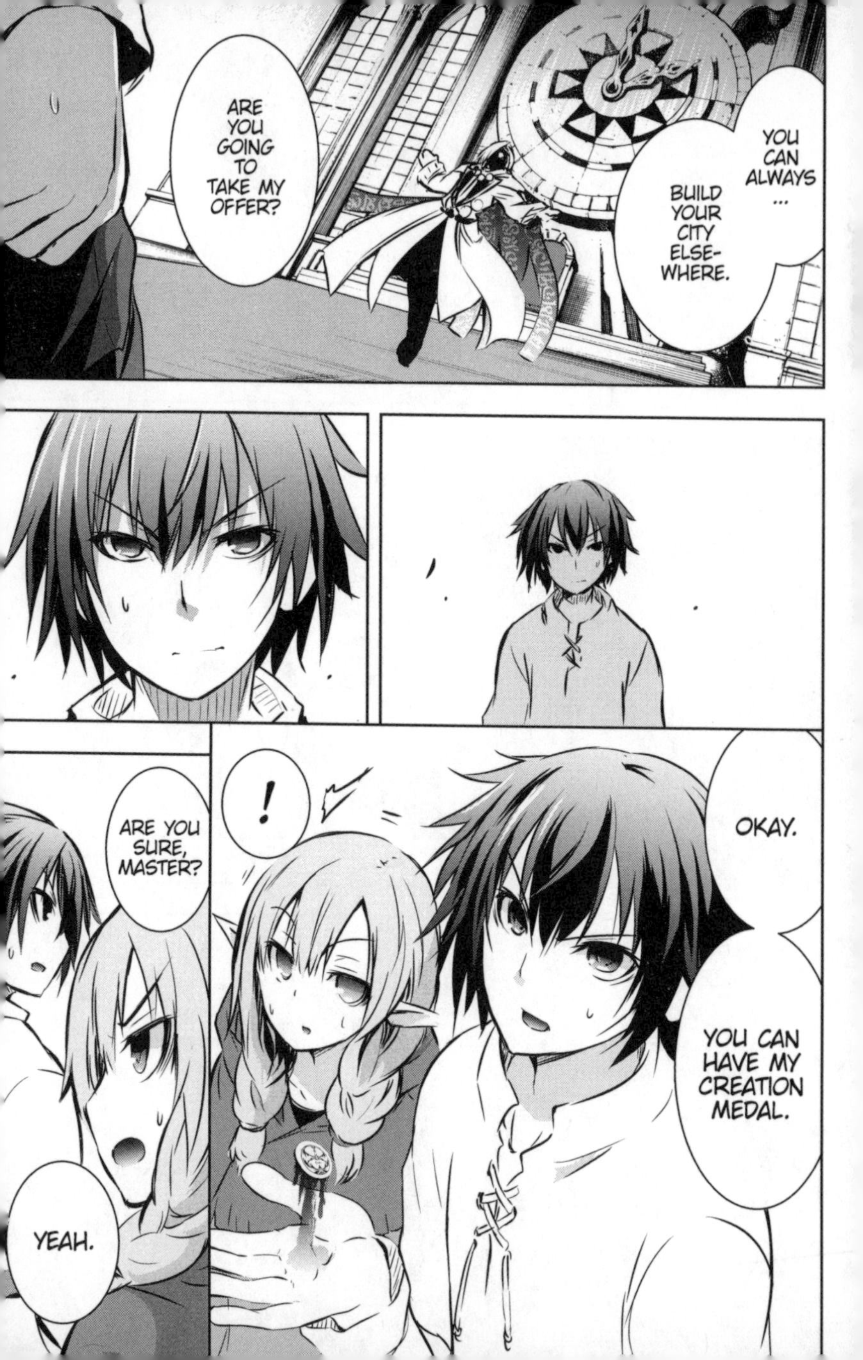
YOU CAN ALWAYS ...
BUILD YOUR CITY ELSEWHERE.
ARE YOU GOING TO TAKE MY OFFER?
OKAY.
YOU CAN HAVE MY CREATION MEDAL.
!
ARE YOU SURE, MASTER?
YEAH.

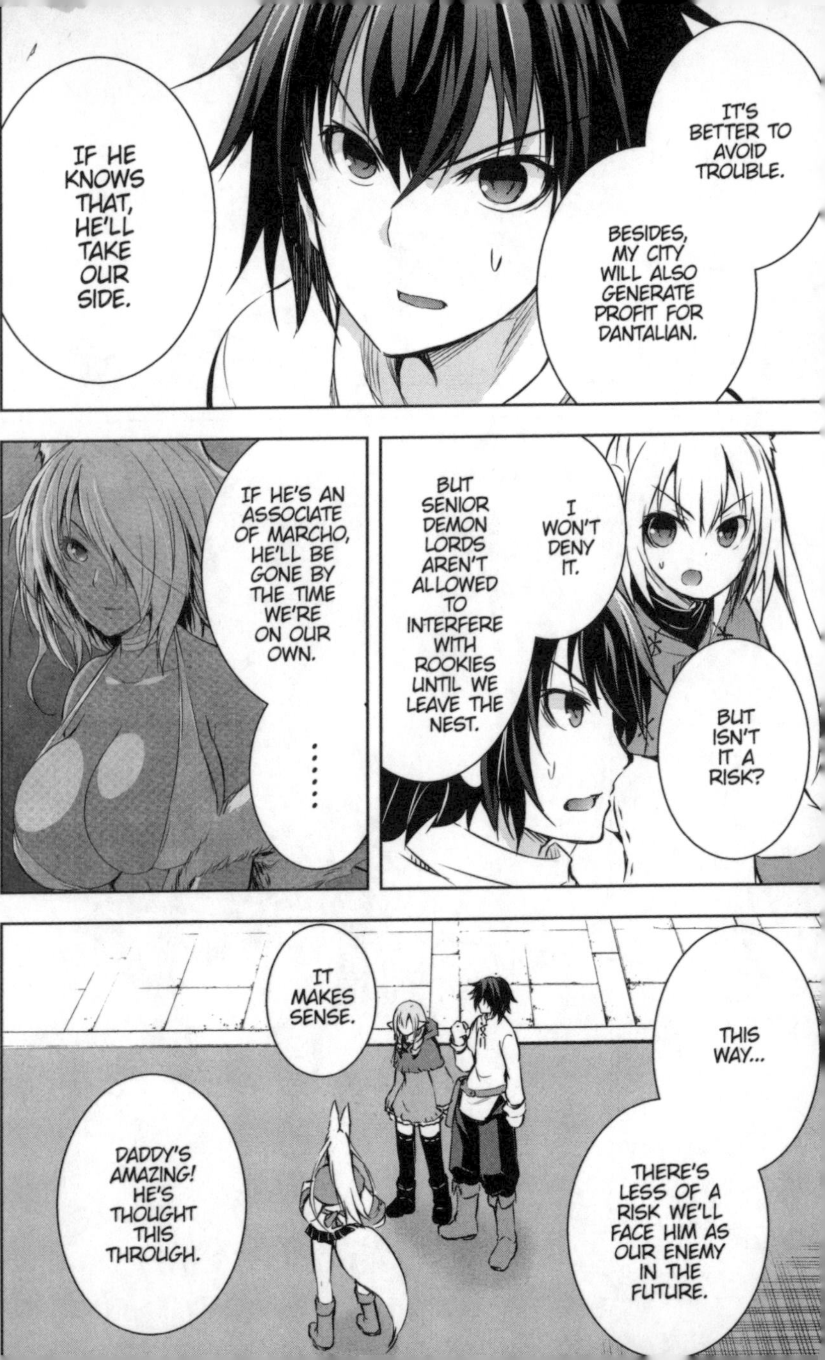
IT'S BETTER TO AVOID TROUBLE.
BESIDES, MY CITY WILL ALSO GENERATE PROFIT FOR DANTALIAN.
IF HE KNOWS THAT, HE'LL TAKE OUR SIDE.
BUT ISN'T IT A RISK?
I WON'T DENY IT.
BUT SENIOR DEMON LORDS AREN'T ALLOWED TO INTERFERE WITH ROOKIES UNTIL WE LEAVE THE NEST.
IF HE'S AN ASSOCIATE OF MARCHO, HE'LL BE GONE BY THE TIME WE'RE ON OUR OWN.
......
THIS WAY...
THERE'S LESS OF A RISK WE'LL FACE HIM AS OUR ENEMY IN THE FUTURE.
IT MAKES SENSE.
DADDY'S AMAZING! HE'S THOUGHT THIS THROUGH.

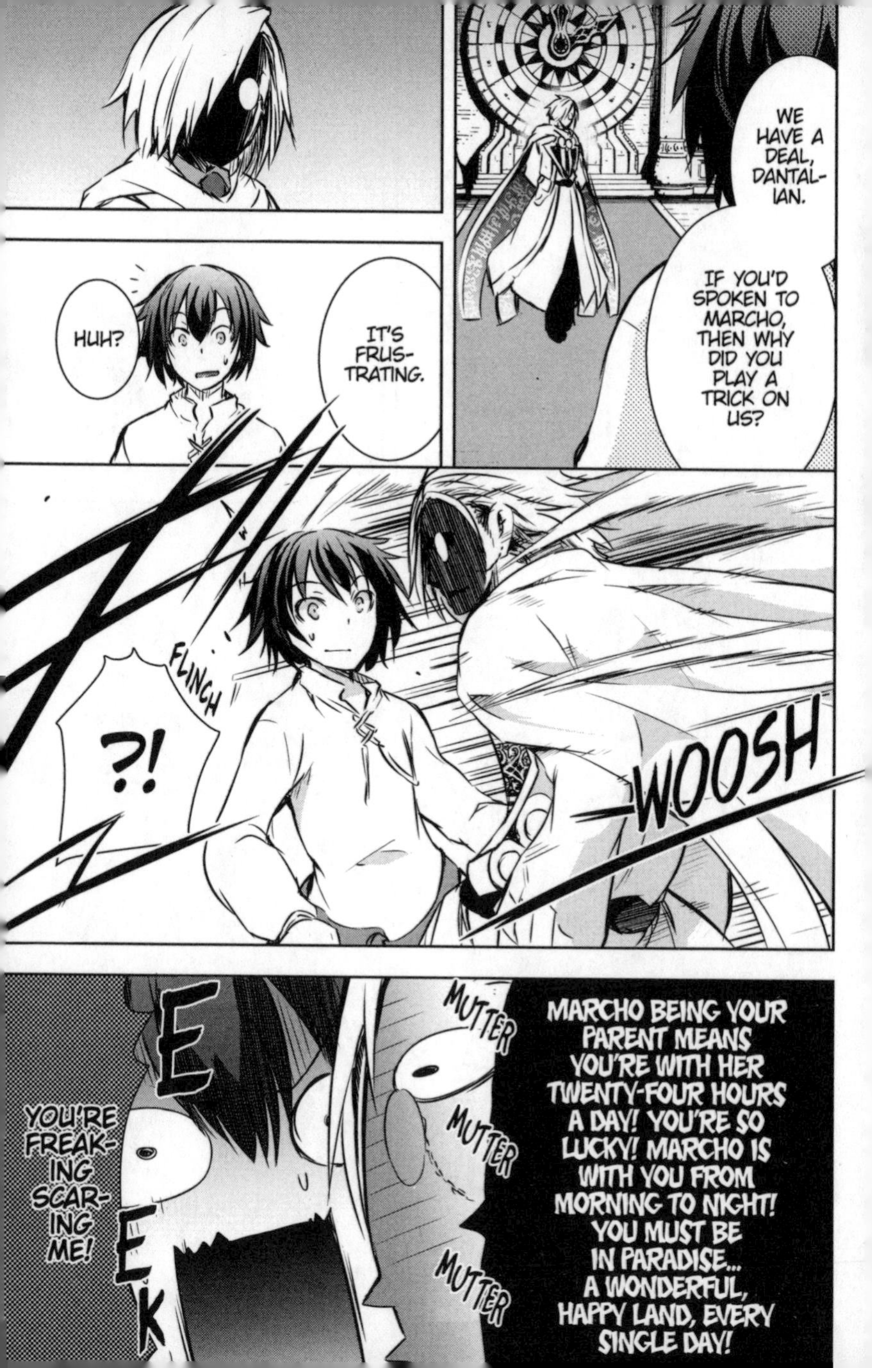
WE HAVE A DEAL, DANTALIAN.
IF YOU'D SPOKEN TO MARCHO, THEN WHY DID YOU PLAY A TRICK ON US?
IT'S FRUSTRATING.
HUH?
WOOSH
FLINCH
?!
MARCHO BEING YOUR PARENT MEANS YOU'RE WITH HER TWENTY-FOUR HOURS A DAY! YOU'RE SO LUCKY! MARCHO IS WITH YOU FROM MORNING TO NIGHT! YOU MUST BE IN PARADISE... A WONDERFUL, HAPPY LAND, EVERY SINGLE DAY!
MUTTER
MUTTER
MUTTER
EEK
YOU'RE FREAKING SCARING ME!

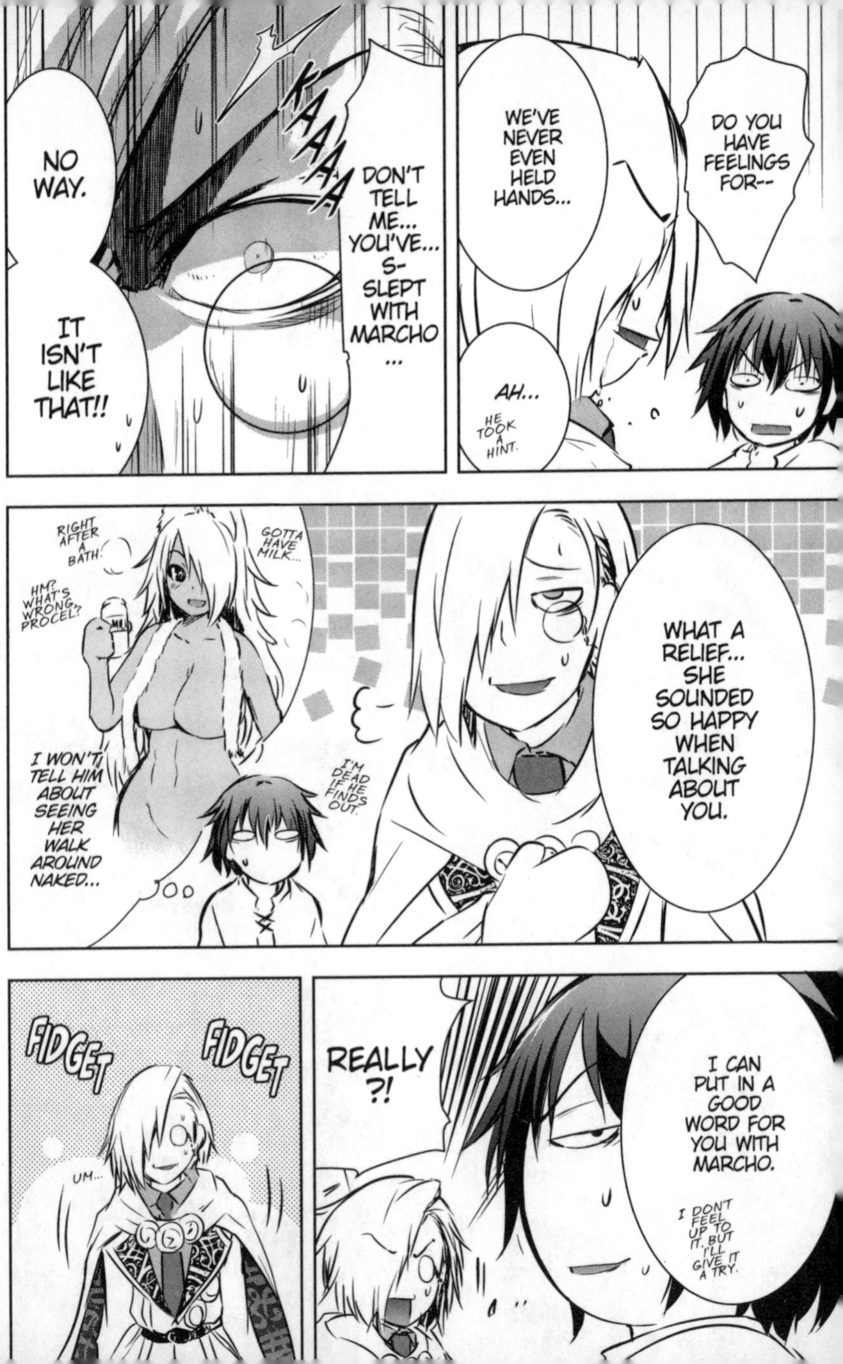
DO YOU HAVE FEELINGS FOR--
WE'VE NEVER EVEN HELD HANDS...
AH...
HE TOOK A HINT.
KAAAAA
DON'T TELL ME... YOU'VE... S-SLEPT WITH MARCHO...
NO WAY.
IT ISN'T LIKE THAT!!
WHAT A RELIEF... SHE SOUNDED SO HAPPY WHEN TALKING ABOUT YOU.
GOTTA HAVE MILK...
RIGHT AFTER A BATH!
HM? WHAT'S WRONG PROCEL?
I'M DEAD IF HE FINDS OUT.
I WON'T TELL HIM ABOUT SEEING HER WALK AROUND NAKED...
I CAN PUT IN A GOOD WORD FOR YOU WITH MARCHO.
I DON'T FEEL UP TO IT, BUT I'LL GIVE IT A TRY.
REALLY?!
FIDGET
FIDGET
UM...

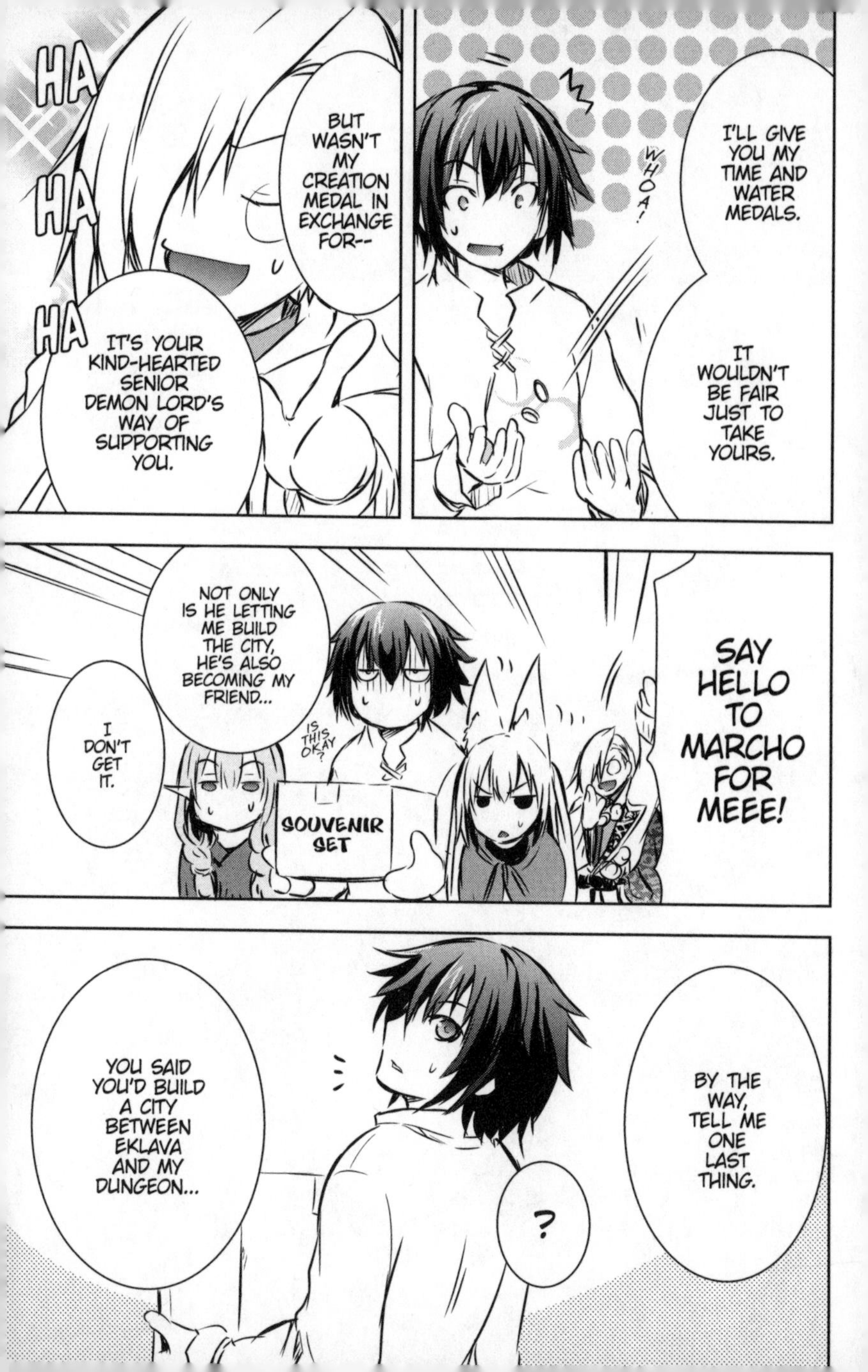
I'LL GIVE YOU MY TIME AND WATER MEDALS.
WHOA!
IT WOULDN'T BE FAIR JUST TO TAKE YOURS.
BUT WASN'T MY CREATION MEDAL IN EXCHANGE FOR--
HA HA HA
IT'S YOUR KIND-HEARTED SENIOR DEMON LORD'S WAY OF SUPPORTING YOU.
SAY HELLO TO MARCHO FOR MEEE!
NOT ONLY IS HE LETTING ME BUILD THE CITY, HE'S ALSO BECOMING MY FRIEND...
IS THIS OKAY?
SOUVENIR SET
I DON'T GET IT.
BY THE WAY, TELL ME ONE LAST THING.
?
YOU SAID YOU'D BUILD A CITY BETWEEN EKLAVA AND MY DUNGEON...

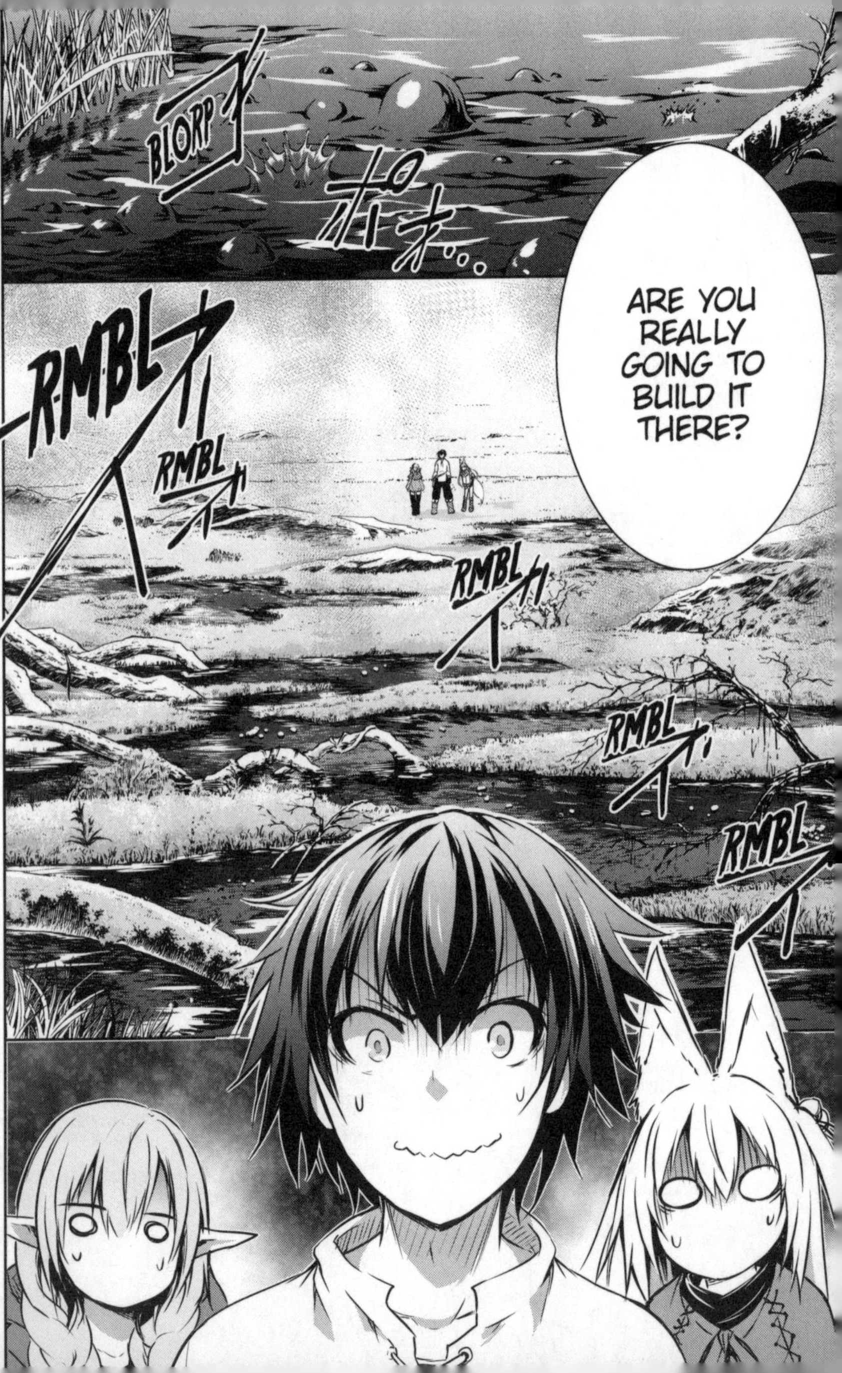
BLORP
ARE YOU REALLY GOING TO BUILD IT THERE?
R-M-B-L
RMBL
RMBL
RMBL
RMBL

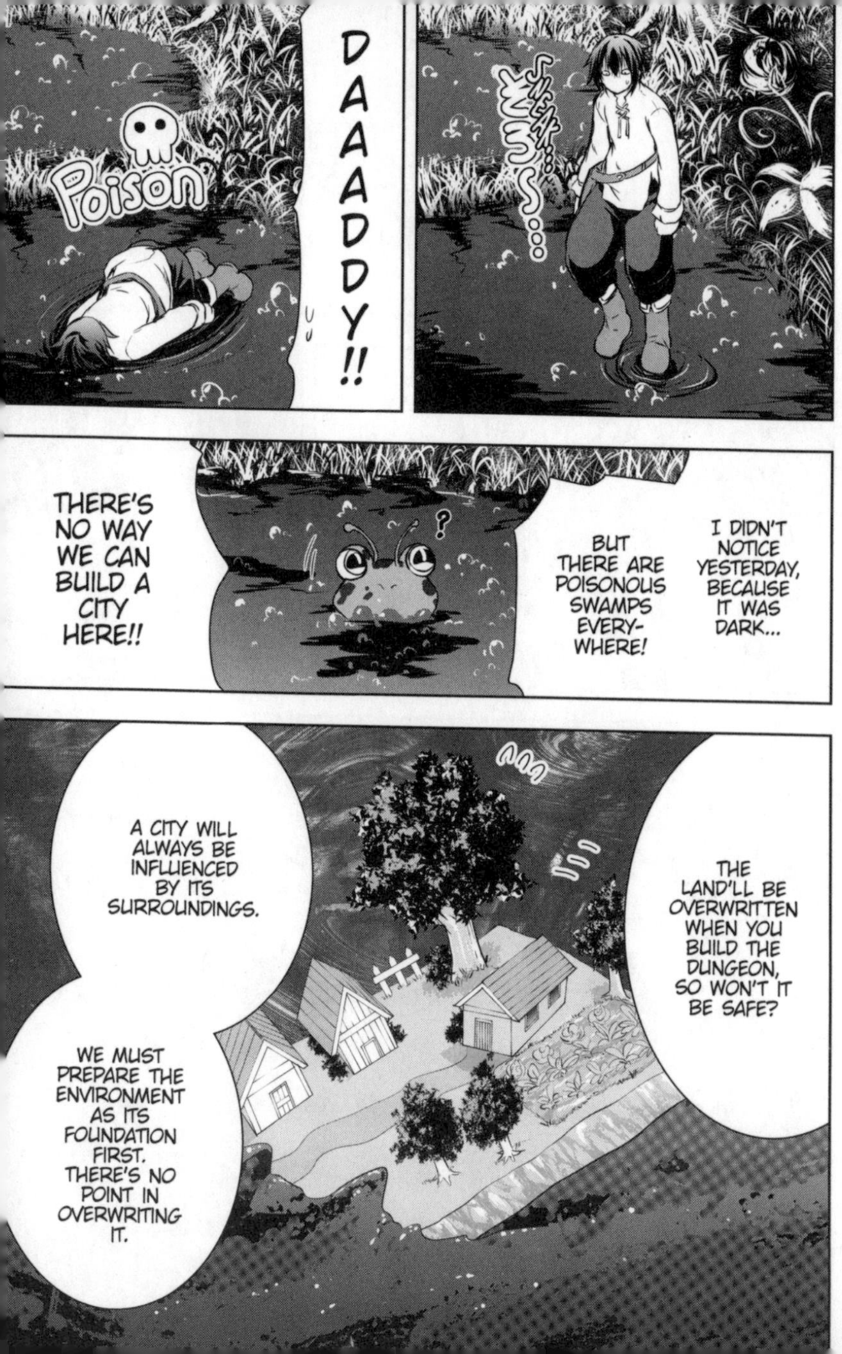
SNEAK...
DAAAADDY!!
Poison
I DIDN'T NOTICE YESTERDAY, BECAUSE IT WAS DARK...
BUT THERE ARE POISONOUS SWAMPS EVERY-WHERE!
THERE'S NO WAY WE CAN BUILD A CITY HERE!!
THE LAND'LL BE OVERWRITTEN WHEN YOU BUILD THE DUNGEON, SO WON'T IT BE SAFE?
A CITY WILL ALWAYS BE INFLUENCED BY ITS SURROUNDINGS.
WE MUST PREPARE THE ENVIRONMENT AS ITS FOUNDATION FIRST. THERE'S NO POINT IN OVERWRITING IT.

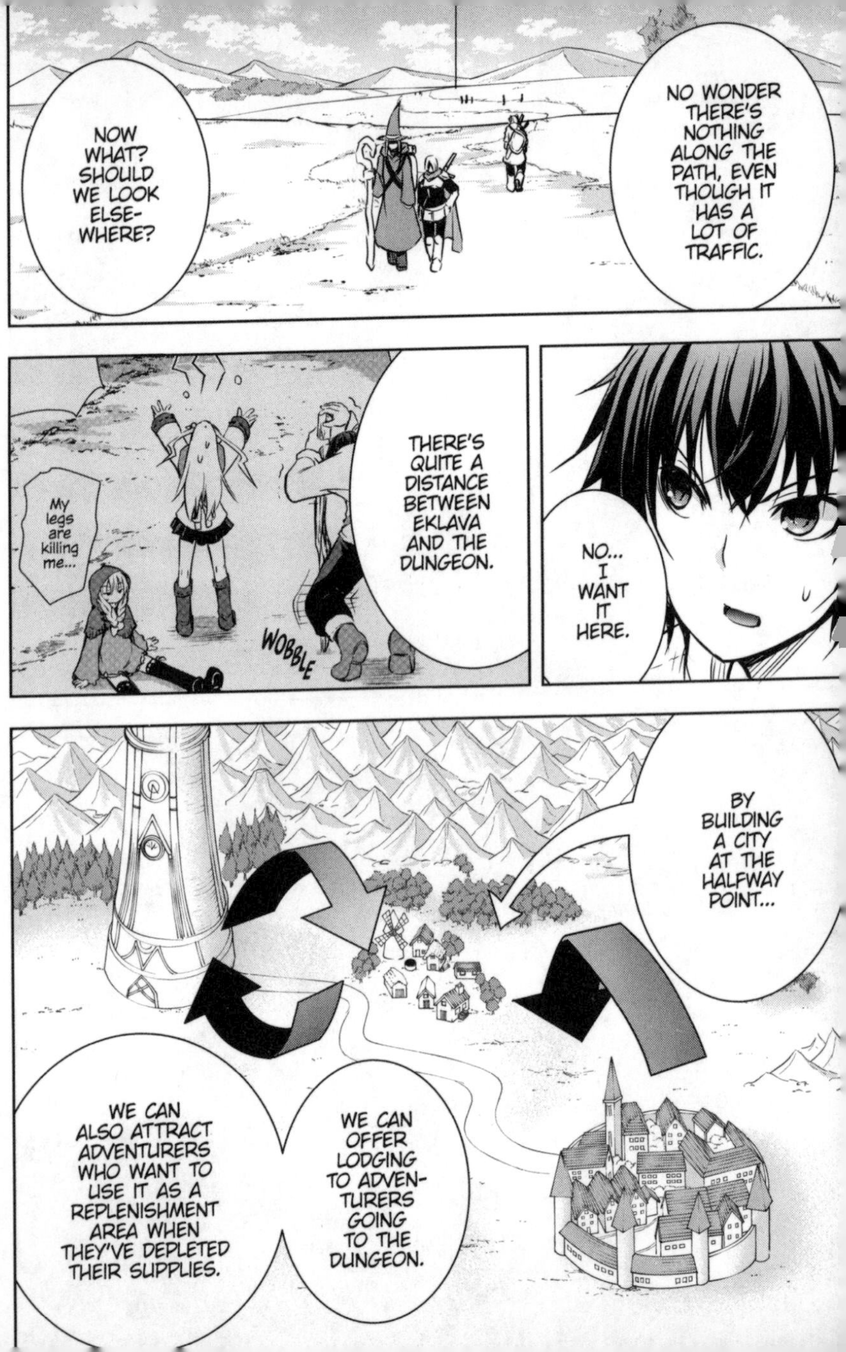
NO WONDER THERE'S NOTHING ALONG THE PATH, EVEN THOUGH IT HAS A LOT OF TRAFFIC.
NOW WHAT? SHOULD WE LOOK ELSE-WHERE?
NO... I WANT IT HERE.
THERE'S QUITE A DISTANCE BETWEEN EKLAVA AND THE DUNGEON.
My legs are killing me...
WOBBLE
BY BUILDING A CITY AT THE HALFWAY POINT...
WE CAN OFFER LODGING TO ADVEN-TURERS GOING TO THE DUNGEON.
WE CAN ALSO ATTRACT ADVENTURERS WHO WANT TO USE IT AS A REPLENISHMENT AREA WHEN THEY'VE DEPLETED THEIR SUPPLIES.

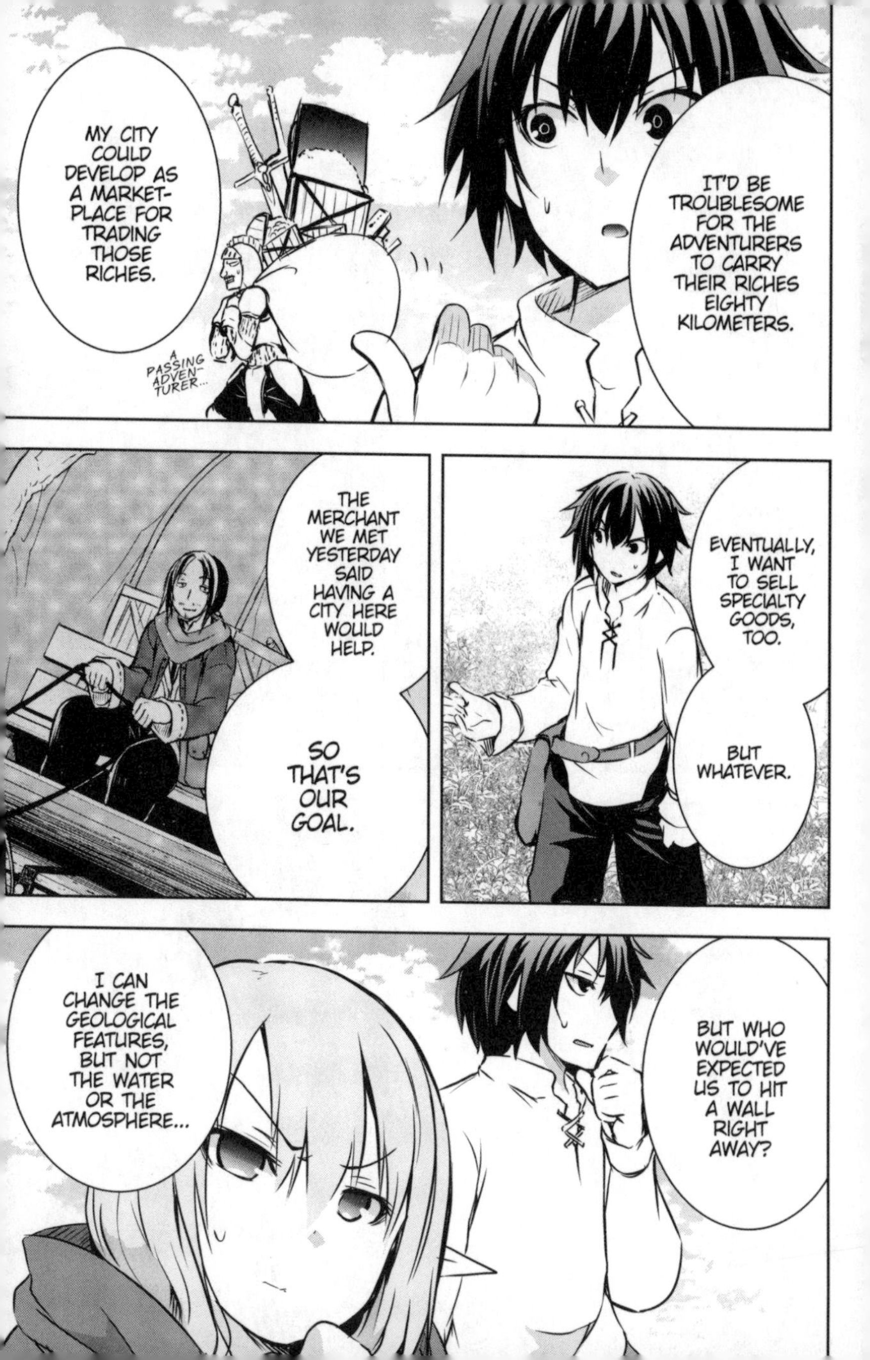
IT'D BE TROUBLESOME FOR THE ADVENTURERS TO CARRY THEIR RICHES EIGHTY KILOMETERS.
MY CITY COULD DEVELOP AS A MARKET-PLACE FOR TRADING THOSE RICHES.
A PASSING ADVENTURER...
EVENTUALLY, I WANT TO SELL SPECIALTY GOODS, TOO.
BUT WHATEVER.
THE MERCHANT WE MET YESTERDAY SAID HAVING A CITY HERE WOULD HELP.
SO THAT'S OUR GOAL.
BUT WHO WOULD'VE EXPECTED US TO HIT A WALL RIGHT AWAY?
I CAN CHANGE THE GEOLOGICAL FEATURES, BUT NOT THE WATER OR THE ATMOSPHERE...

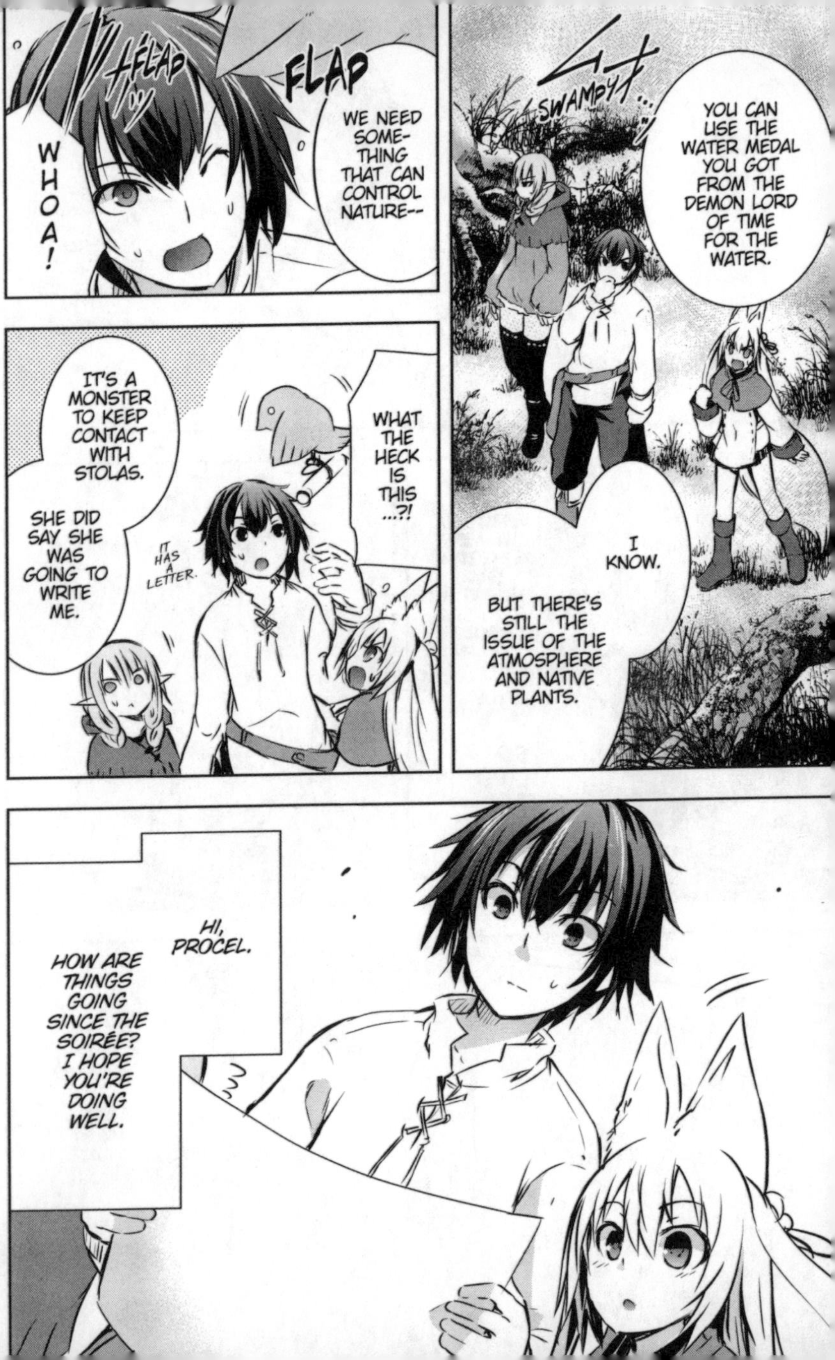
SWAMPY...
YOU CAN USE THE WATER MEDAL YOU GOT FROM THE DEMON LORD OF TIME FOR THE WATER.
I KNOW.
BUT THERE'S STILL THE ISSUE OF THE ATMOSPHERE AND NATIVE PLANTS.
FLAP
WE NEED SOMETHING THAT CAN CONTROL NATURE--
FLAP
WHOA!
WHAT THE HECK IS THIS...?!
IT HAS A LETTER.
IT'S A MONSTER TO KEEP CONTACT WITH STOLAS.
SHE DID SAY SHE WAS GOING TO WRITE ME.
HI, PROCEL.
HOW ARE THINGS GOING SINCE THE SOIRÉE? I HOPE YOU'RE DOING WELL.

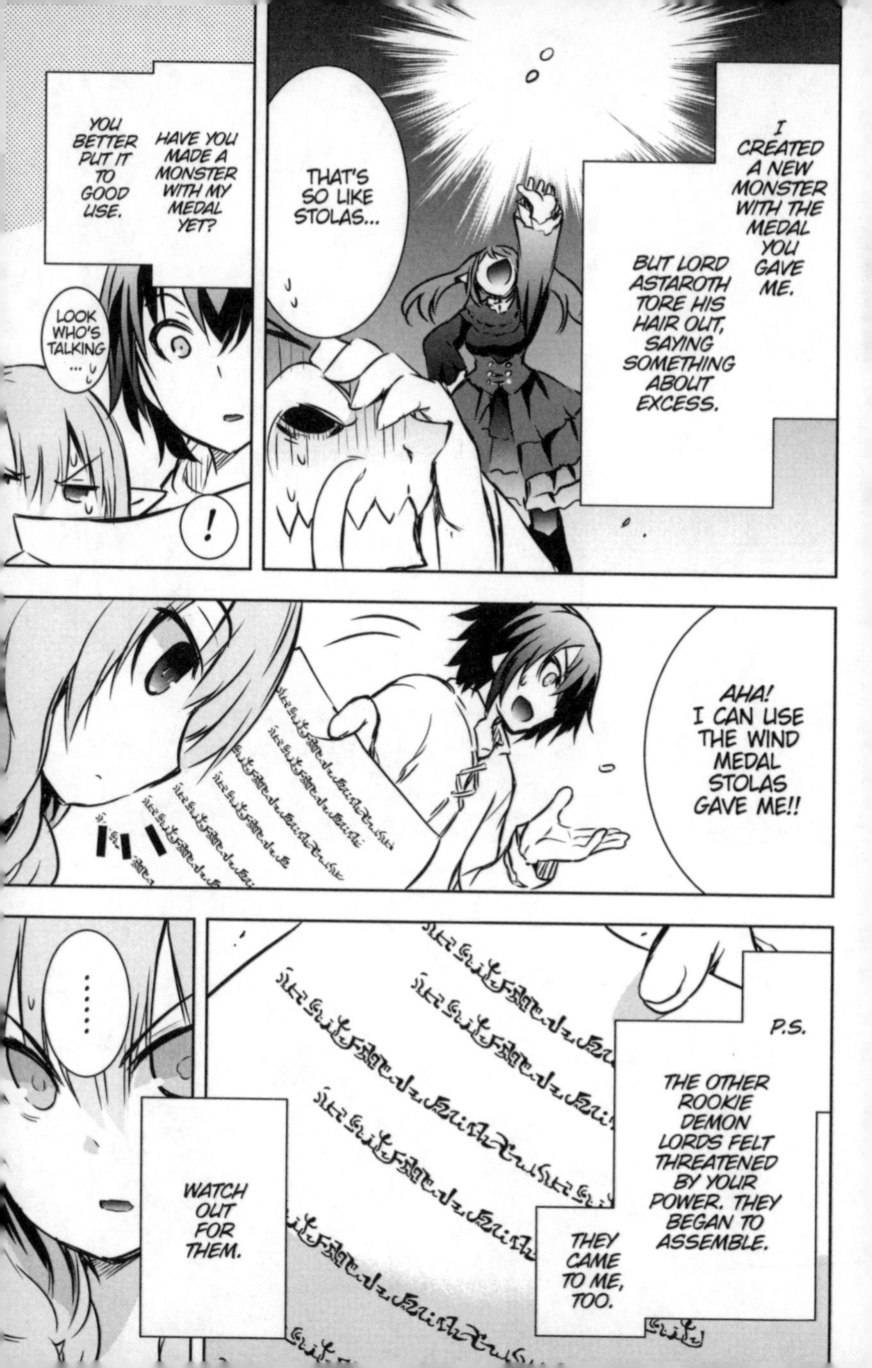
I CREATED A NEW MONSTER WITH THE MEDAL YOU GAVE ME.
BUT LORD ASTAROTH TORE HIS HAIR OUT, SAYING SOMETHING ABOUT EXCESS.
THAT'S SO LIKE STOLAS...
HAVE YOU MADE A MONSTER WITH MY MEDAL YET?
YOU BETTER PUT IT TO GOOD USE.
!
LOOK WHO'S TALKING...
AHA! I CAN USE THE WIND MEDAL STOLAS GAVE ME!!
P.S.
THE OTHER ROOKIE DEMON LORDS FELT THREATENED BY YOUR POWER. THEY BEGAN TO ASSEMBLE.
THEY CAME TO ME, TOO.
WATCH OUT FOR THEM.
......

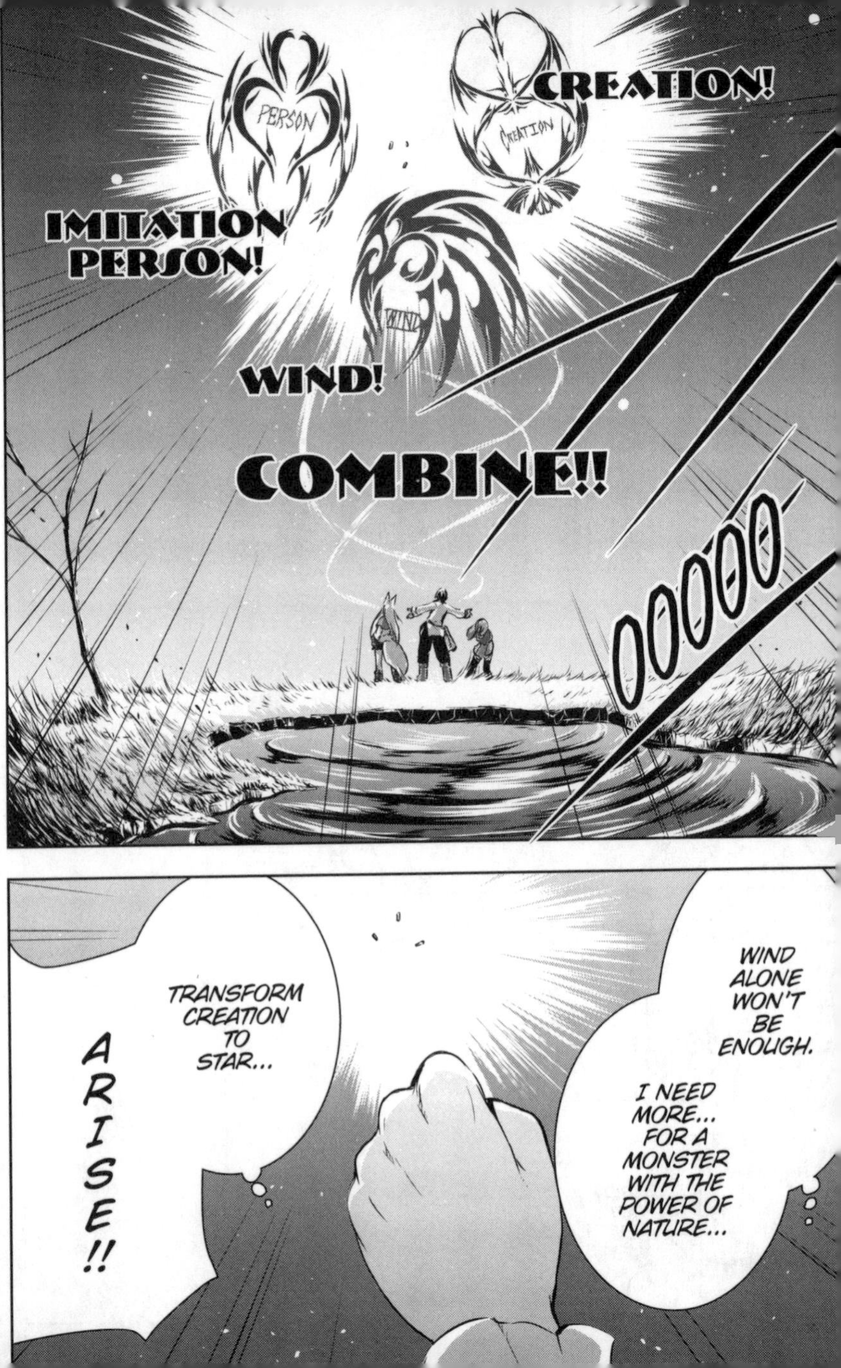
CREATION!
CREATION
PERSON
IMITATION PERSON!
WIND
WIND!
COMBINE!!
OOOOO
WIND ALONE WON'T BE ENOUGH.
I NEED MORE... FOR A MONSTER WITH THE POWER OF NATURE...
TRANSFORM CREATION TO STAR...
ARISE!!

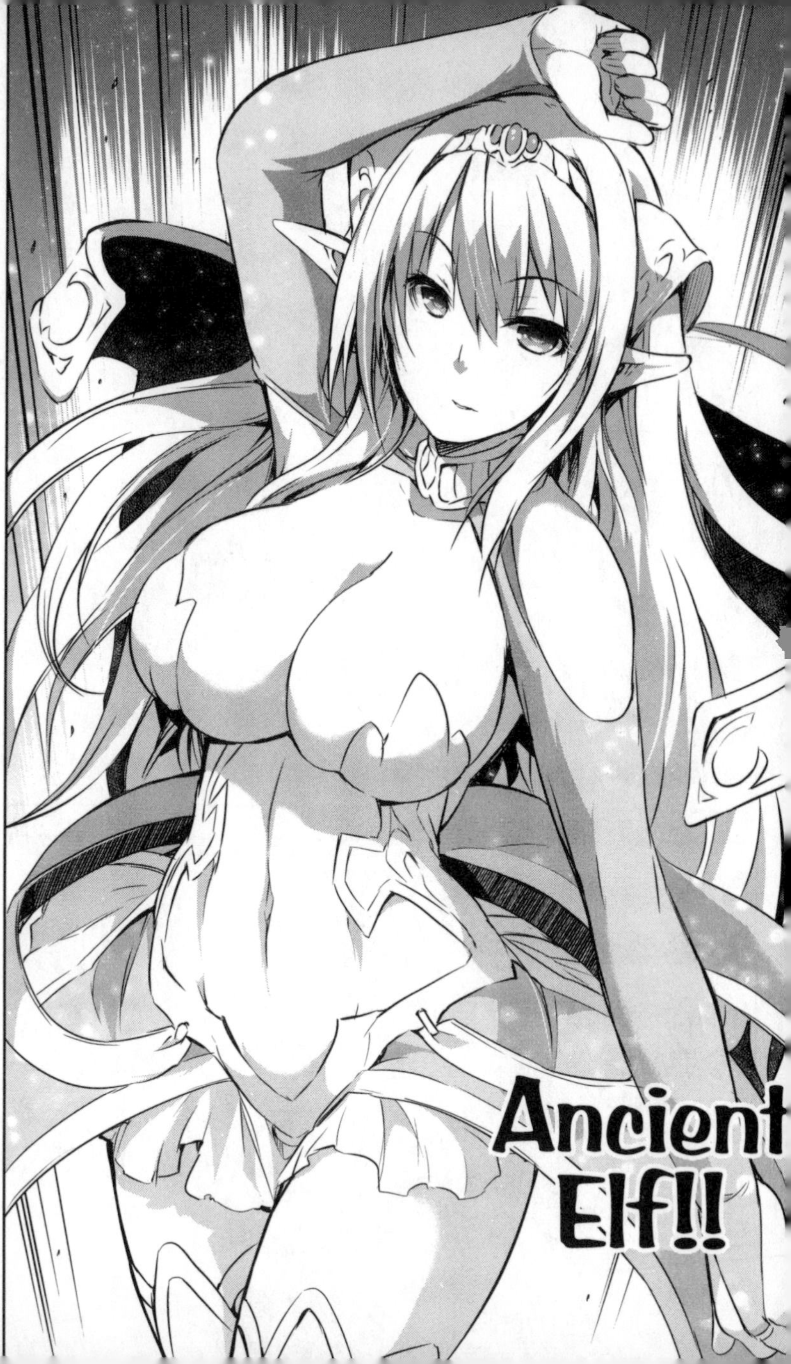
Ancient
Elf!!

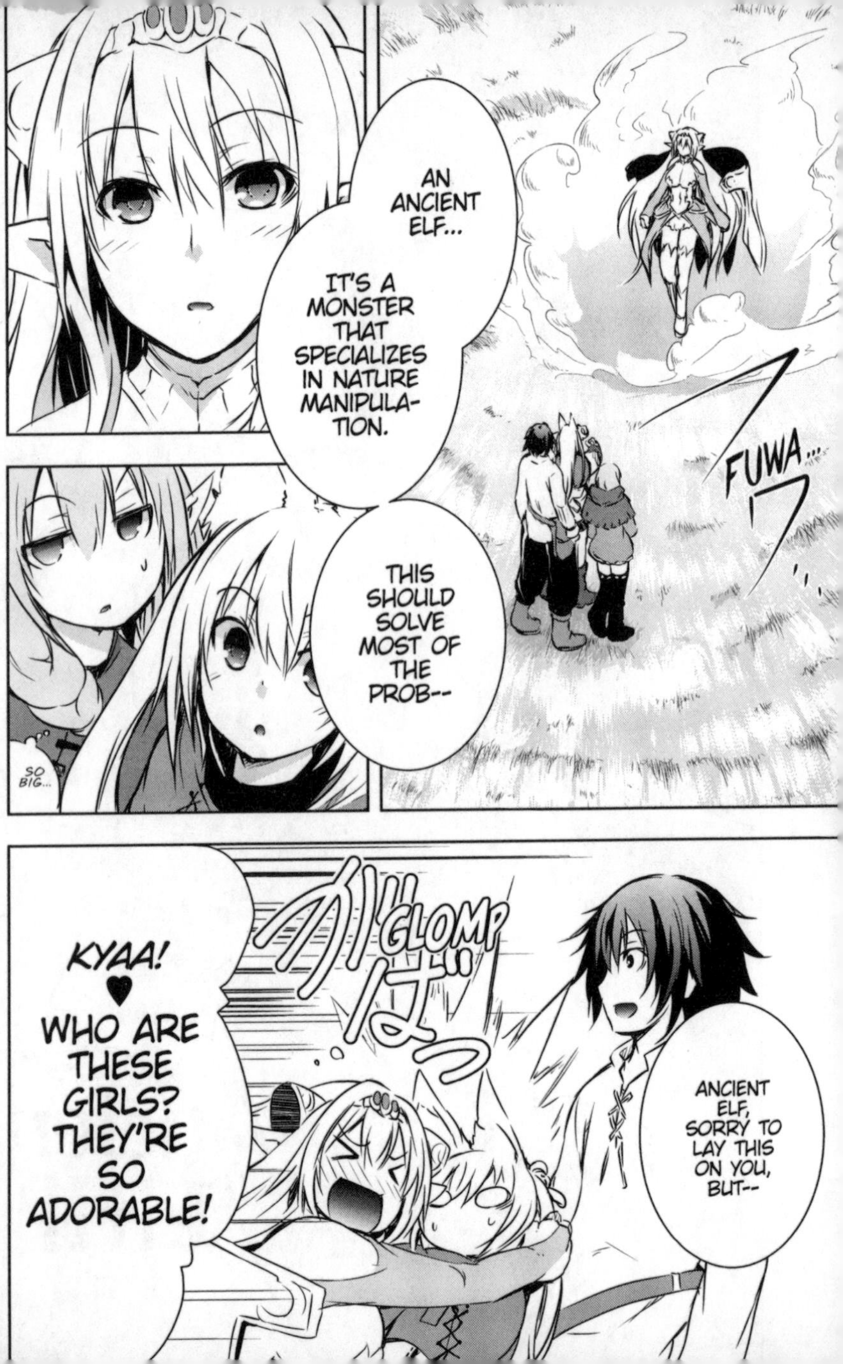
FUWA...
AN ANCIENT ELF...
IT'S A MONSTER THAT SPECIALIZES IN NATURE MANIPULA-TION.
THIS SHOULD SOLVE MOST OF THE PROB--
SO BIG...
ANCIENT ELF, SORRY TO LAY THIS ON YOU, BUT--
GLOMP
KYAA! ♥ WHO ARE THESE GIRLS? THEY'RE SO ADORABLE!

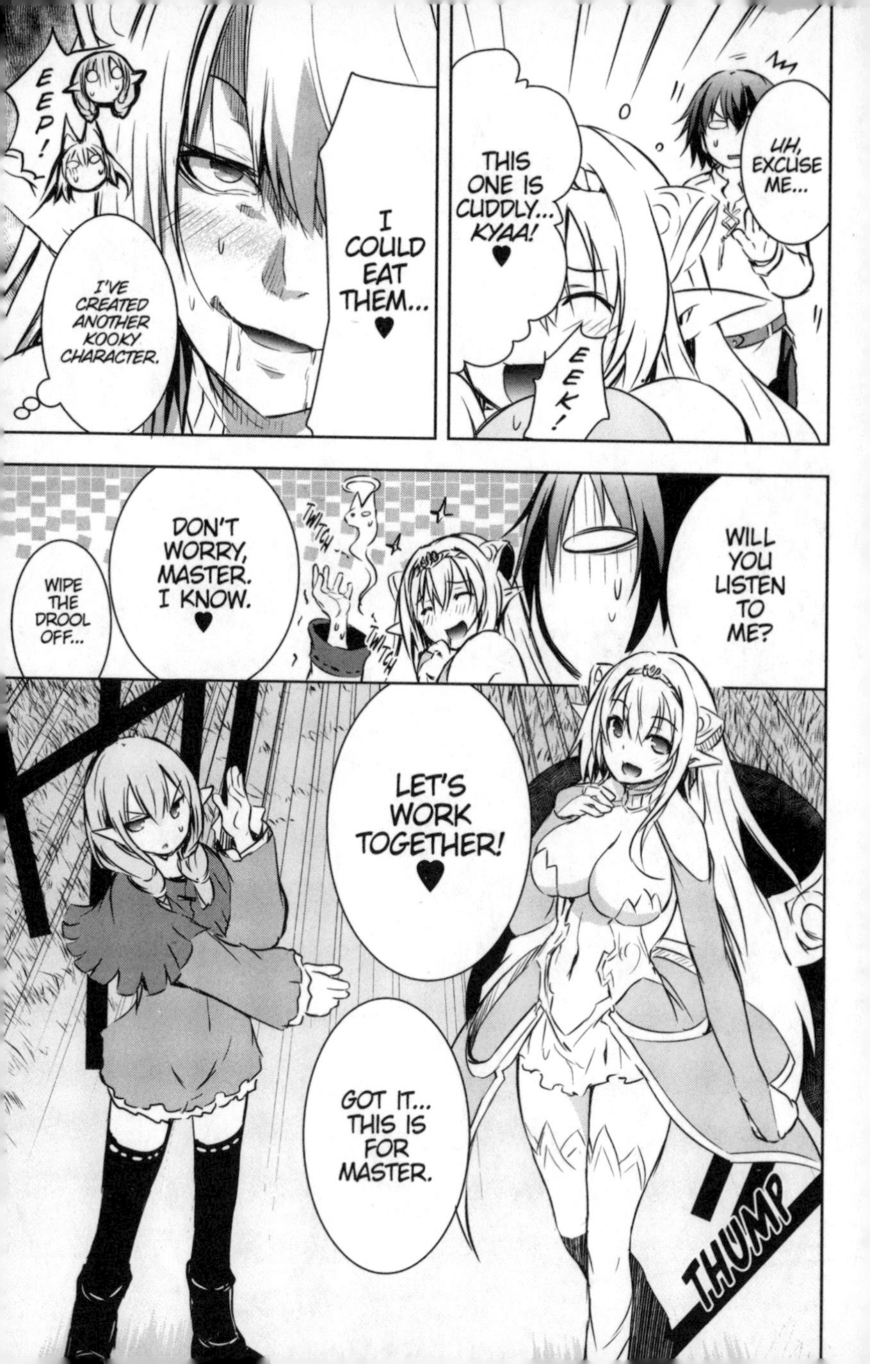
UH, EXCUSE ME...
THIS ONE IS CUDDLY... KYAA! ♥
EEEK!
I COULD EAT THEM... ♥
EEP!
I'VE CREATED ANOTHER KOOKY CHARACTER.
WILL YOU LISTEN TO ME?
TWITCH TWITCH
DON'T WORRY, MASTER. I KNOW. ♥
WIPE THE DROOL OFF...
LET'S WORK TOGETHER! ♥
THUMP
GOT IT... THIS IS FOR MASTER.

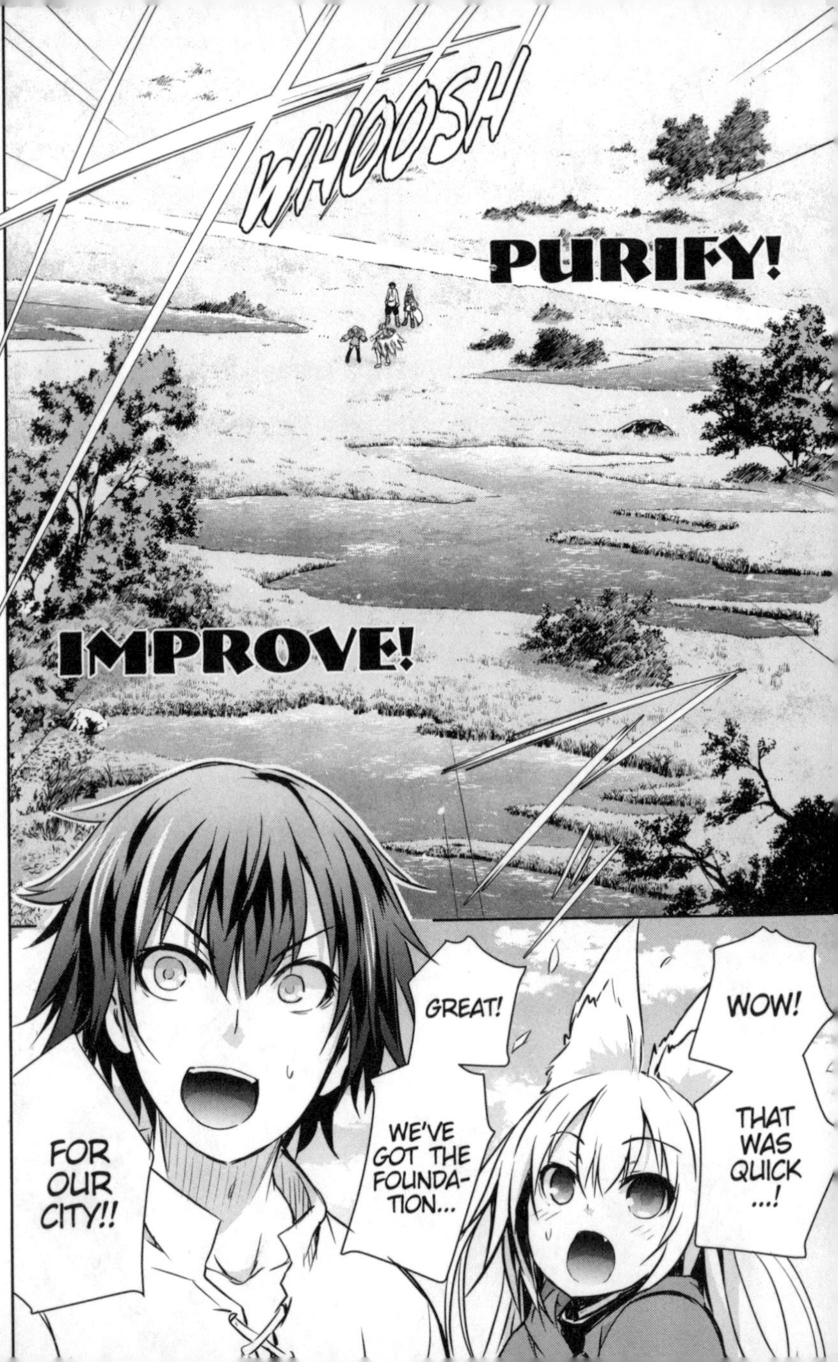
WHOOSH
PURIFY!
IMPROVE!
WOW!
THAT WAS QUICK...!
GREAT!
WE'VE GOT THE FOUNDATION...
FOR OUR CITY!!

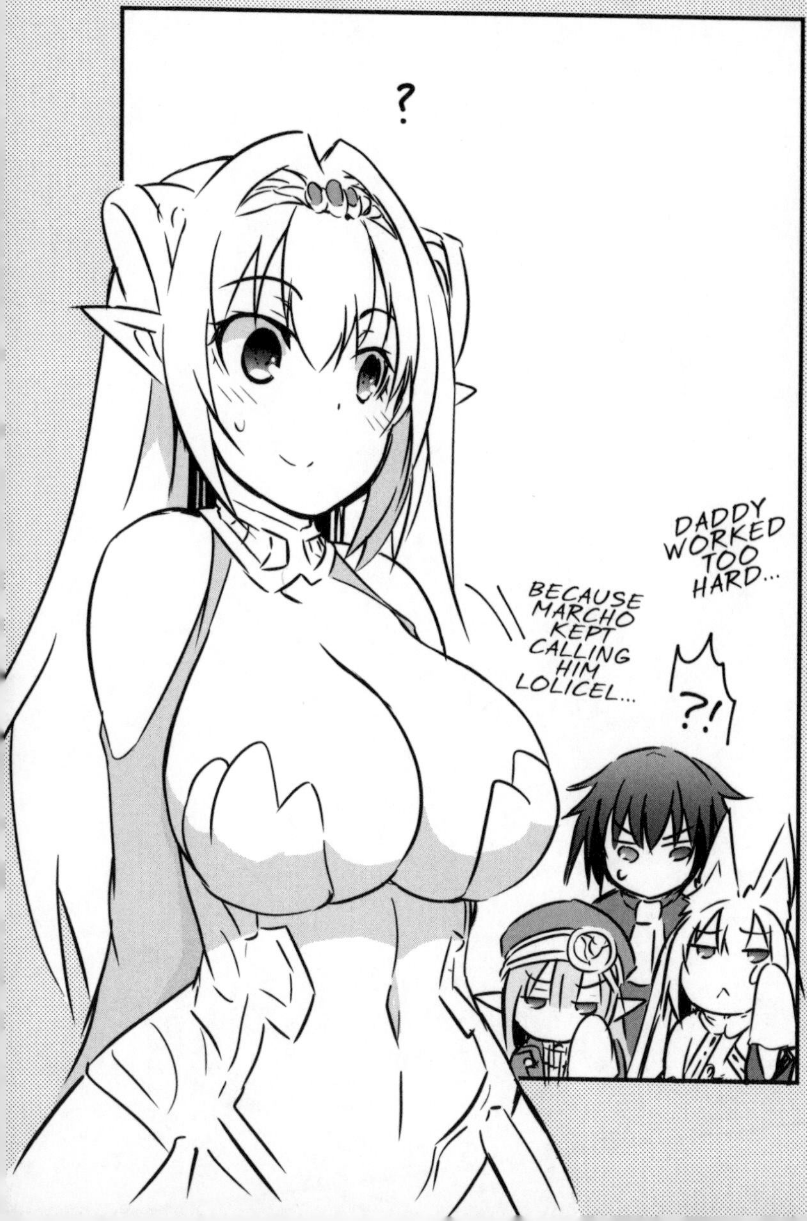
?
DADDY WORKED TOO HARD...
BECAUSE MARCHO KEPT CALLING HIM LOLICEL...
?!

DUNGEON BUILDER:

THE DEMON KING'S LABYRINTH IS A MODERN CITY!

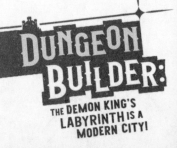

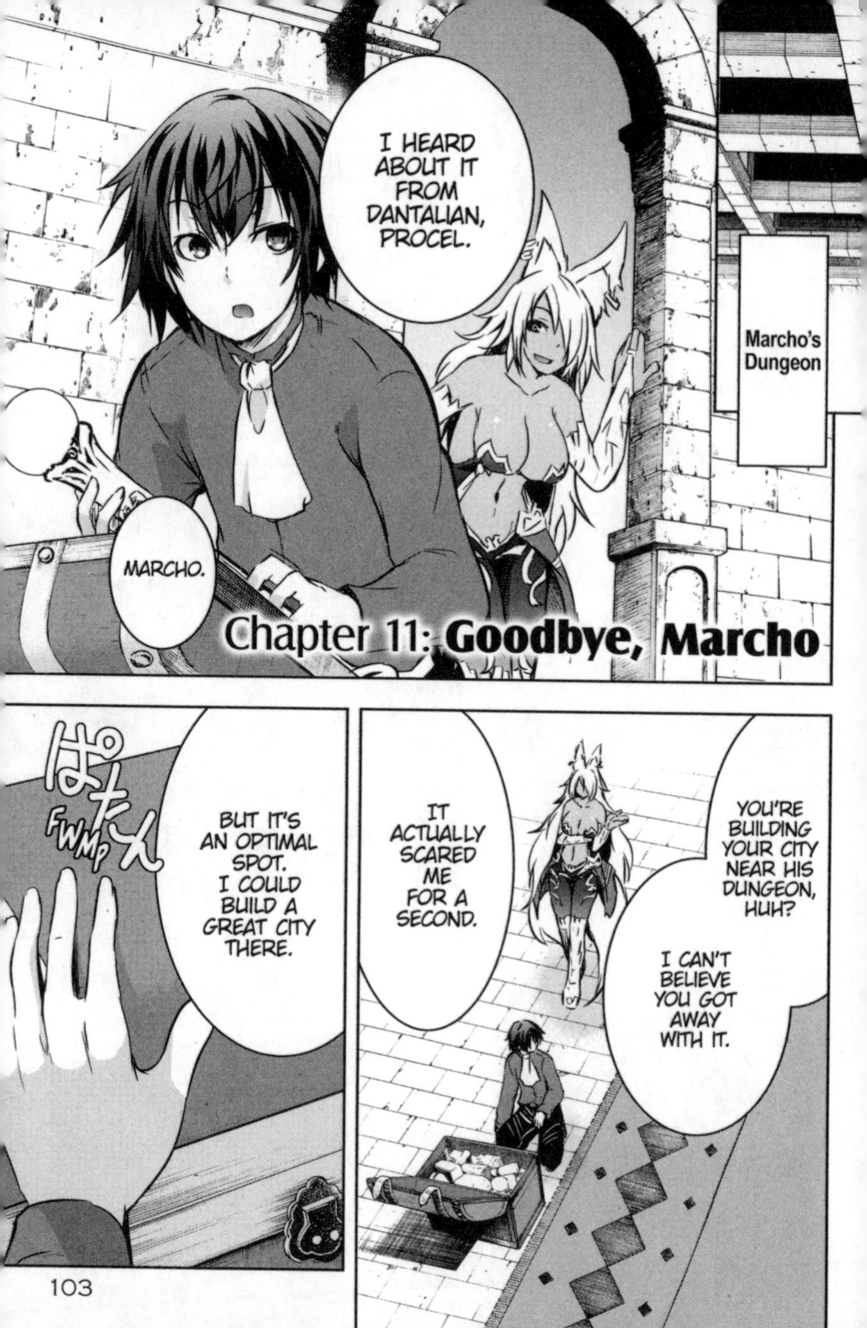
Marcho's Dungeon
I HEARD ABOUT IT FROM DANTALIAN, PROCEL.
MARCHO.
Chapter 11: Goodbye, Marcho
YOU'RE BUILDING YOUR CITY NEAR HIS DUNGEON, HUH?
I CAN'T BELIEVE YOU GOT AWAY WITH IT.
IT ACTUALLY SCARED ME FOR A SECOND.
BUT IT'S AN OPTIMAL SPOT. I COULD BUILD A GREAT CITY THERE.
ぱたん
FWMP

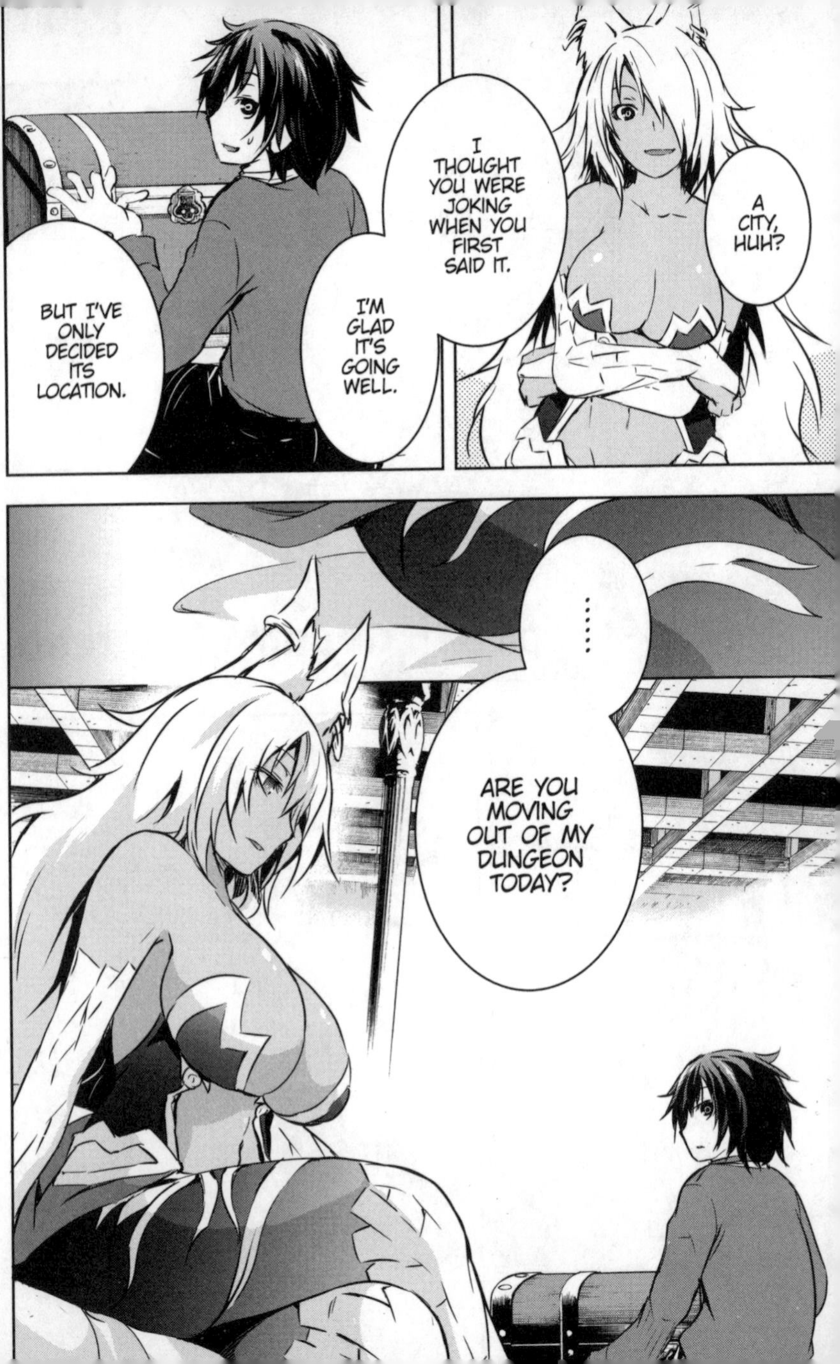
A CITY, HUH?
I THOUGHT YOU WERE JOKING WHEN YOU FIRST SAID IT.
I'M GLAD IT'S GOING WELL.
BUT I'VE ONLY DECIDED ITS LOCATION.
......
ARE YOU MOVING OUT OF MY DUNGEON TODAY?

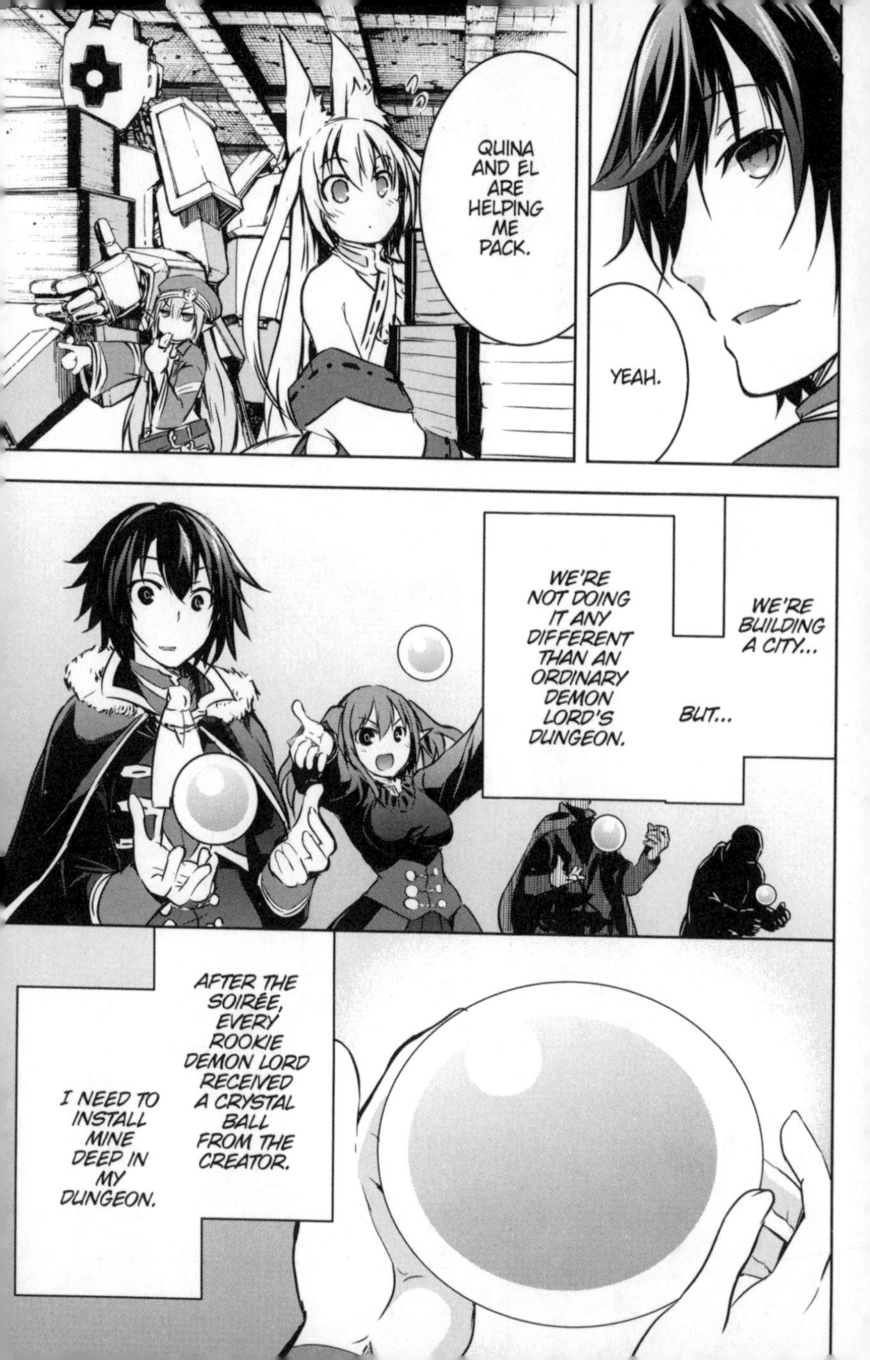
YEAH.
QUINA AND EL ARE HELPING ME PACK.
WE'RE BUILDING A CITY...
BUT...
WE'RE NOT DOING IT ANY DIFFERENT THAN AN ORDINARY DEMON LORD'S DUNGEON.
AFTER THE SOIRÉE, EVERY ROOKIE DEMON LORD RECEIVED A CRYSTAL BALL FROM THE CREATOR.
I NEED TO INSTALL MINE DEEP IN MY DUNGEON.

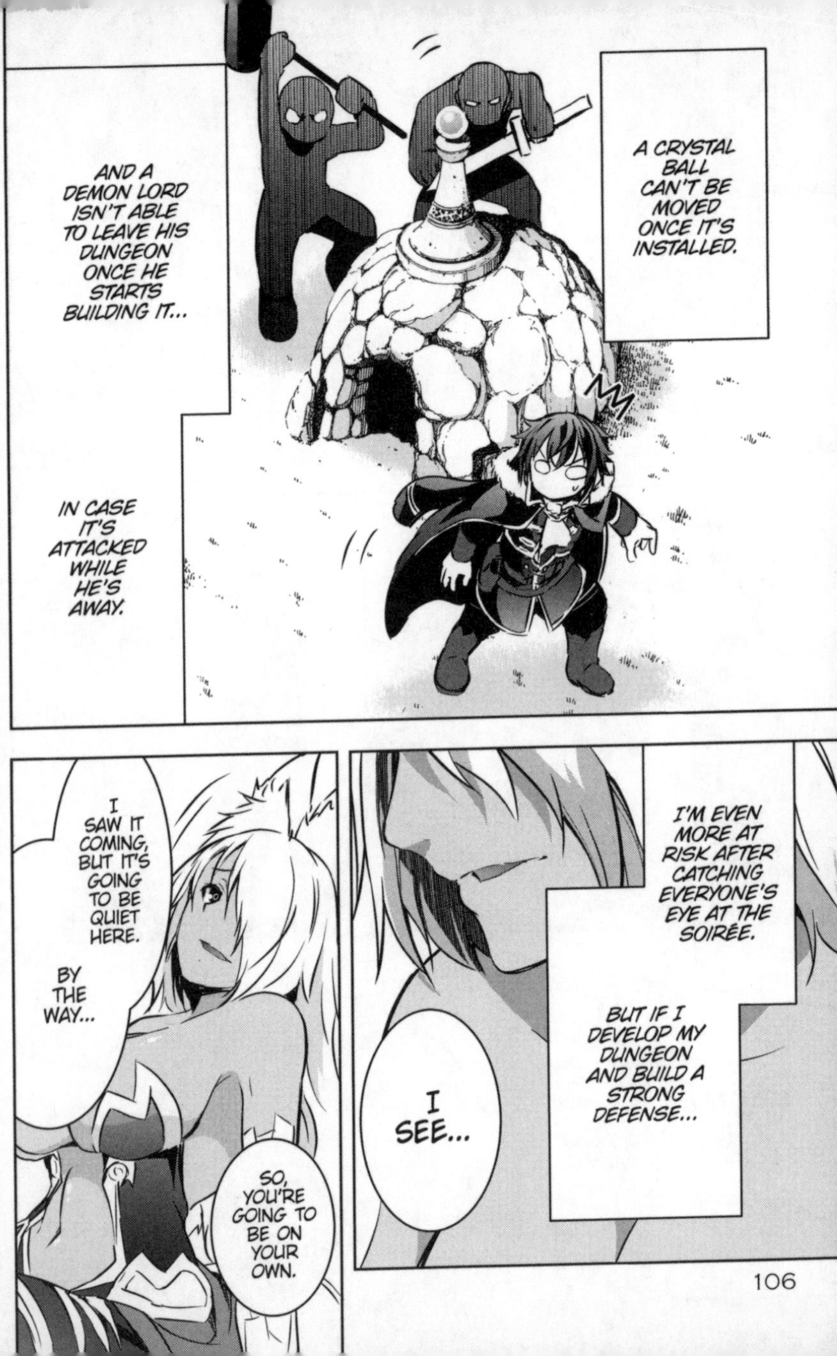
A CRYSTAL BALL CAN'T BE MOVED ONCE IT'S INSTALLED.
AND A DEMON LORD ISN'T ABLE TO LEAVE HIS DUNGEON ONCE HE STARTS BUILDING IT...
IN CASE IT'S ATTACKED WHILE HE'S AWAY.
I'M EVEN MORE AT RISK AFTER CATCHING EVERYONE'S EYE AT THE SOIRÉE.
BUT IF I DEVELOP MY DUNGEON AND BUILD A STRONG DEFENSE...
I SEE...
I SAW IT COMING, BUT IT'S GOING TO BE QUIET HERE.
BY THE WAY...
SO, YOU'RE GOING TO BE ON YOUR OWN.

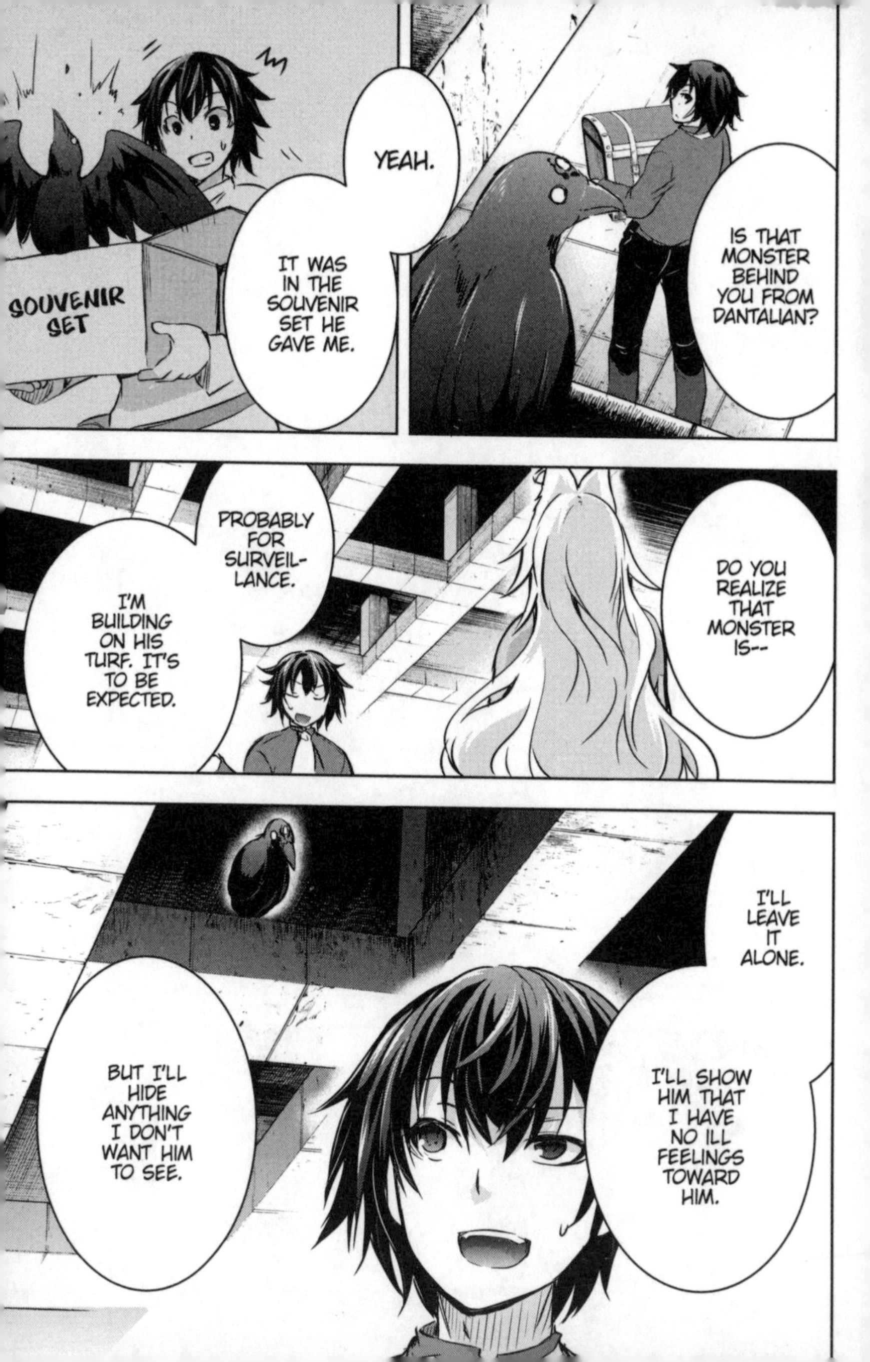
IS THAT MONSTER BEHIND YOU FROM DANTALIAN?
YEAH.
IT WAS IN THE SOUVENIR SET HE GAVE ME.
SOUVENIR SET
DO YOU REALIZE THAT MONSTER IS--
PROBABLY FOR SURVEIL-LANCE.
I'M BUILDING ON HIS TURF. IT'S TO BE EXPECTED.
I'LL LEAVE IT ALONE.
I'LL SHOW HIM THAT I HAVE NO ILL FEELINGS TOWARD HIM.
BUT I'LL HIDE ANYTHING I DON'T WANT HIM TO SEE.

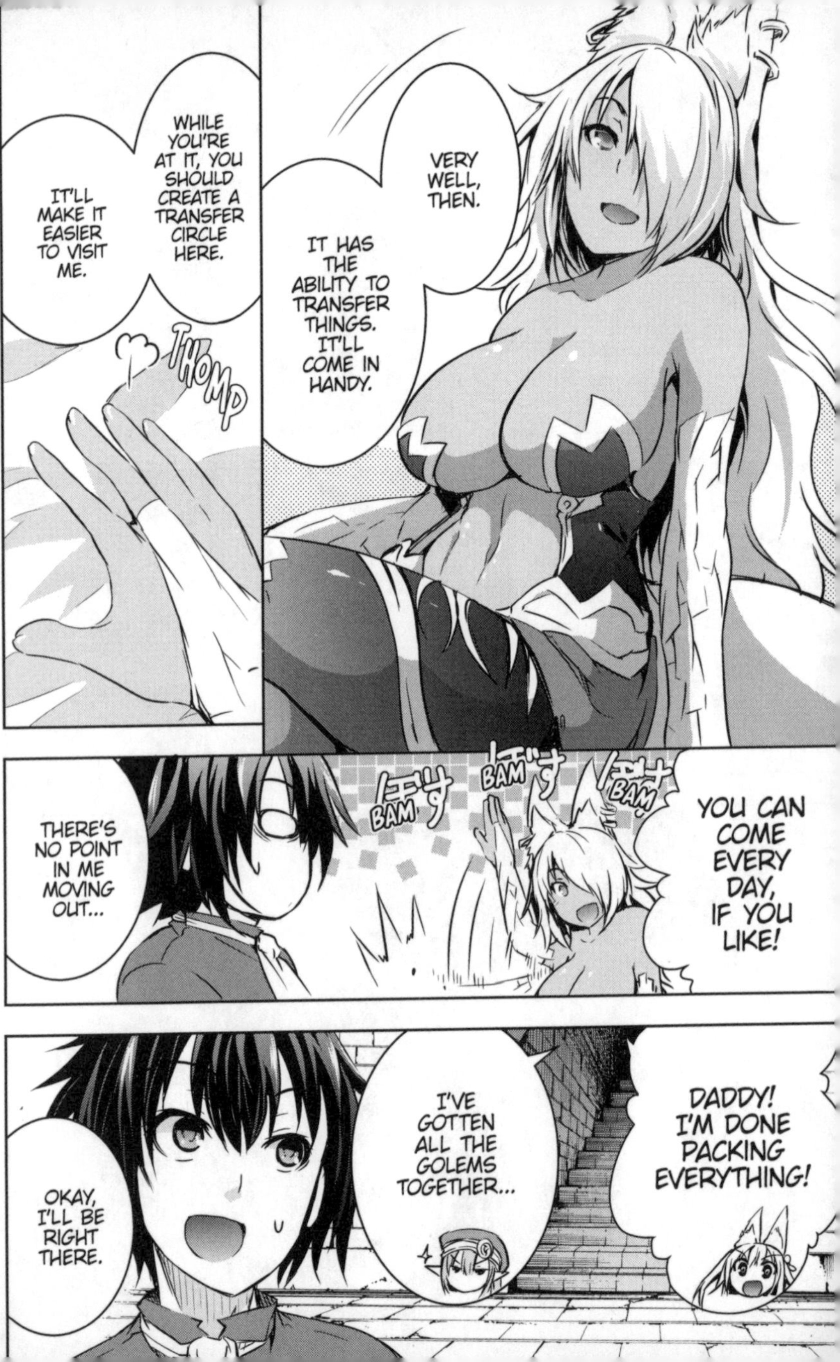
VERY WELL, THEN.
IT HAS THE ABILITY TO TRANSFER THINGS. IT'LL COME IN HANDY.
WHILE YOU'RE AT IT, YOU SHOULD CREATE A TRANSFER CIRCLE HERE.
IT'LL MAKE IT EASIER TO VISIT ME.
THOMP
BAM
YOU CAN COME EVERY DAY, IF YOU LIKE!
BAM
BAM
THERE'S NO POINT IN ME MOVING OUT...
DADDY! I'M DONE PACKING EVERYTHING!
I'VE GOTTEN ALL THE GOLEMS TOGETHER...
OKAY, I'LL BE RIGHT THERE.

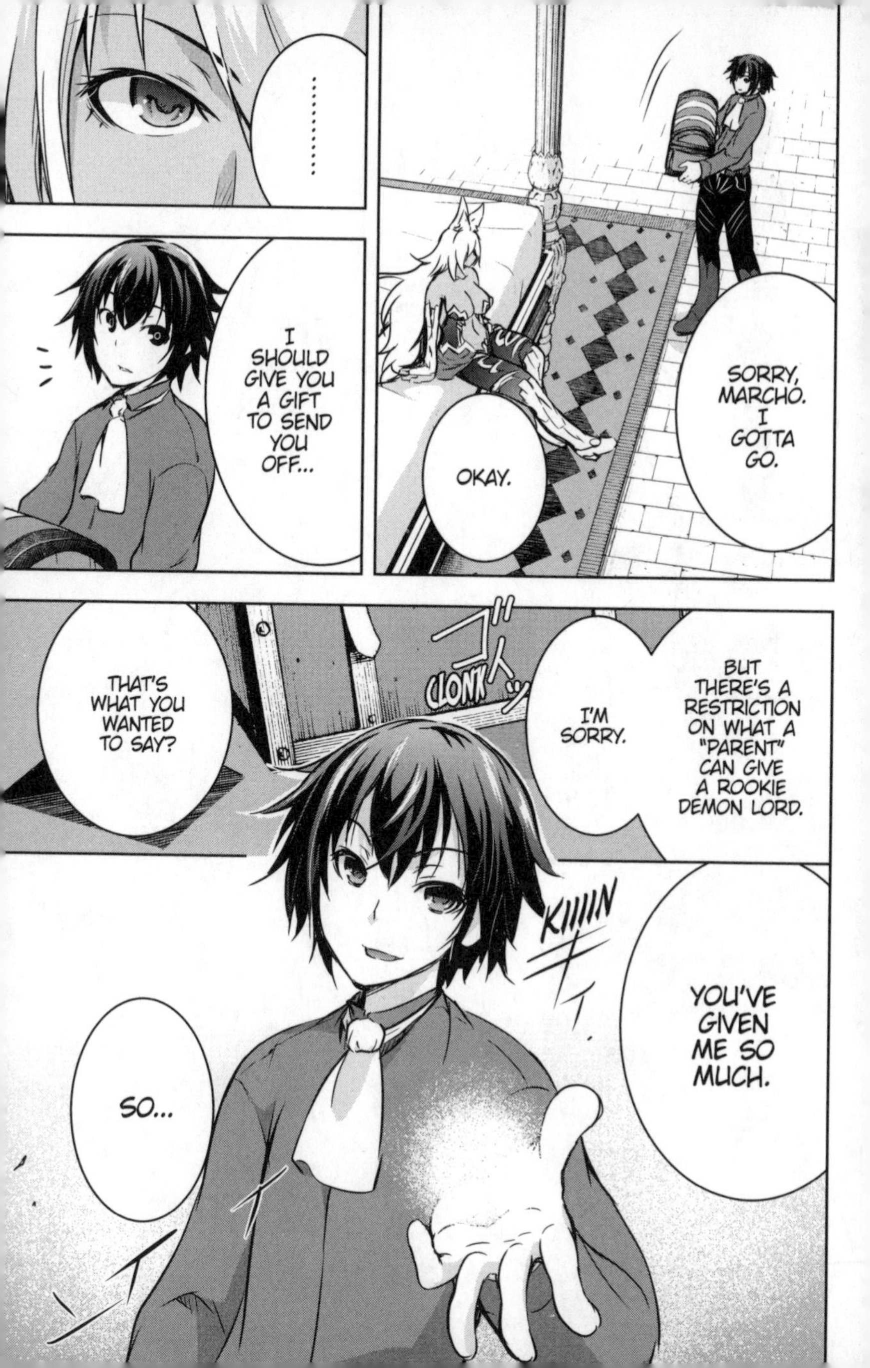
SORRY, MARCHO. I GOTTA GO.
OKAY.
......
I SHOULD GIVE YOU A GIFT TO SEND YOU OFF...
BUT THERE'S A RESTRICTION ON WHAT A "PARENT" CAN GIVE A ROOKIE DEMON LORD.
I'M SORRY.
CLONK
THAT'S WHAT YOU WANTED TO SAY?
KIIIIN
YOU'VE GIVEN ME SO MUCH.
SO...

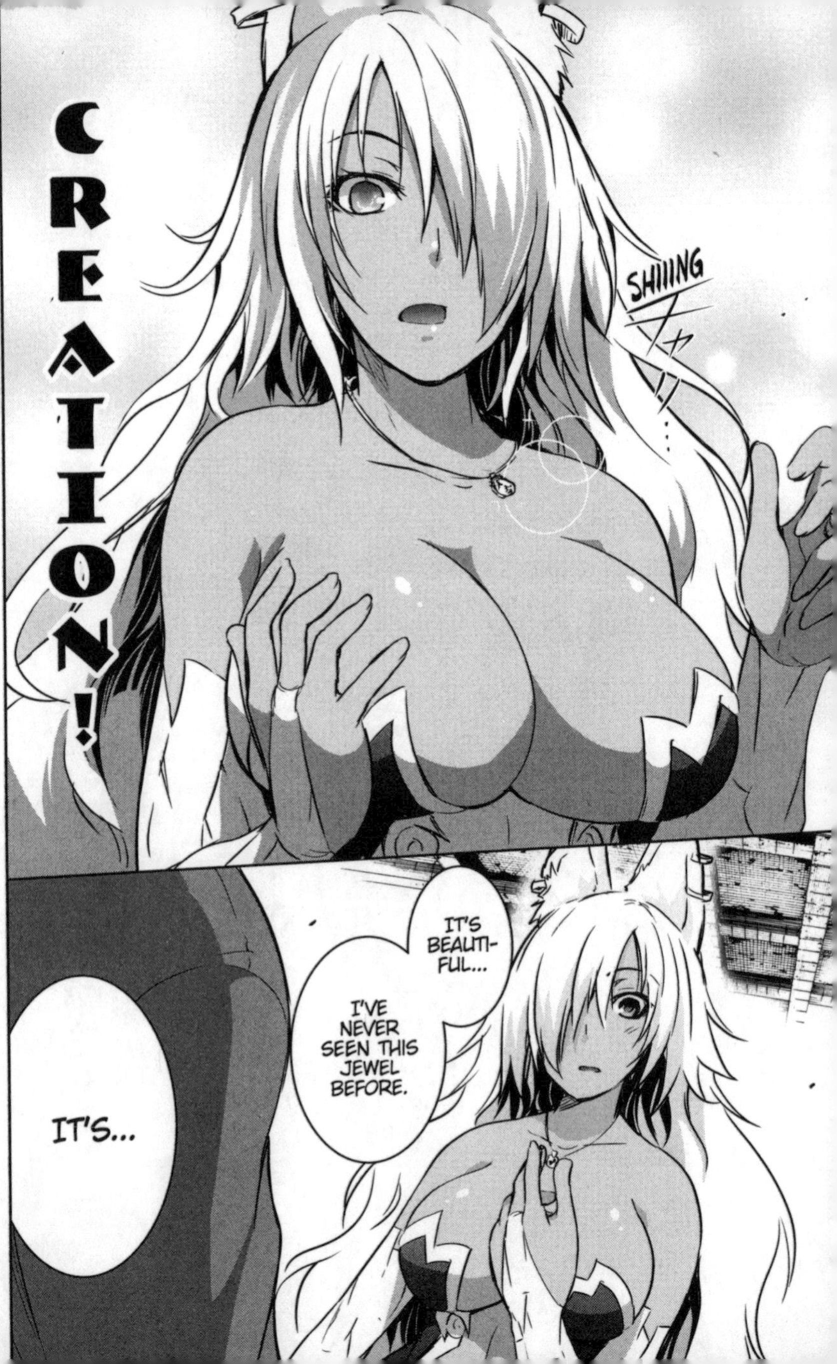
CREATION!
SHIIING
IT'S BEAUTI-FUL...
I'VE NEVER SEEN THIS JEWEL BEFORE.
IT'S...

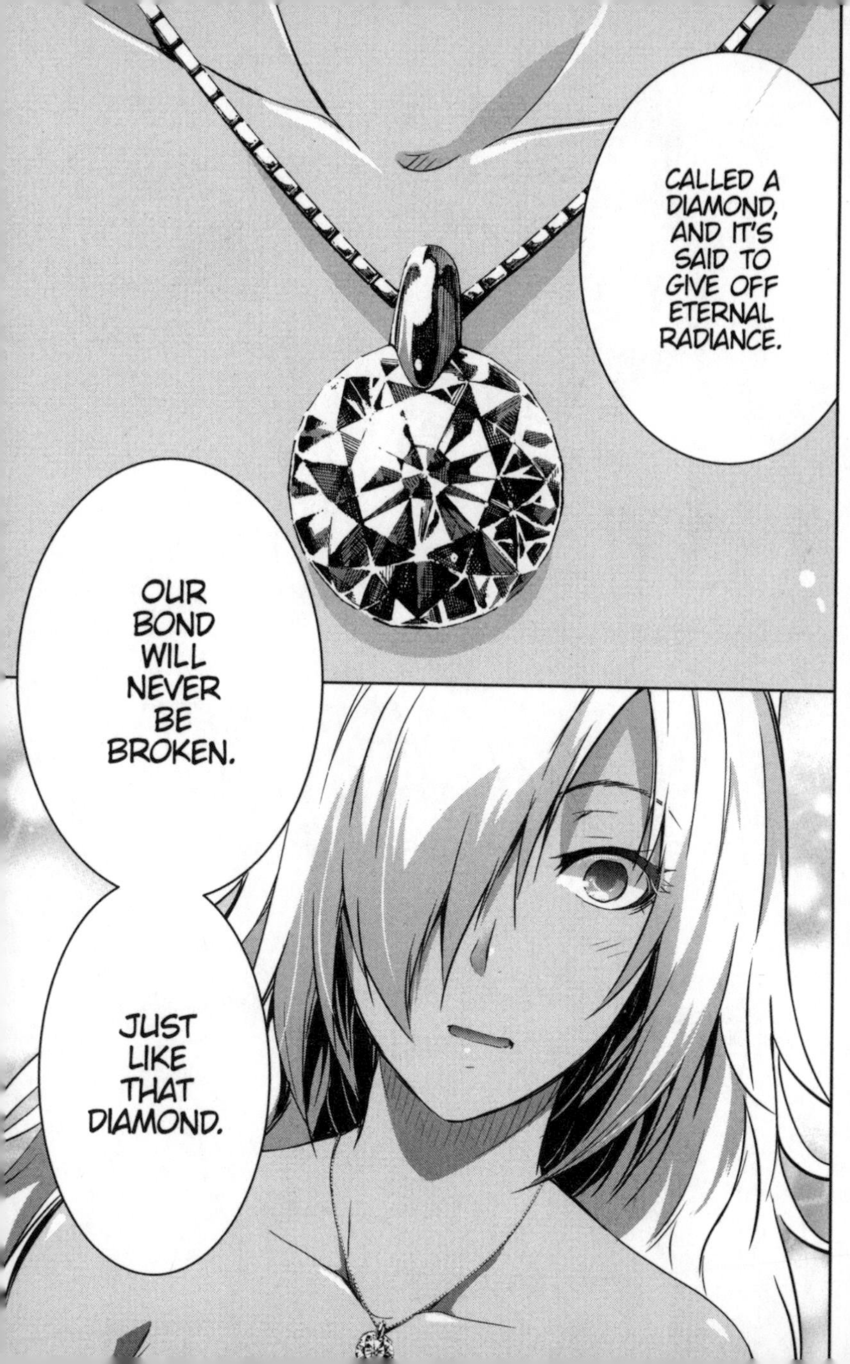
CALLED A DIAMOND, AND IT'S SAID TO GIVE OFF ETERNAL RADIANCE.
OUR BOND WILL NEVER BE BROKEN.
JUST LIKE THAT DIAMOND.

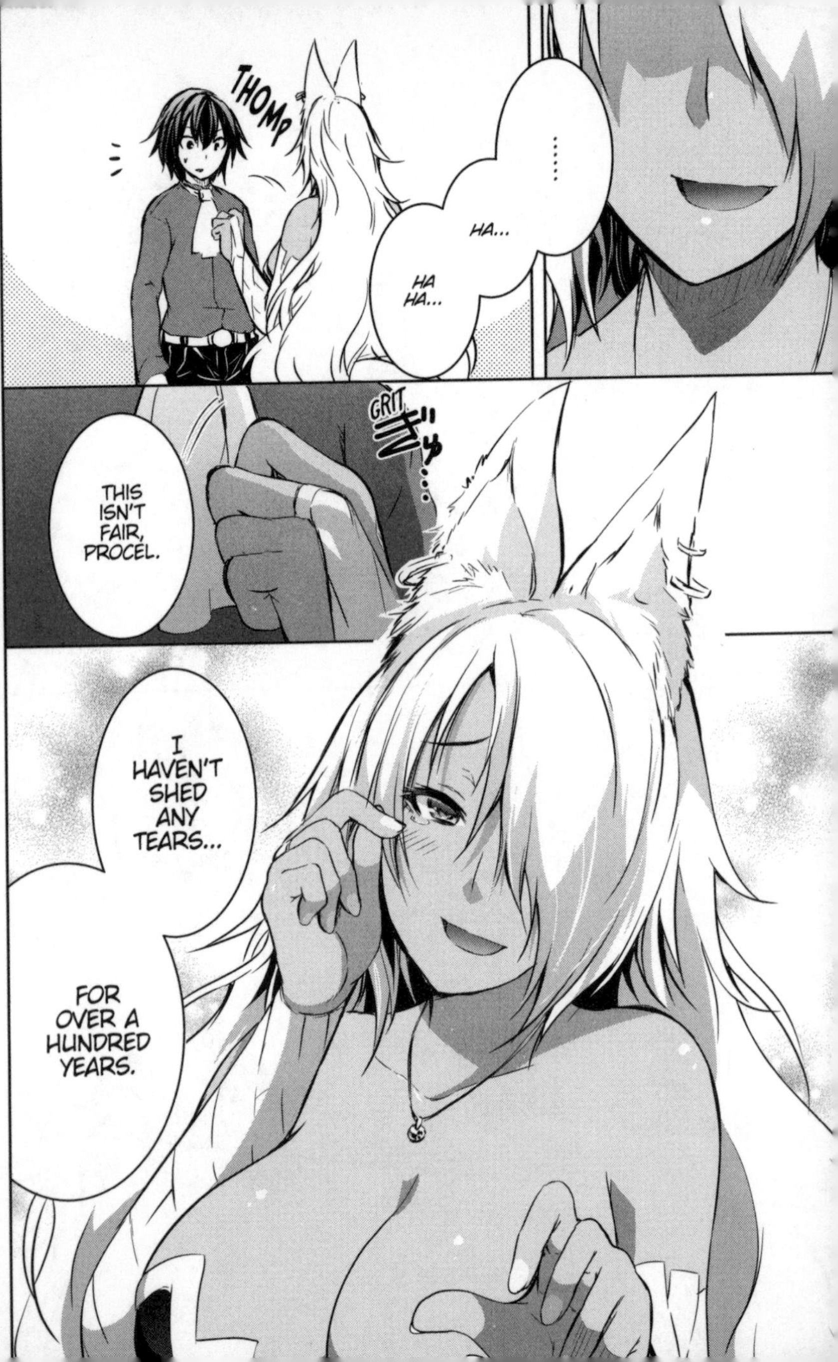
……
HA…
HA HA…
THOMP
GRIT
THIS ISN'T FAIR, PROCEL.
I HAVEN'T SHED ANY TEARS…
FOR OVER A HUNDRED YEARS.

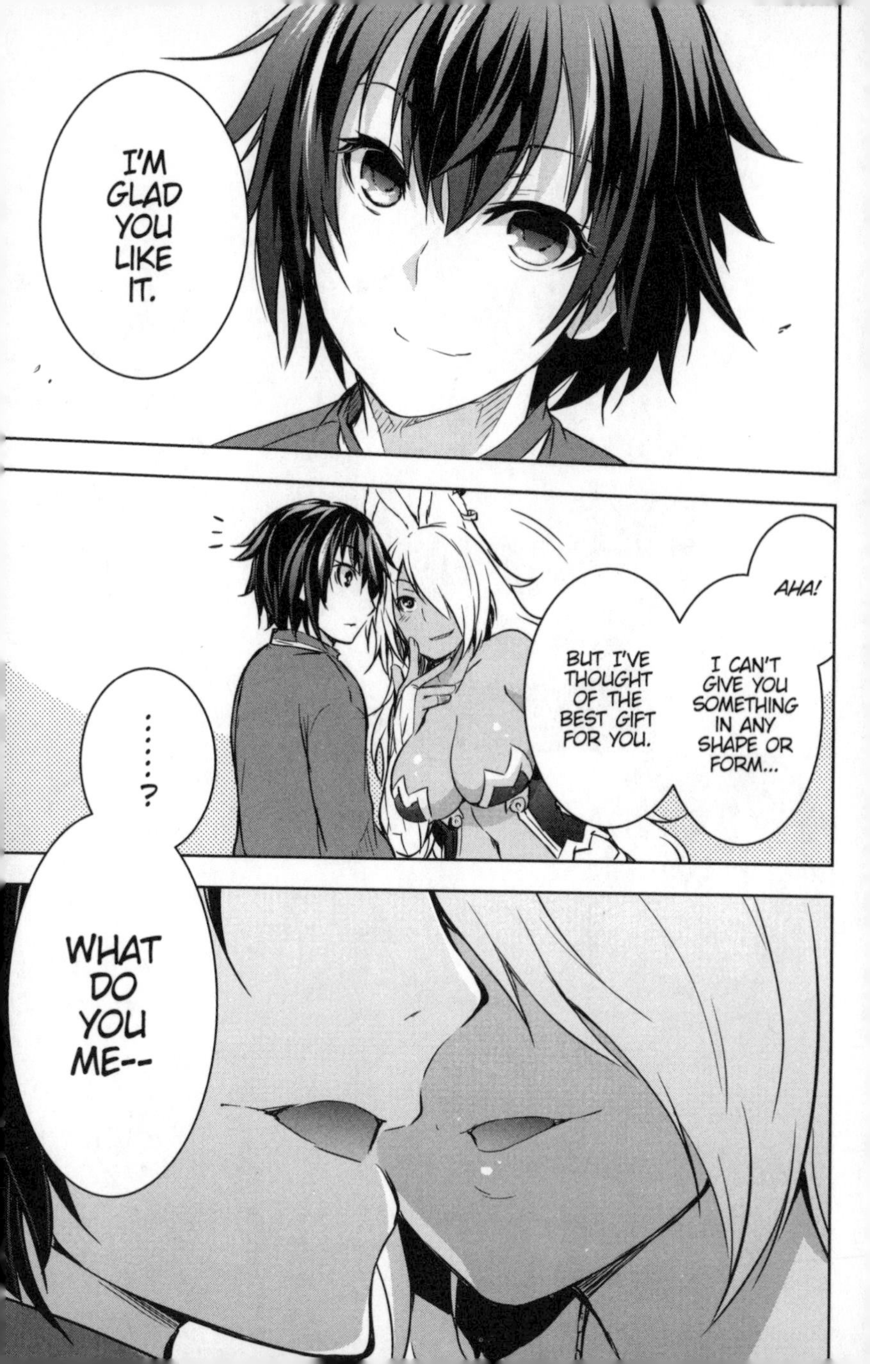
I'M GLAD YOU LIKE IT.
AHA!
I CAN'T GIVE YOU SOMETHING IN ANY SHAPE OR FORM...
BUT I'VE THOUGHT OF THE BEST GIFT FOR YOU.
......?
WHAT DO YOU ME--

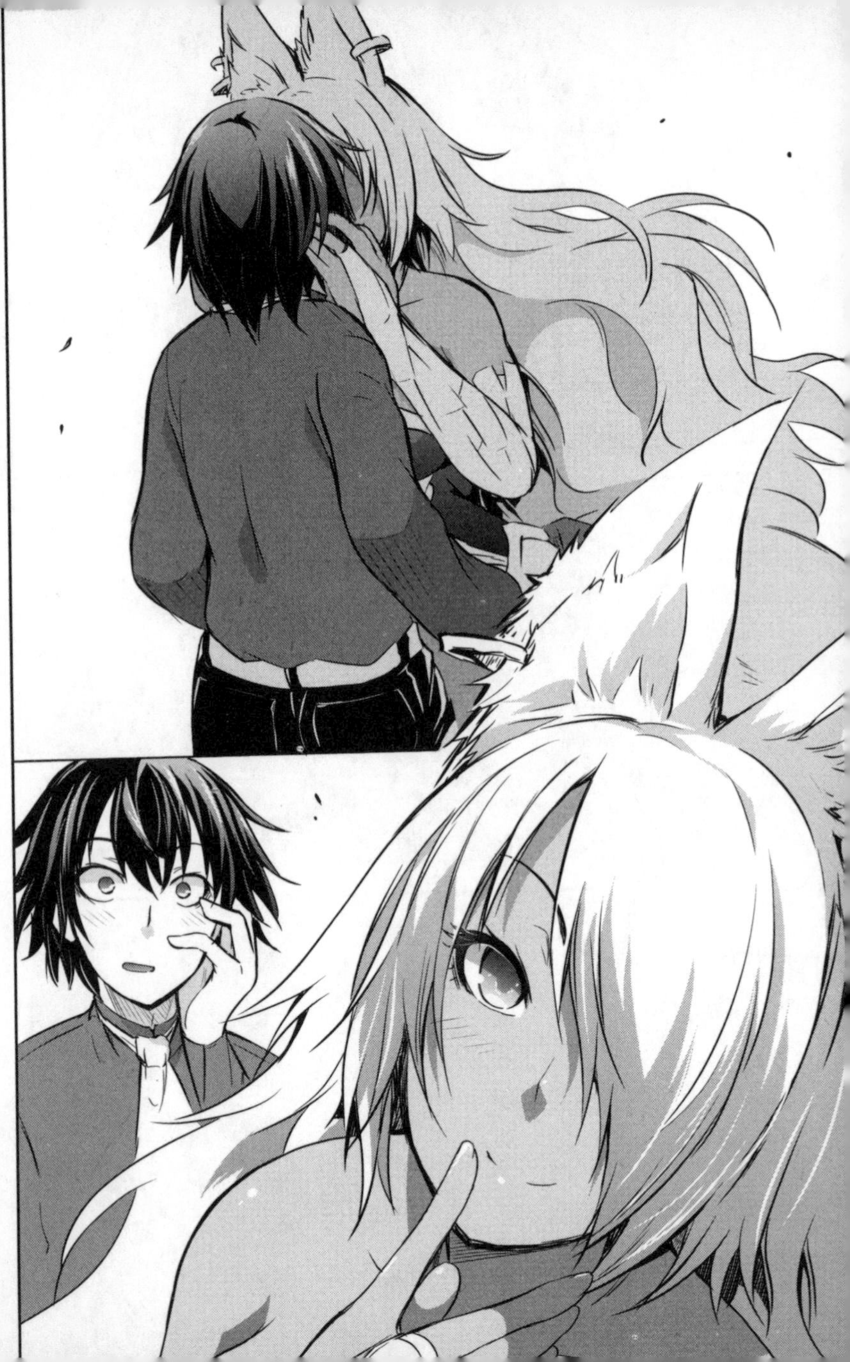

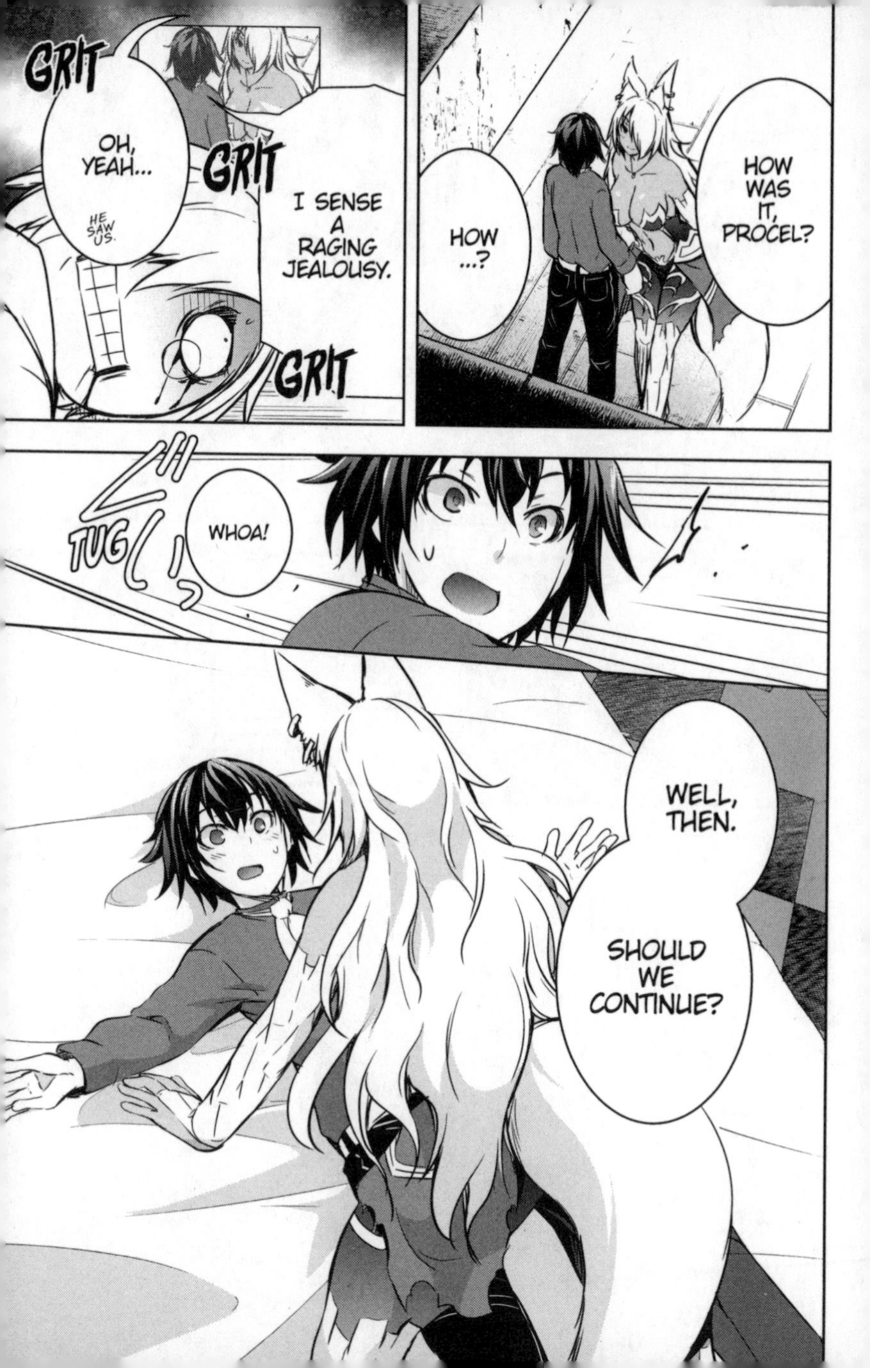
HOW WAS IT, PROCEL?
HOW ...?
I SENSE A RAGING JEALOUSY.
GRIT
GRIT
OH, YEAH...
HE SAW US.
GRIT
TUG
WHOA!
WELL, THEN.
SHOULD WE CONTINUE?

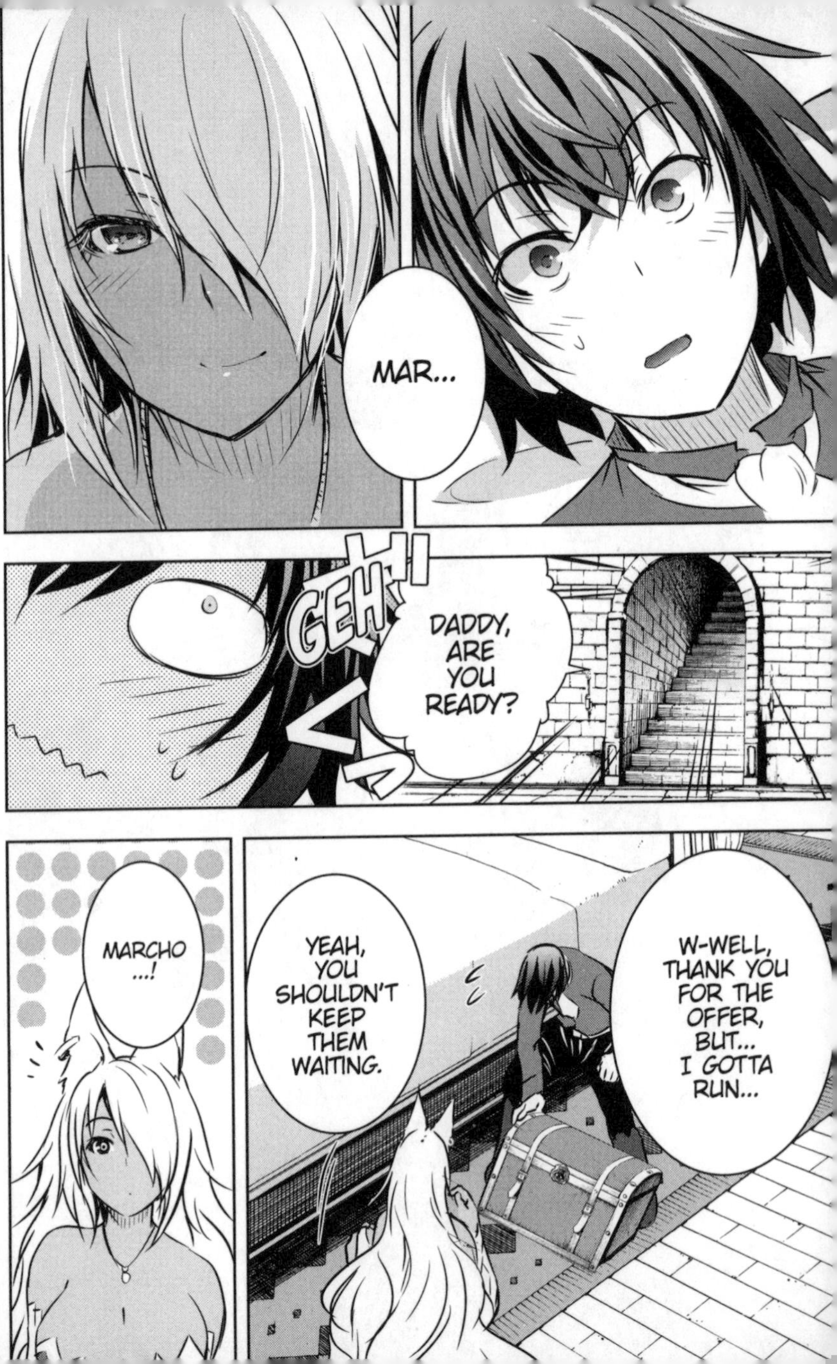
MAR...
DADDY, ARE YOU READY?
GEH
W-WELL, THANK YOU FOR THE OFFER, BUT... I GOTTA RUN...
YEAH, YOU SHOULDN'T KEEP THEM WAITING.
MARCHO ...!

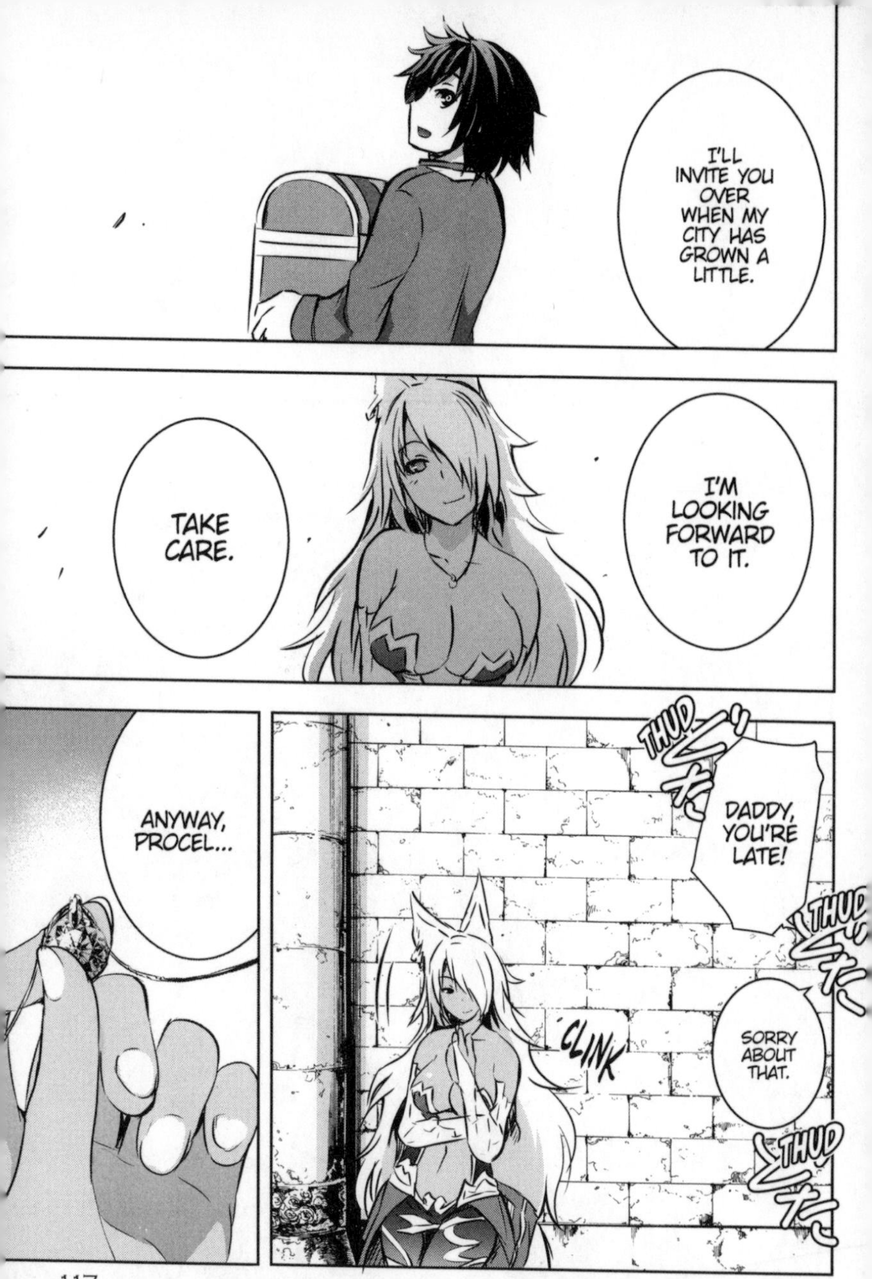
I'LL INVITE YOU OVER WHEN MY CITY HAS GROWN A LITTLE.
I'M LOOKING FORWARD TO IT.
TAKE CARE.
THUD
DADDY, YOU'RE LATE!
THUD
SORRY ABOUT THAT.
THUD
CLINK
ANYWAY, PROCEL...

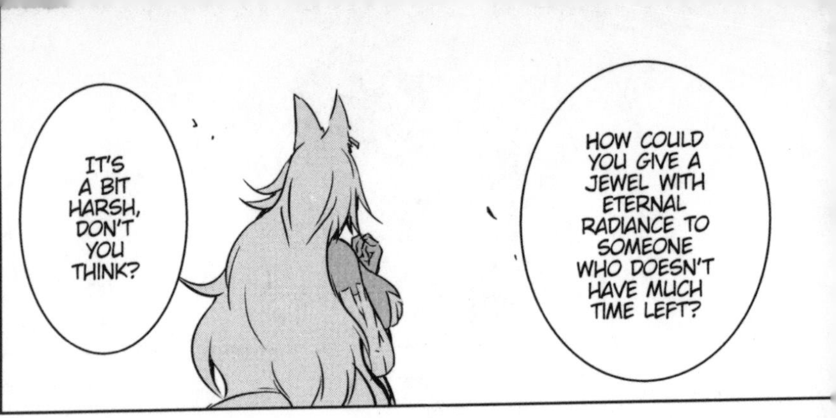
HOW COULD YOU GIVE A JEWEL WITH ETERNAL RADIANCE TO SOMEONE WHO DOESN'T HAVE MUCH TIME LEFT?
IT'S A BIT HARSH, DON'T YOU THINK?

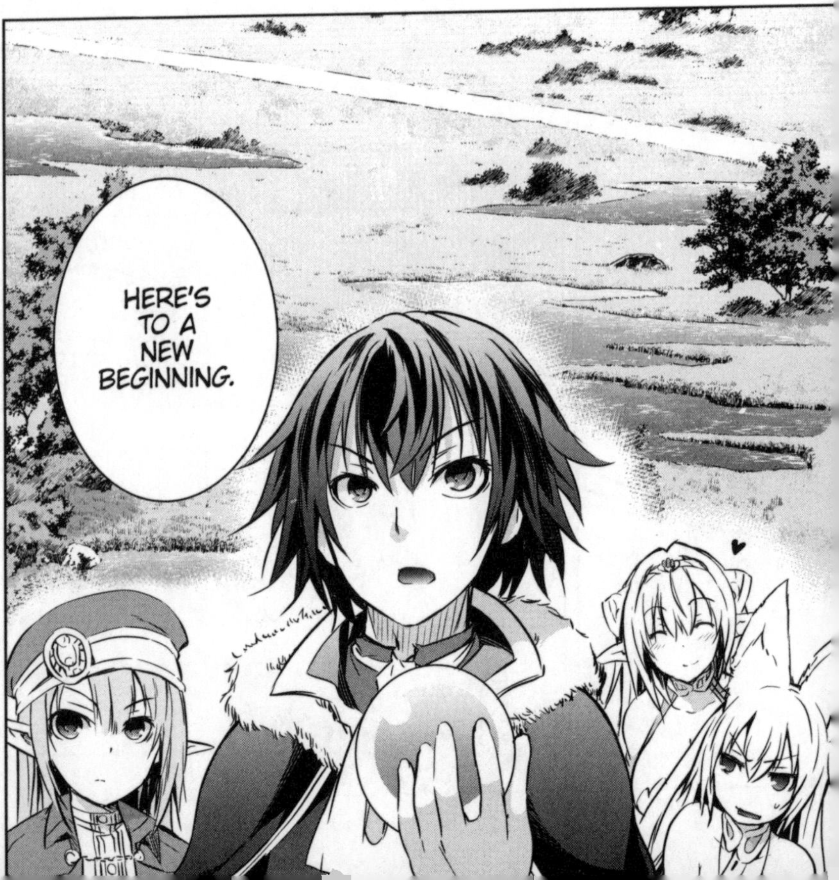
HERE'S TO A NEW BEGINNING.

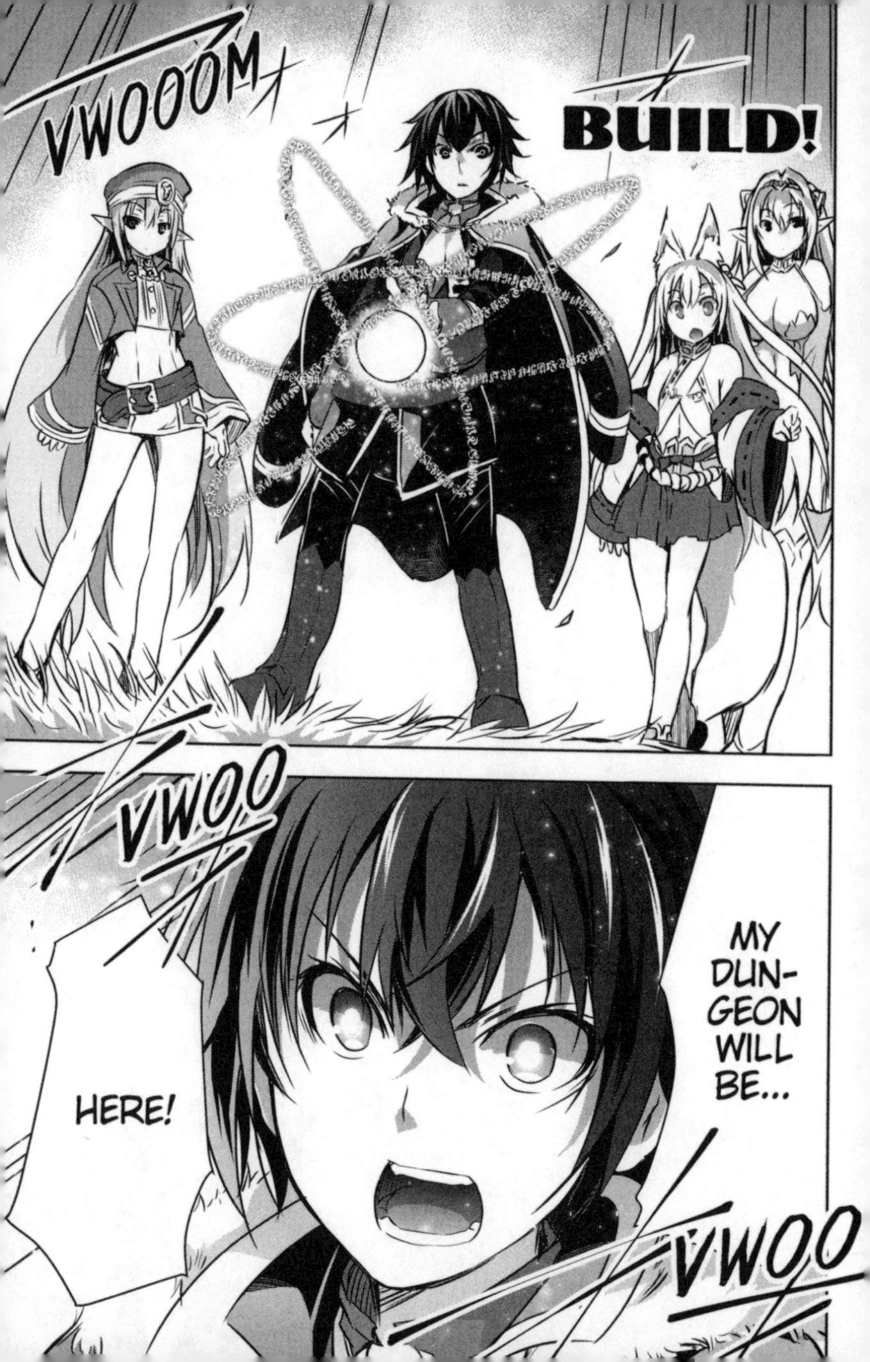
BUILD!
VWOOOM
VWOO
MY DUN-GEON WILL BE...
HERE!
VWOO

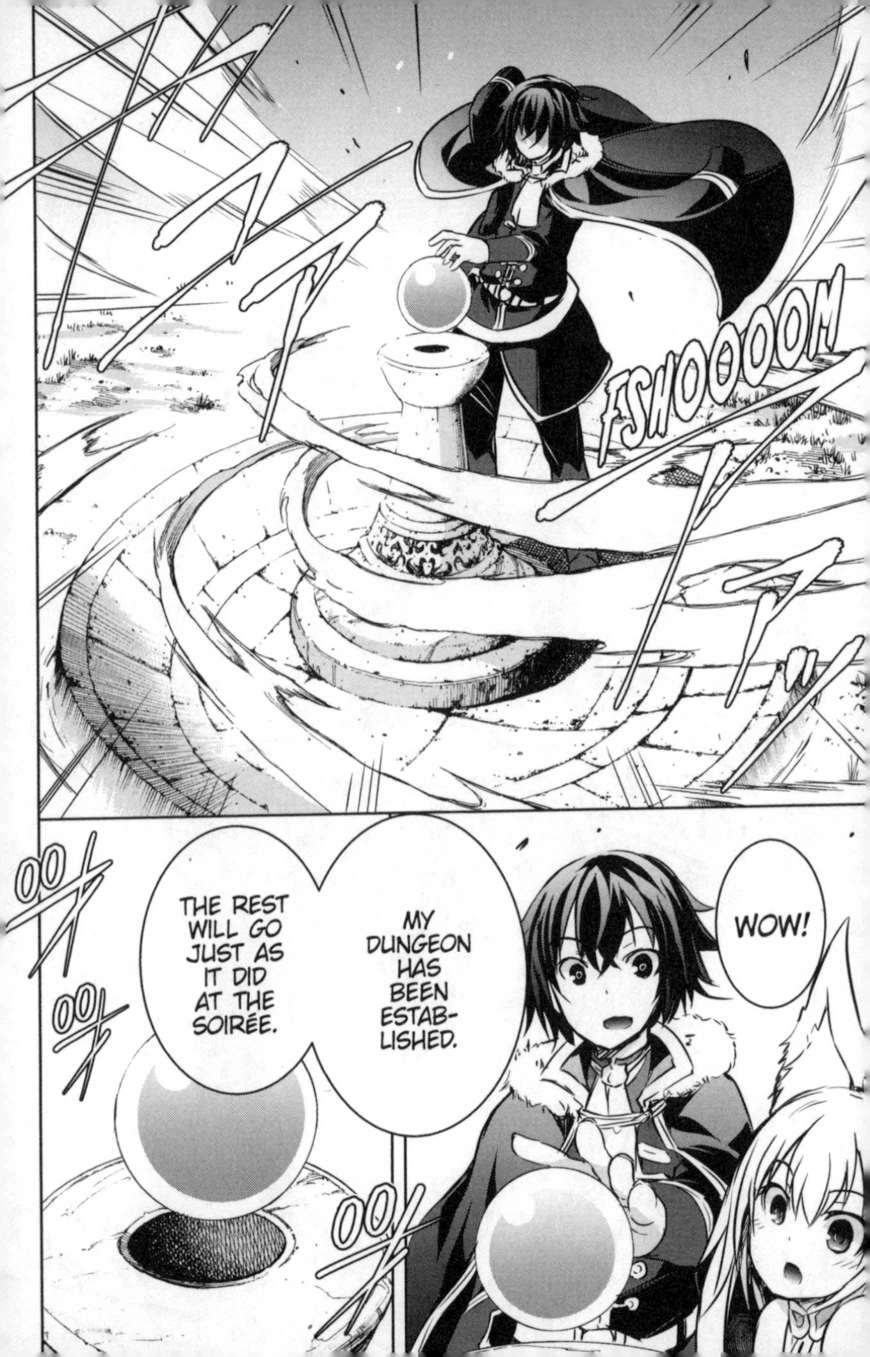
FSHOOOOM
WOW!
MY DUNGEON HAS BEEN ESTABLISHED.
THE REST WILL GO JUST AS IT DID AT THE SOIRÉE.

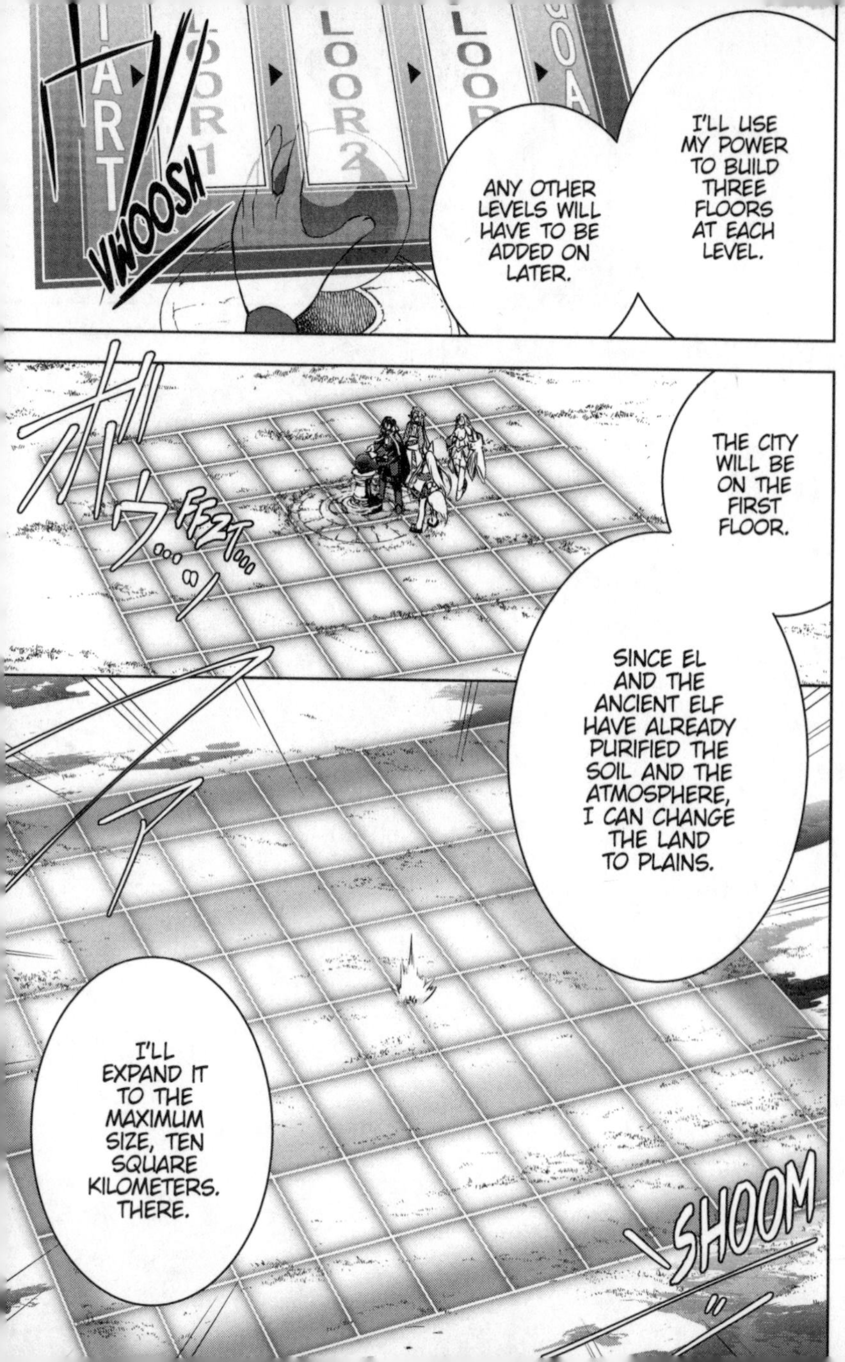
I'LL USE MY POWER TO BUILD THREE FLOORS AT EACH LEVEL.
ANY OTHER LEVELS WILL HAVE TO BE ADDED ON LATER.
VWOOSH
THE CITY WILL BE ON THE FIRST FLOOR.
FFZZT...
SINCE EL AND THE ANCIENT ELF HAVE ALREADY PURIFIED THE SOIL AND THE ATMOSPHERE, I CAN CHANGE THE LAND TO PLAINS.
I'LL EXPAND IT TO THE MAXIMUM SIZE, TEN SQUARE KILOMETERS. THERE.
SHOOM

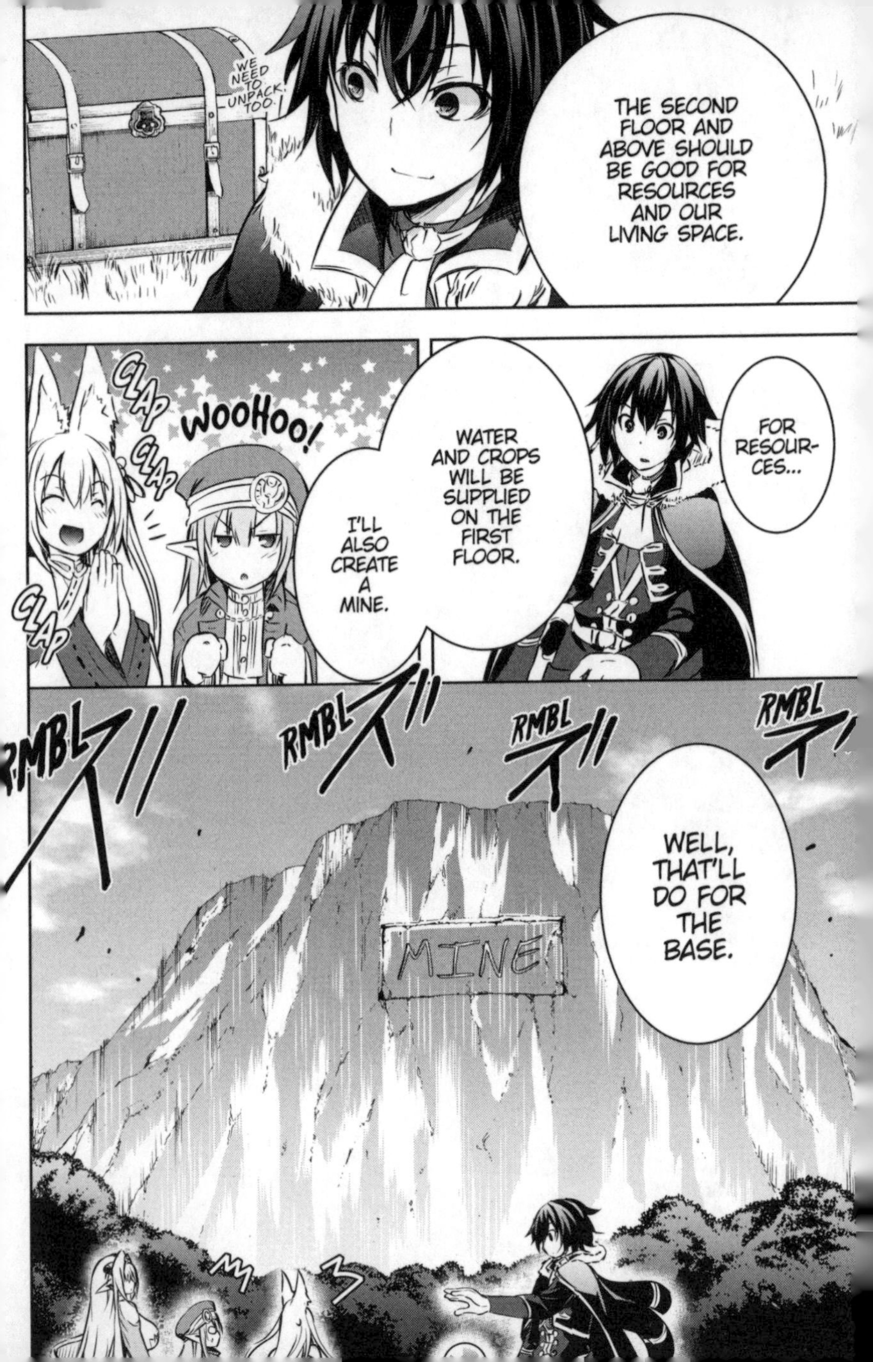
THE SECOND FLOOR AND ABOVE SHOULD BE GOOD FOR RESOURCES AND OUR LIVING SPACE.
WE NEED TO UNPACK, TOO.
FOR RESOUR-CES...
WATER AND CROPS WILL BE SUPPLIED ON THE FIRST FLOOR.
I'LL ALSO CREATE A MINE.
WOOHOO!
CLAP
CLAP
CLAP
RMBL
RMBL
RMBL
RMBL
WELL, THAT'LL DO FOR THE BASE.
MINE

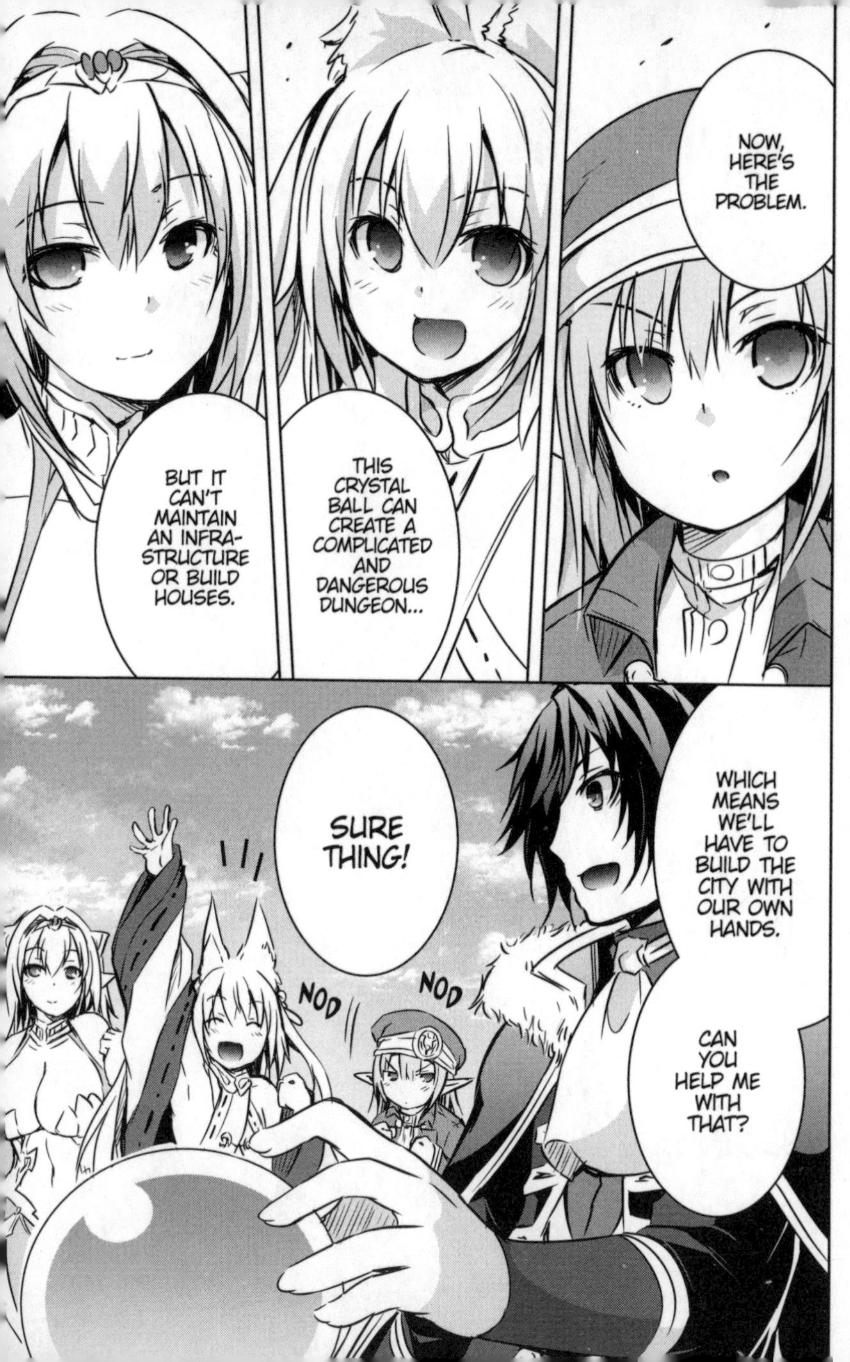
NOW, HERE'S THE PROBLEM.
THIS CRYSTAL BALL CAN CREATE A COMPLICATED AND DANGEROUS DUNGEON...
BUT IT CAN'T MAINTAIN AN INFRA-STRUCTURE OR BUILD HOUSES.
WHICH MEANS WE'LL HAVE TO BUILD THE CITY WITH OUR OWN HANDS.
CAN YOU HELP ME WITH THAT?
SURE THING!
NOD
NOD

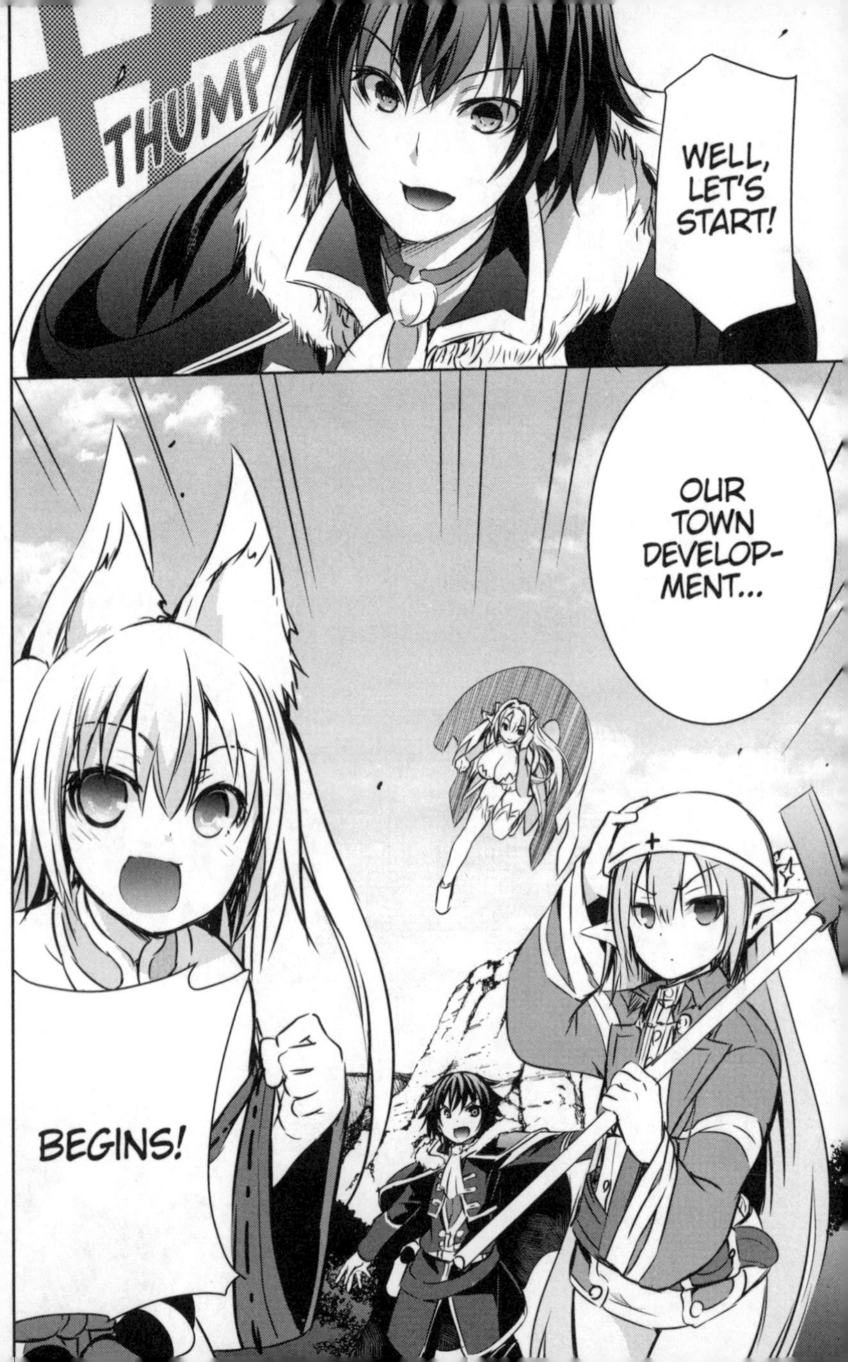
THUMP
WELL, LET'S START!
OUR TOWN DEVELOPMENT...
BEGINS!

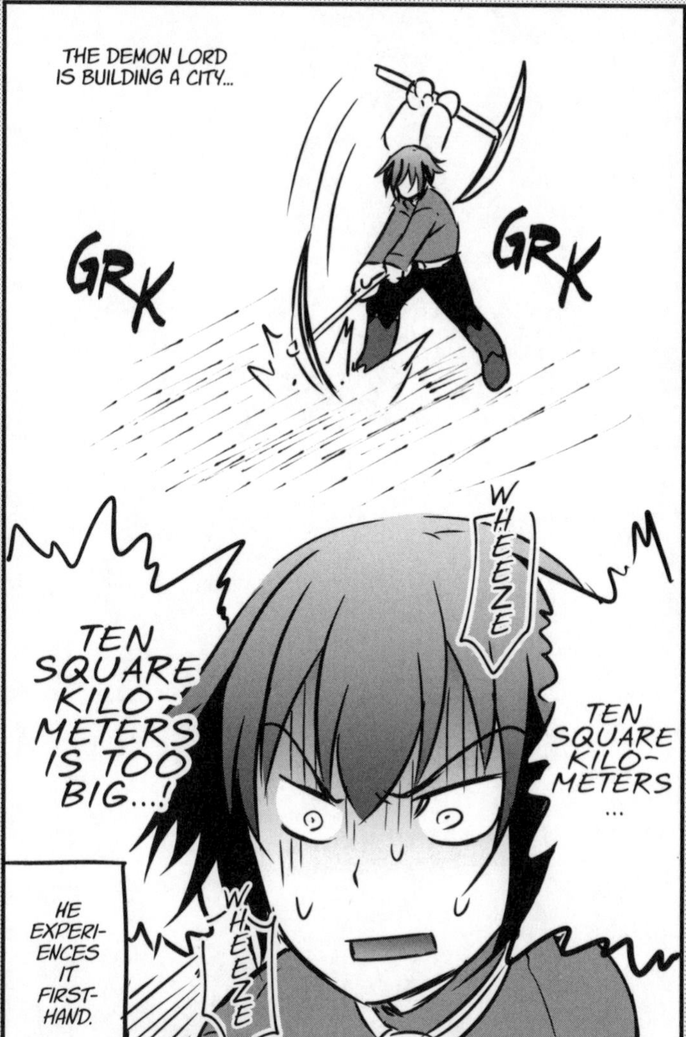
THE DEMON LORD IS BUILDING A CITY...
GRK
GRK
WHEEZE
TEN SQUARE KILO-METERS...
TEN SQUARE KILO-METERS IS TOO BIG...!
WHEEZE
HE EXPERIENCES IT FIRST-HAND.

DUNGEON BUILDER:
THE DEMON KING'S LABYRINTH IS A MODERN CITY!

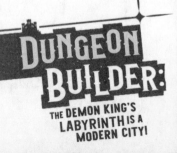

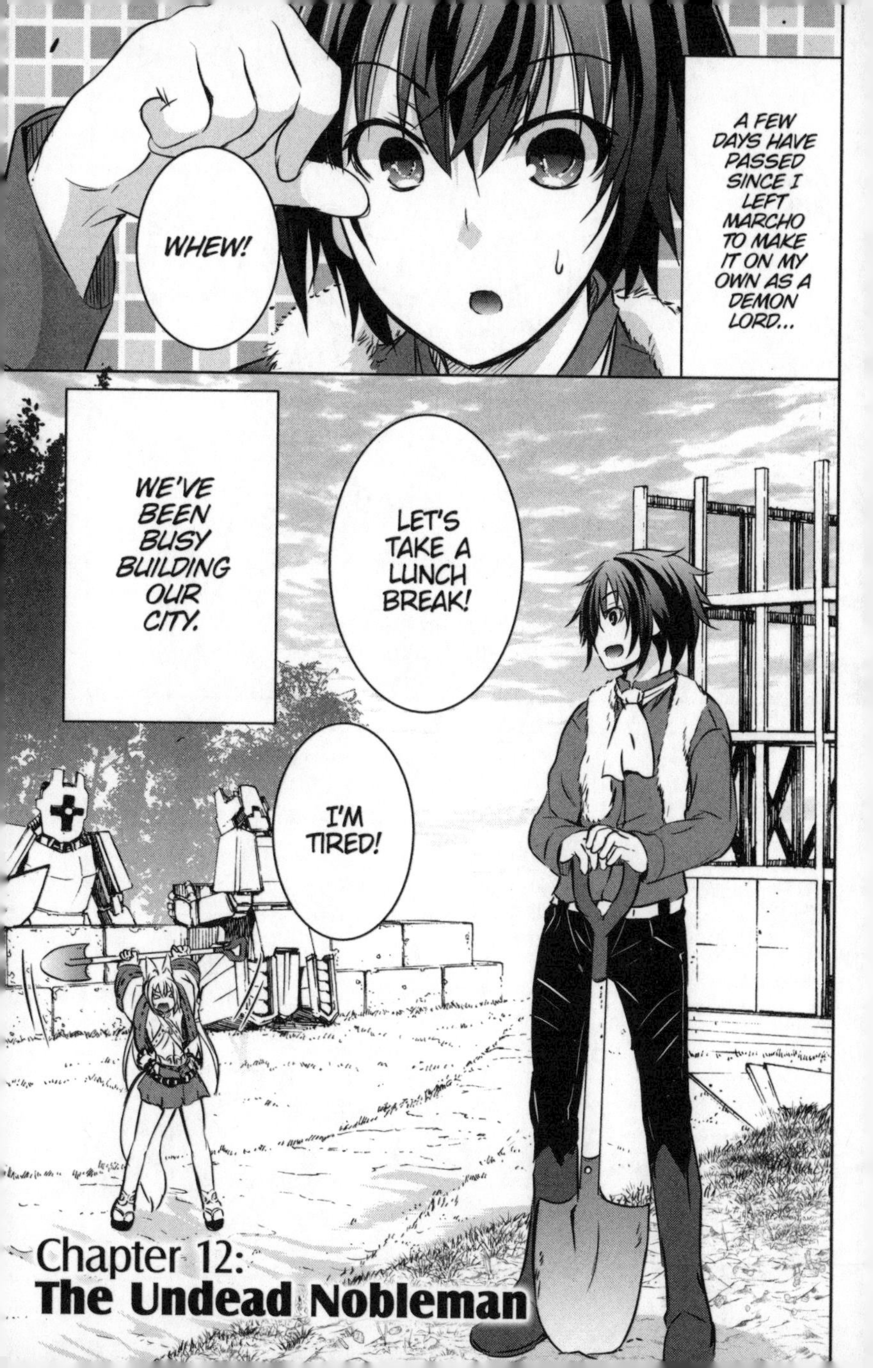
A FEW DAYS HAVE PASSED SINCE I LEFT MARCHO TO MAKE IT ON MY OWN AS A DEMON LORD...
WHEW!
WE'VE BEEN BUSY BUILDING OUR CITY.
LET'S TAKE A LUNCH BREAK!
I'M TIRED!
Chapter 12:
The Undead Nobleman

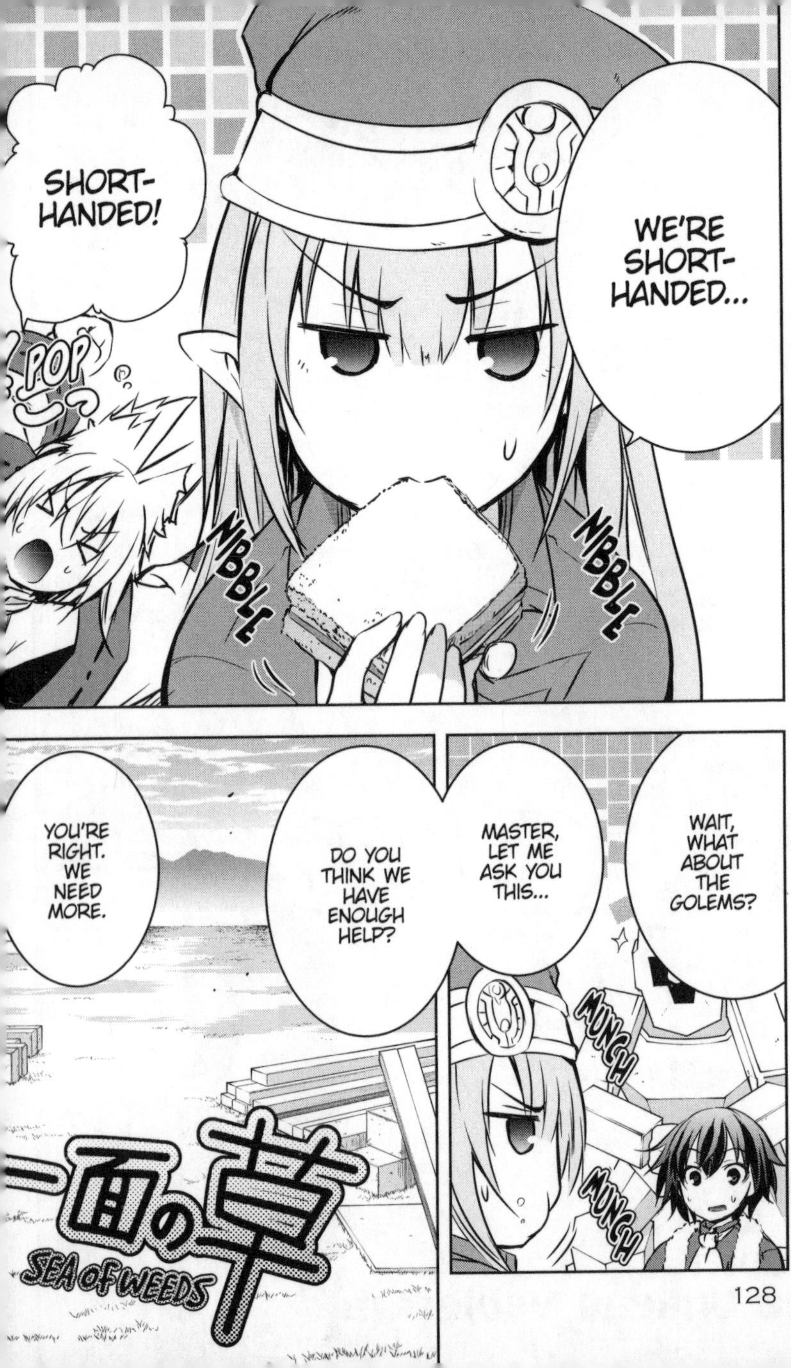
WE'RE SHORT-HANDED...
SHORT-HANDED!
POP
NIBBLE
NIBBLE
WAIT, WHAT ABOUT THE GOLEMS?
MASTER, LET ME ASK YOU THIS...
DO YOU THINK WE HAVE ENOUGH HELP?
MUNCH
MUNCH
YOU'RE RIGHT. WE NEED MORE.
一面の草
SEA OF WEEDS

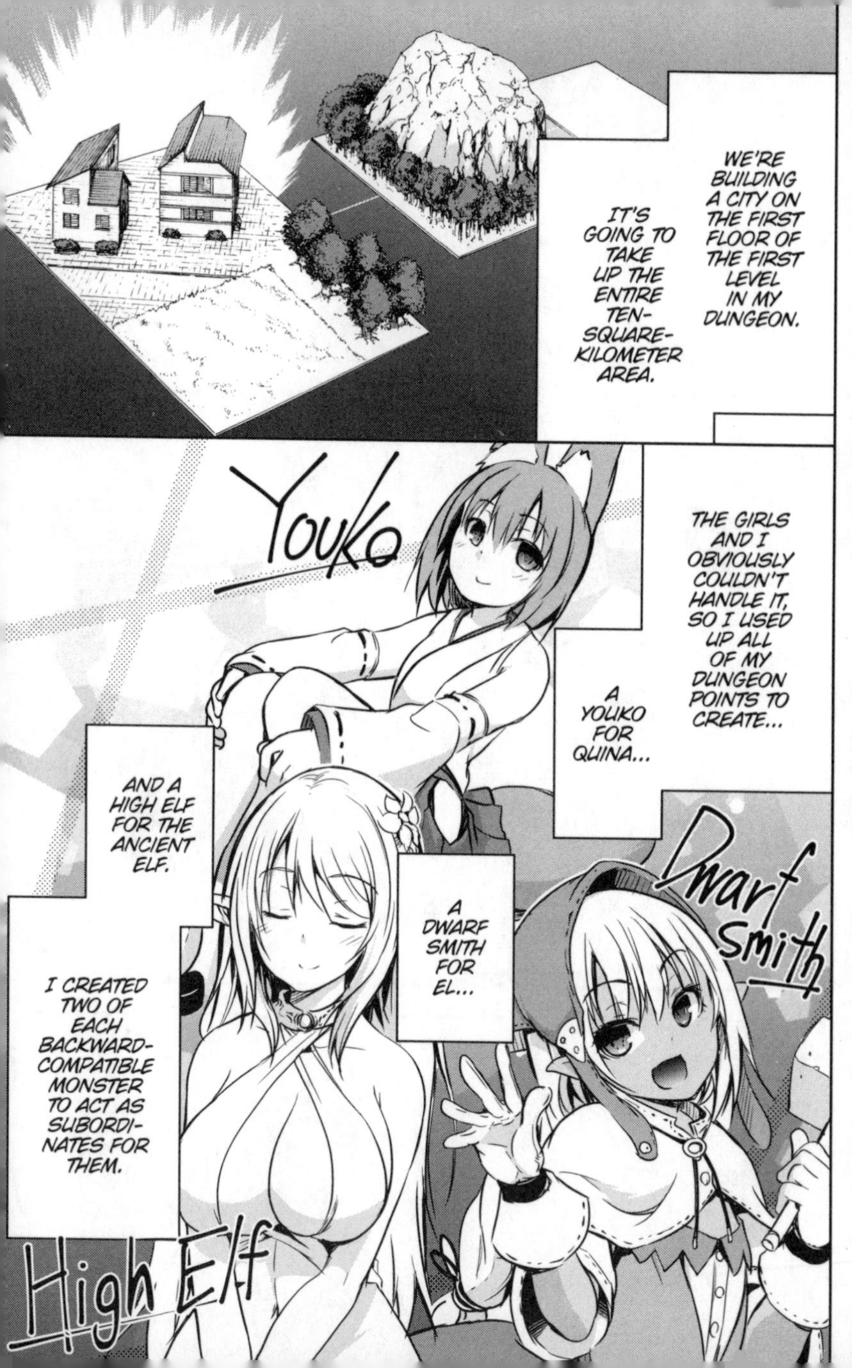
WE'RE BUILDING A CITY ON THE FIRST FLOOR OF THE FIRST LEVEL IN MY DUNGEON.
IT'S GOING TO TAKE UP THE ENTIRE TEN-SQUARE-KILOMETER AREA.
THE GIRLS AND I OBVIOUSLY COULDN'T HANDLE IT, SO I USED UP ALL OF MY DUNGEON POINTS TO CREATE...
Youko
A YOUKO FOR QUINA...
A DWARF SMITH FOR EL...
Dwarf Smith
AND A HIGH ELF FOR THE ANCIENT ELF.
I CREATED TWO OF EACH BACKWARD-COMPATIBLE MONSTER TO ACT AS SUBORDINATES FOR THEM.
High Elf

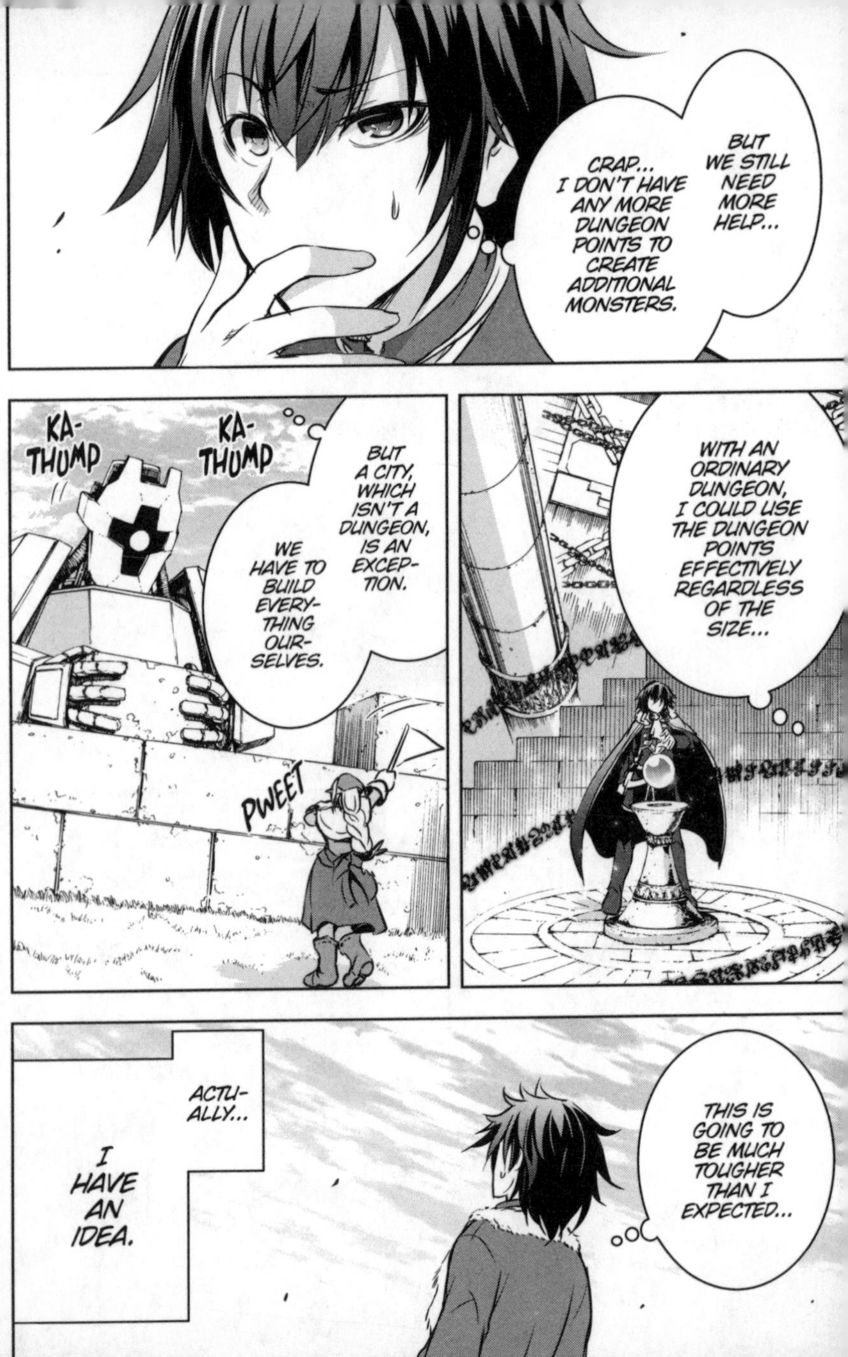
CRAP... I DON'T HAVE ANY MORE DUNGEON POINTS TO CREATE ADDITIONAL MONSTERS.
BUT WE STILL NEED MORE HELP...
WITH AN ORDINARY DUNGEON, I COULD USE THE DUNGEON POINTS EFFECTIVELY REGARDLESS OF THE SIZE...
KA-THUMP
KA-THUMP
BUT A CITY, WHICH ISN'T A DUNGEON, IS AN EXCEPTION.
WE HAVE TO BUILD EVERYTHING OURSELVES.
PWEET
THIS IS GOING TO BE MUCH TOUGHER THAN I EXPECTED...
ACTUALLY...
I HAVE AN IDEA.

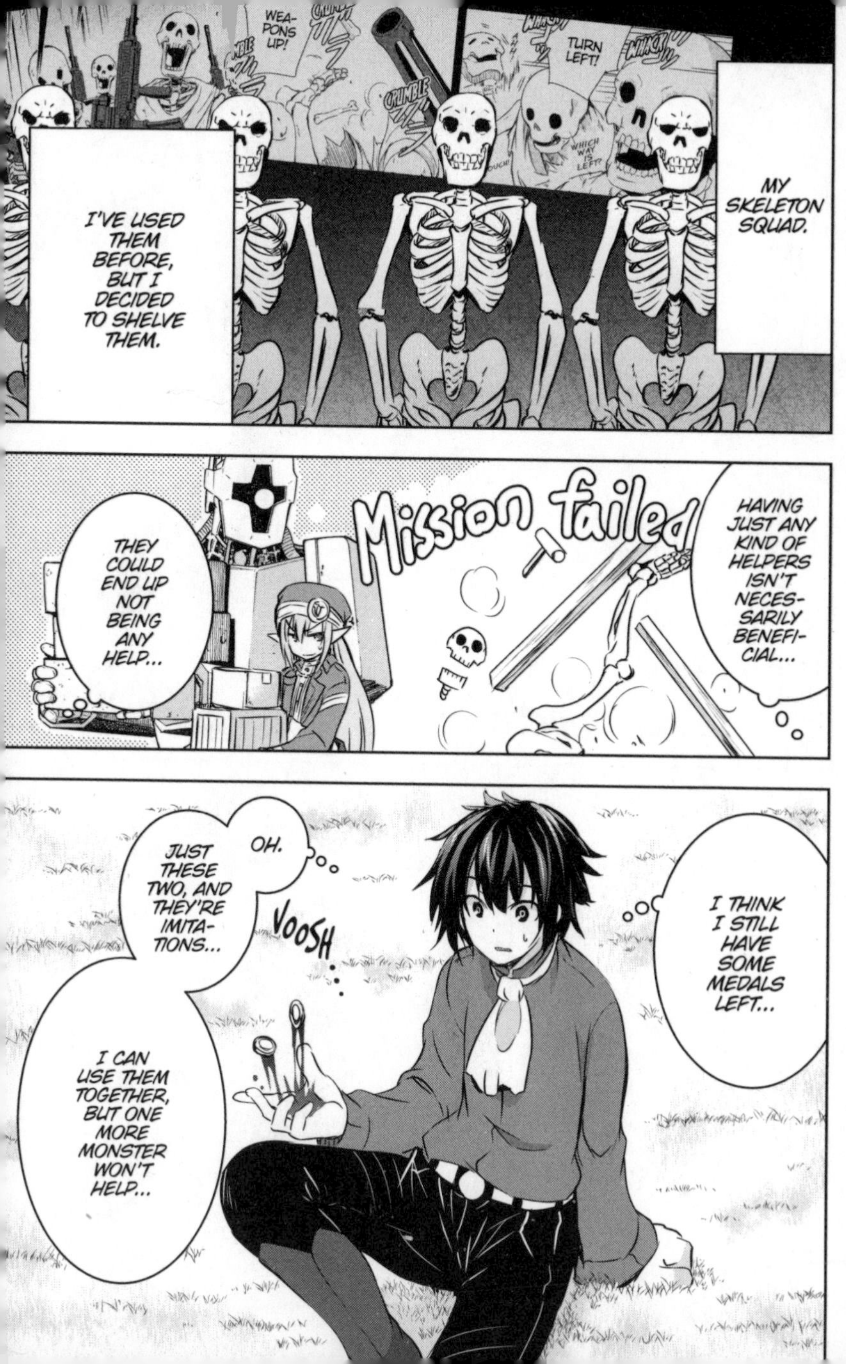
MY SKELETON SQUAD.
TURN LEFT!
WHICH WAY IS LEFT?
CRUMBLE
WEA-PONS UP!
I'VE USED THEM BEFORE, BUT I DECIDED TO SHELVE THEM.
HAVING JUST ANY KIND OF HELPERS ISN'T NECES-SARILY BENEFI-CIAL...
Mission failed
THEY COULD END UP NOT BEING ANY HELP...
I THINK I STILL HAVE SOME MEDALS LEFT...
OH.
JUST THESE TWO, AND THEY'RE IMITA-TIONS...
VOOSH
I CAN USE THEM TOGETHER, BUT ONE MORE MONSTER WON'T HELP...

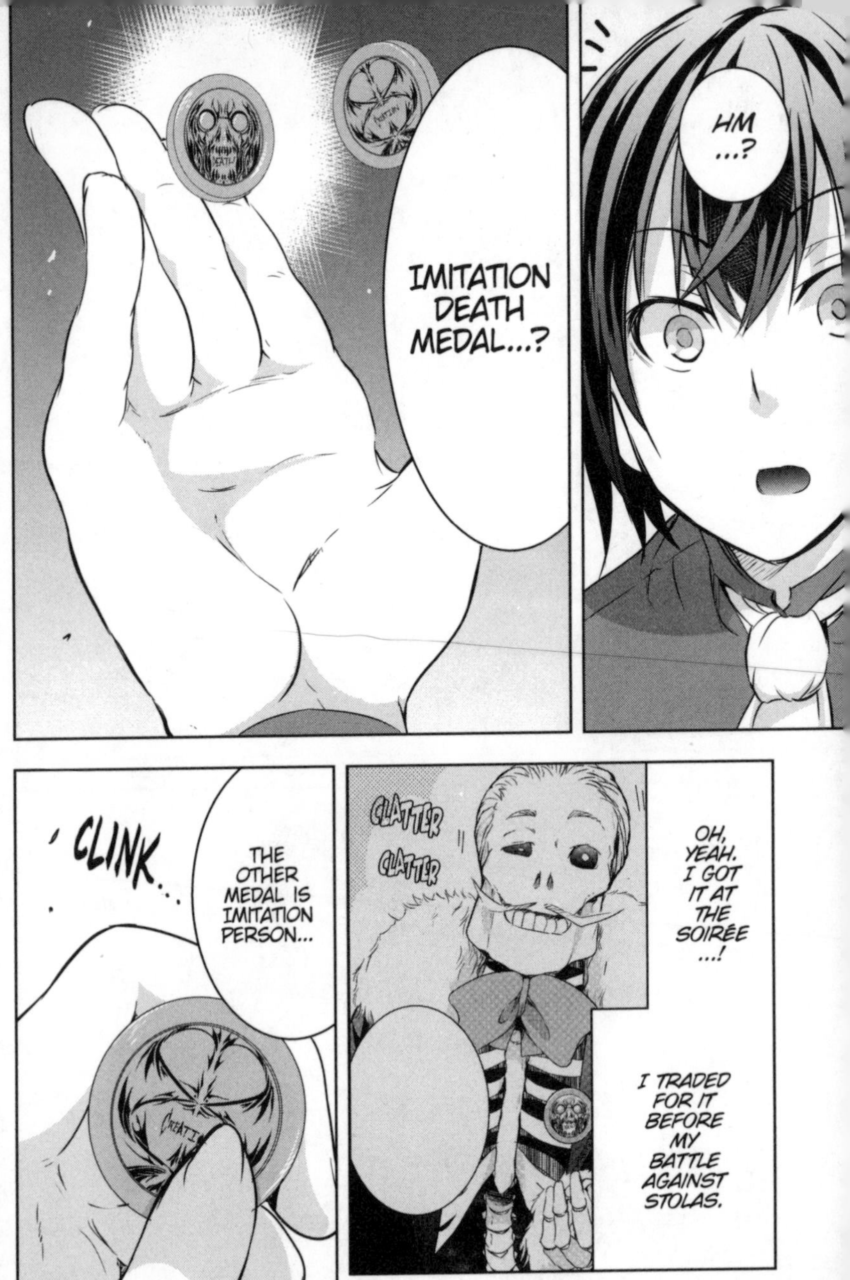
HM ...?
IMITATION DEATH MEDAL...?
OH, YEAH. I GOT IT AT THE SOIRÉE ...!
CLATTER
CLATTER
I TRADED FOR IT BEFORE MY BATTLE AGAINST STOLAS.
THE OTHER MEDAL IS IMITATION PERSON...
CLINK...

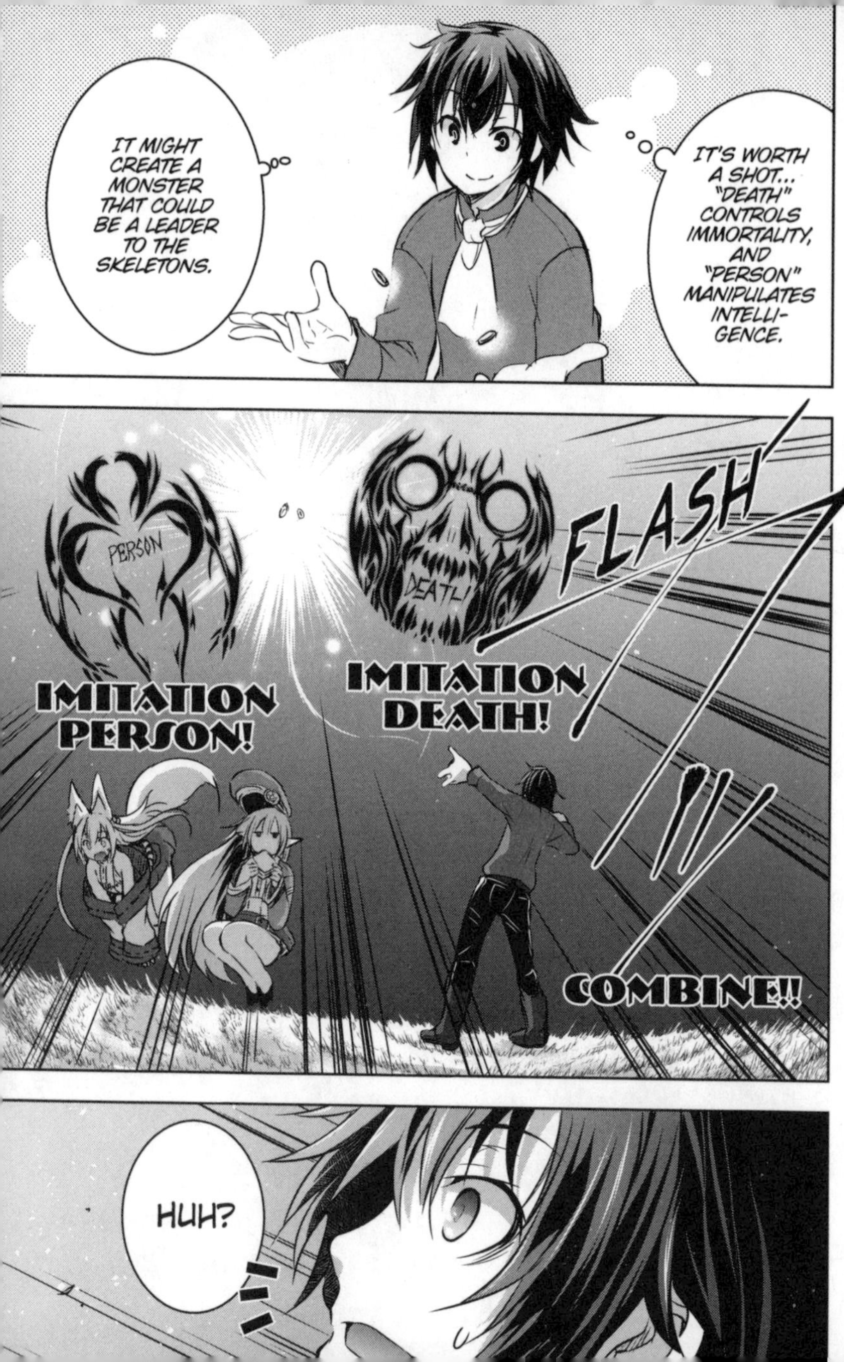
IT'S WORTH A SHOT... "DEATH" CONTROLS IMMORTALITY, AND "PERSON" MANIPULATES INTELLIGENCE.
IT MIGHT CREATE A MONSTER THAT COULD BE A LEADER TO THE SKELETONS.
FLASH
DEATH
IMITATION DEATH!
PERSON
IMITATION PERSON!
COMBINE!!
HUH?

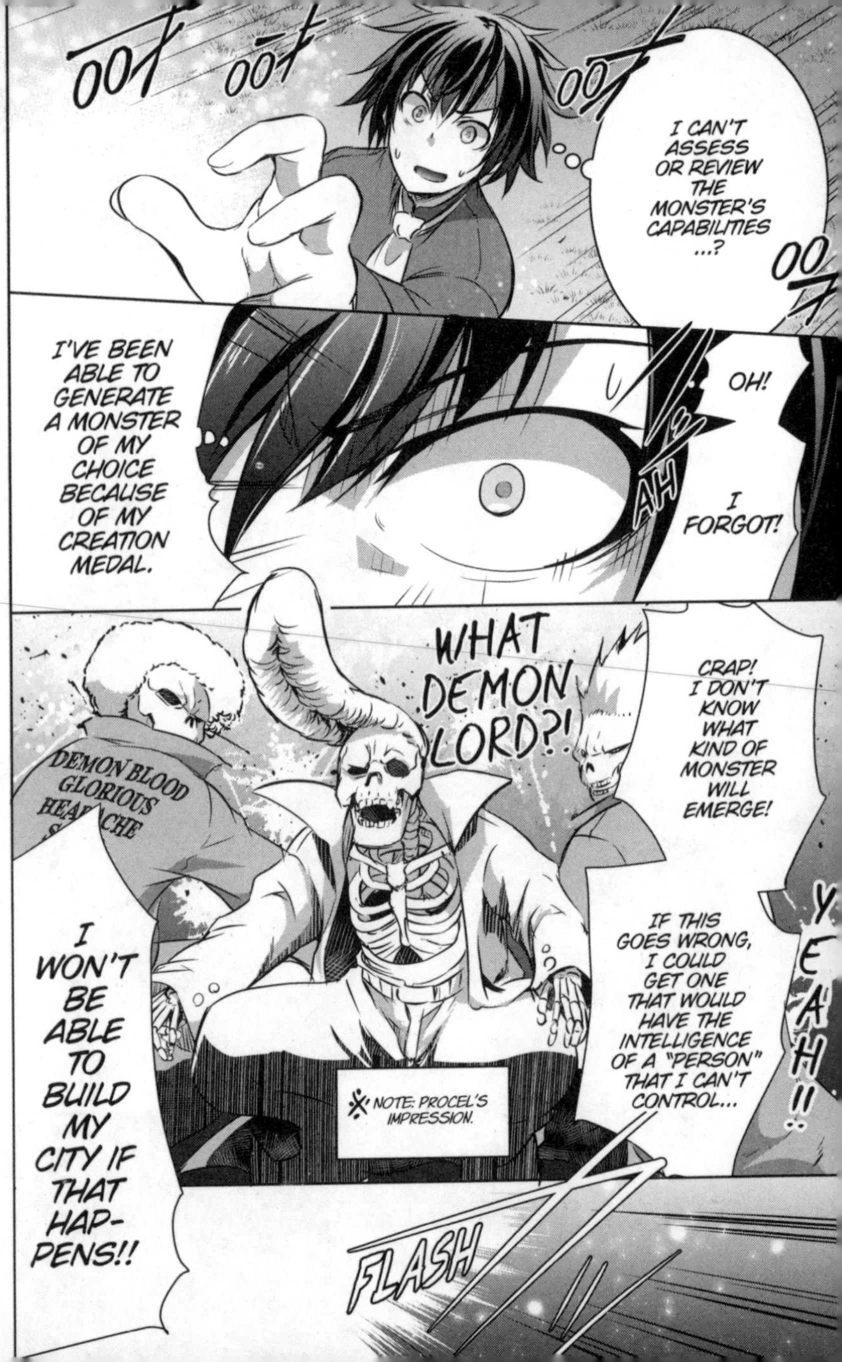

I CAN'T ASSESS OR REVIEW THE MONSTER'S CAPABILITIES ...?
OH!
AH
I FORGOT!
I'VE BEEN ABLE TO GENERATE A MONSTER OF MY CHOICE BECAUSE OF MY CREATION MEDAL.
CRAP! I DON'T KNOW WHAT KIND OF MONSTER WILL EMERGE!
WHAT DEMON LORD?!
DEMON BLOOD GLORIOUS HEADACHE
YEAH!!
IF THIS GOES WRONG, I COULD GET ONE THAT WOULD HAVE THE INTELLIGENCE OF A "PERSON" THAT I CAN'T CONTROL...
※NOTE: PROCEL'S IMPRESSION.
I WON'T BE ABLE TO BUILD MY CITY IF THAT HAP-PENS!!
FLASH

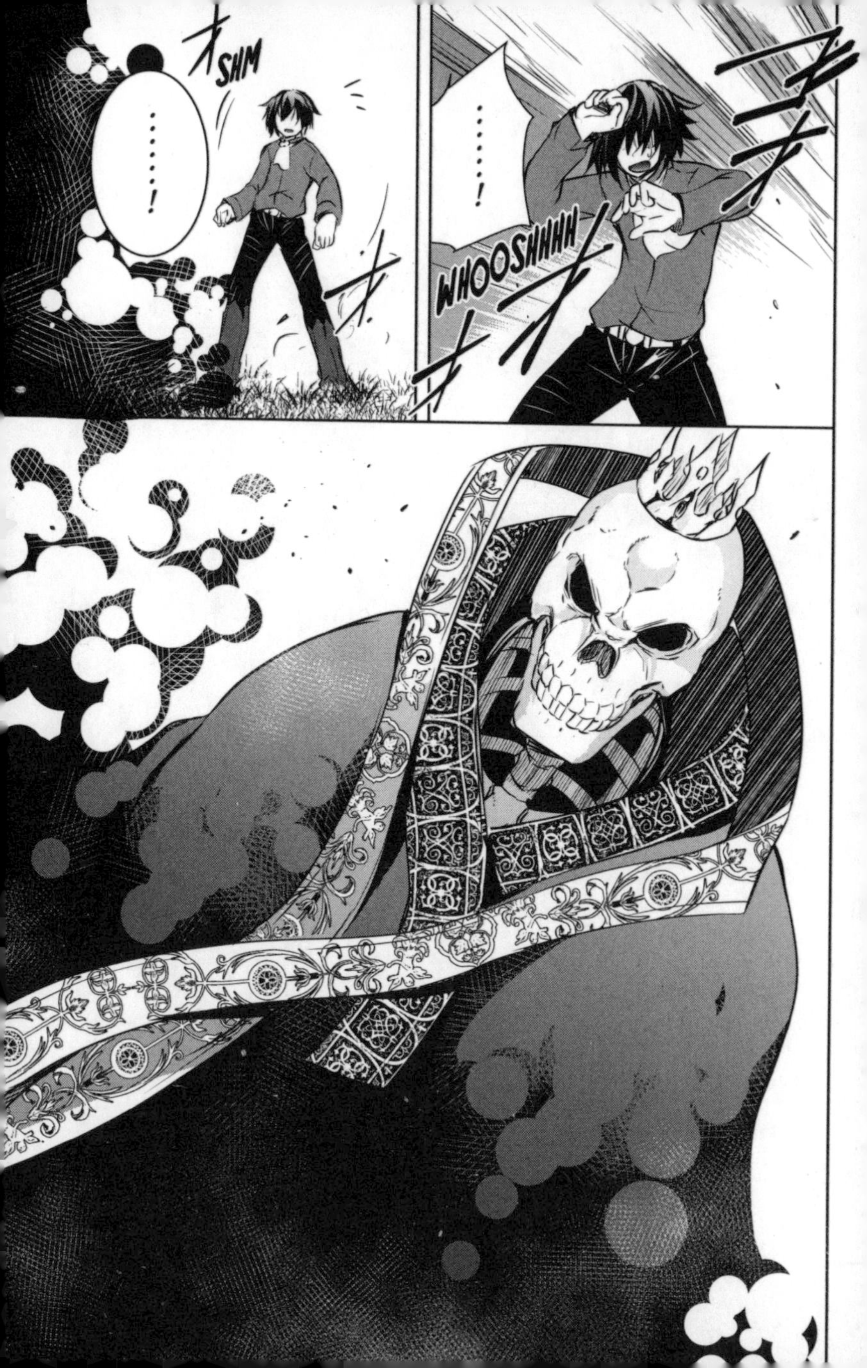

......!
WHOOSHHHH
......!
SHM

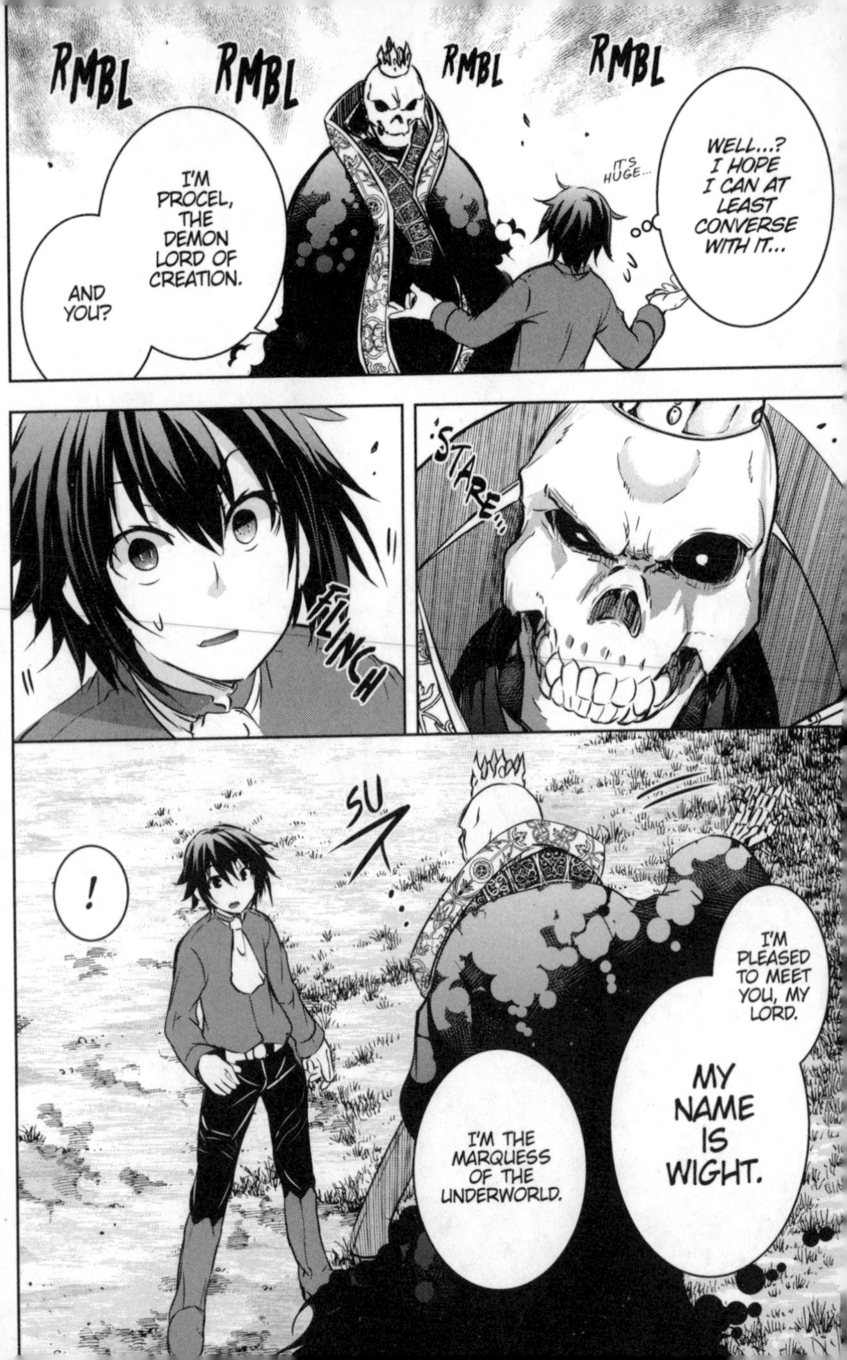
RMBL
RMBL
WELL...? I HOPE I CAN AT LEAST CONVERSE WITH IT...
IT'S HUGE...
RMBL
RMBL
I'M PROCEL, THE DEMON LORD OF CREATION.
AND YOU?
STARE...
FLINCH
SU
!
I'M PLEASED TO MEET YOU, MY LORD.
MY NAME IS WIGHT.
I'M THE MARQUESS OF THE UNDERWORLD.

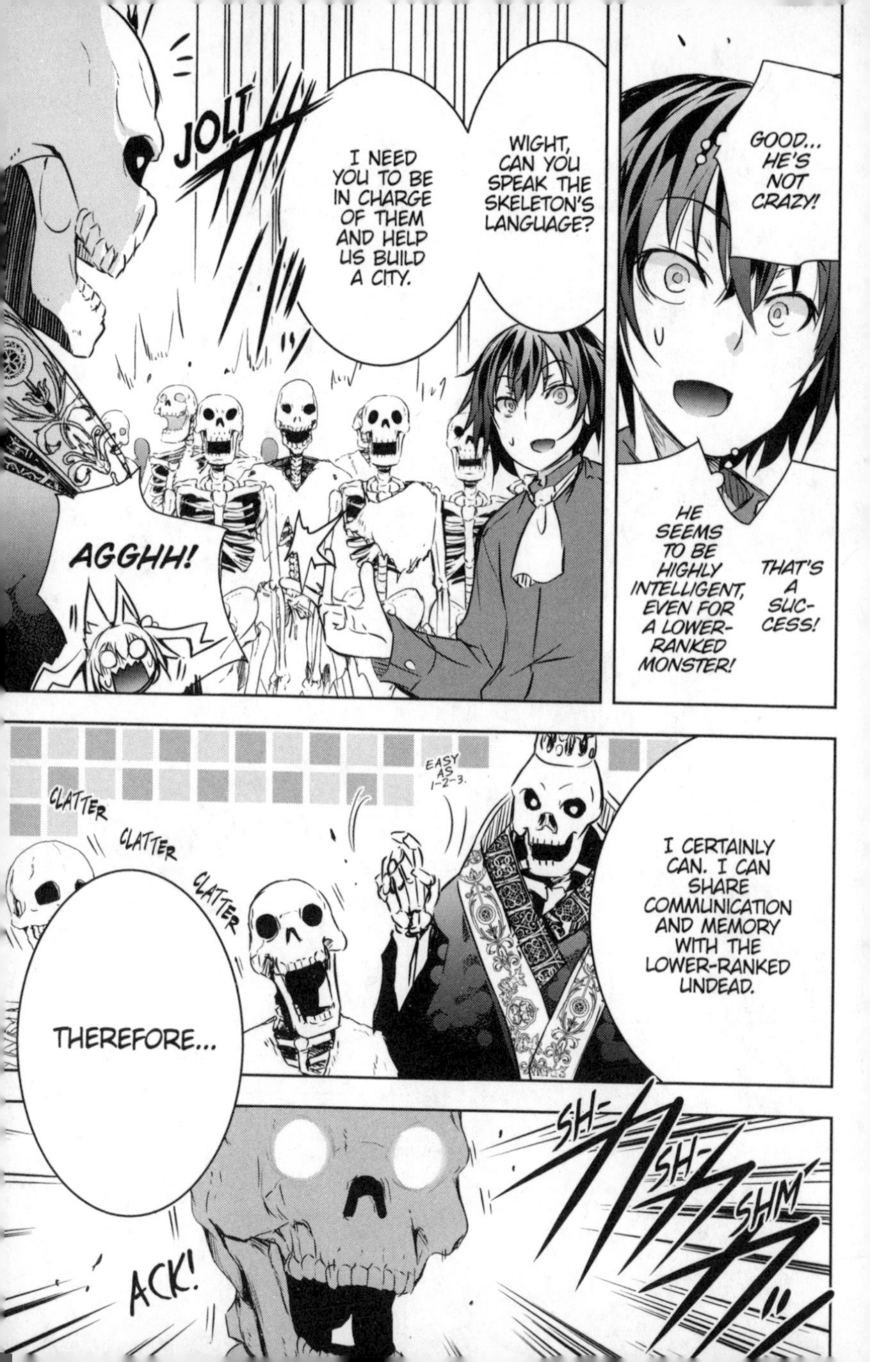
GOOD... HE'S NOT CRAZY!
THAT'S A SUC-CESS!
HE SEEMS TO BE HIGHLY INTELLIGENT, EVEN FOR A LOWER-RANKED MONSTER!
WIGHT, CAN YOU SPEAK THE SKELETON'S LANGUAGE?
I NEED YOU TO BE IN CHARGE OF THEM AND HELP US BUILD A CITY.
JOLT
AGGHH!
I CERTAINLY CAN. I CAN SHARE COMMUNICATION AND MEMORY WITH THE LOWER-RANKED UNDEAD.
EASY AS 1-2-3.
CLATTER
CLATTER
CLATTER
THEREFORE...
SH-
SH-
SHM
ACK!

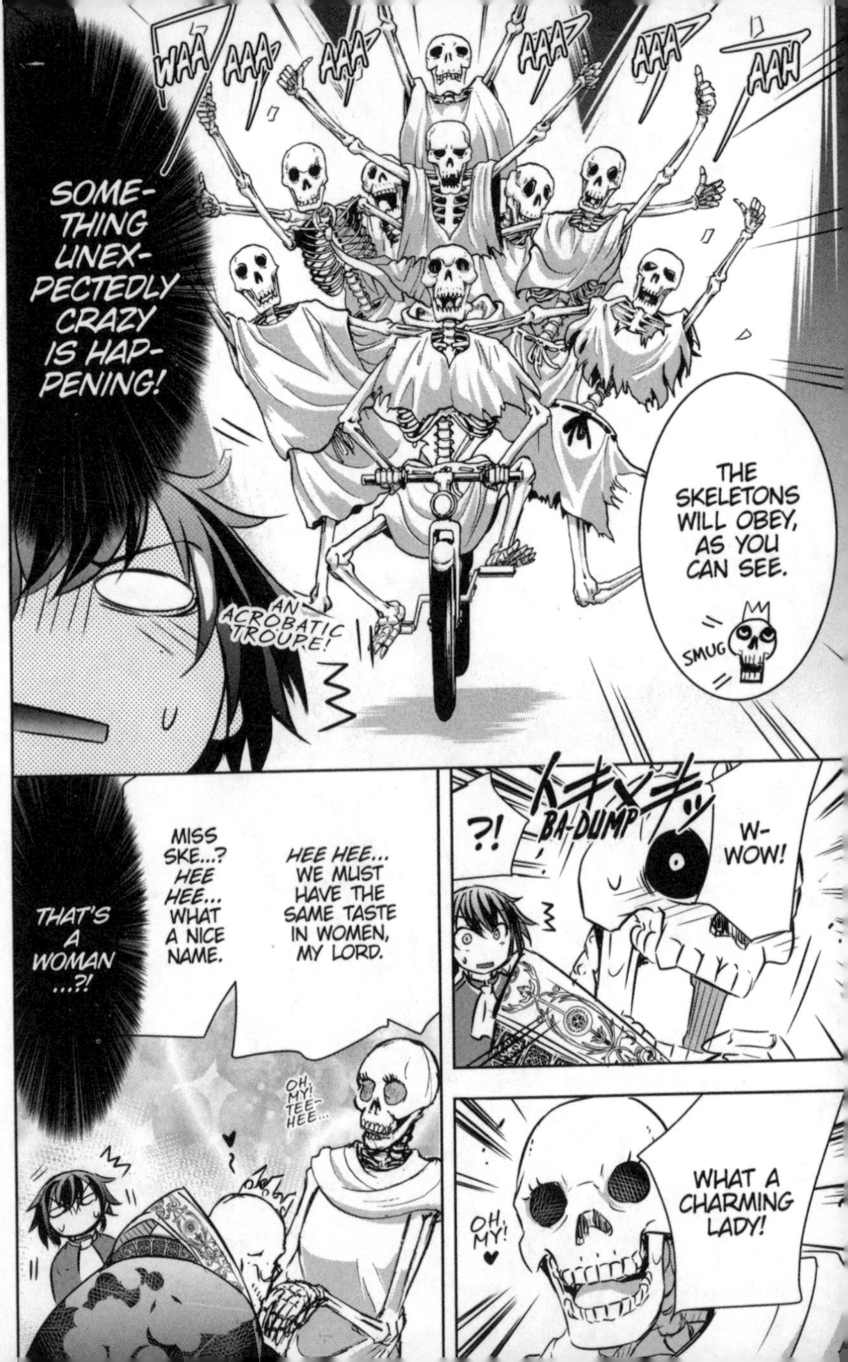
WAA AAA AAA AAA AAA AAH
THE SKELETONS WILL OBEY, AS YOU CAN SEE.
SMUG
SOMETHING UNEXPECTEDLY CRAZY IS HAPPENING!
AN ACROBATIC TROUPE!
BA-DUMP
W-WOW!
?!
WHAT A CHARMING LADY!
OH, MY! ♥
HEE HEE... WE MUST HAVE THE SAME TASTE IN WOMEN, MY LORD.
MISS SKE...? HEE HEE... WHAT A NICE NAME.
THAT'S A WOMAN...?!
OH, MY! TEE-HEE...

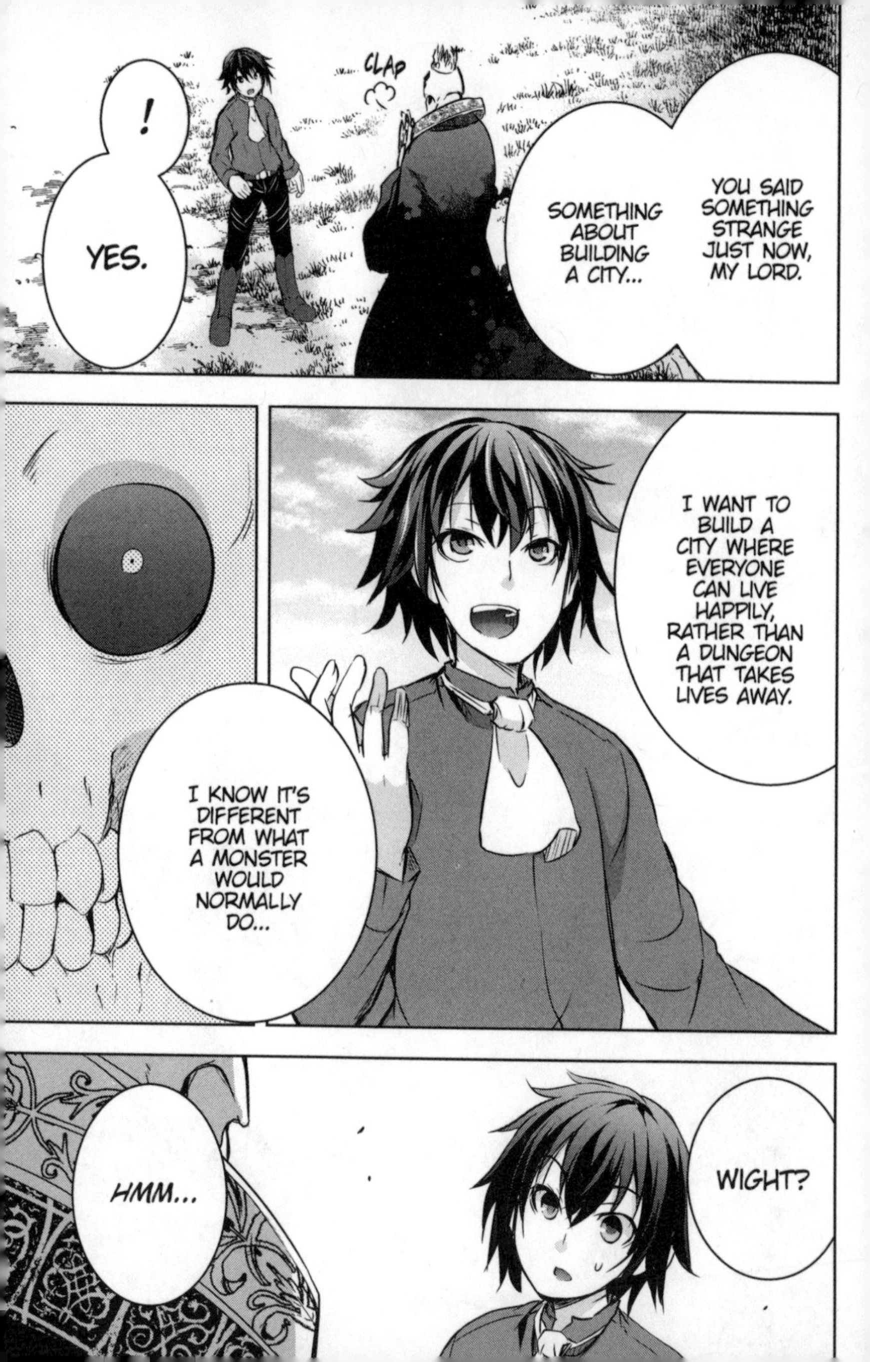
YOU SAID SOMETHING STRANGE JUST NOW, MY LORD.
SOMETHING ABOUT BUILDING A CITY...
CLAP
!
YES.
I WANT TO BUILD A CITY WHERE EVERYONE CAN LIVE HAPPILY, RATHER THAN A DUNGEON THAT TAKES LIVES AWAY.
I KNOW IT'S DIFFERENT FROM WHAT A MONSTER WOULD NORMALLY DO...
WIGHT?
HMM...

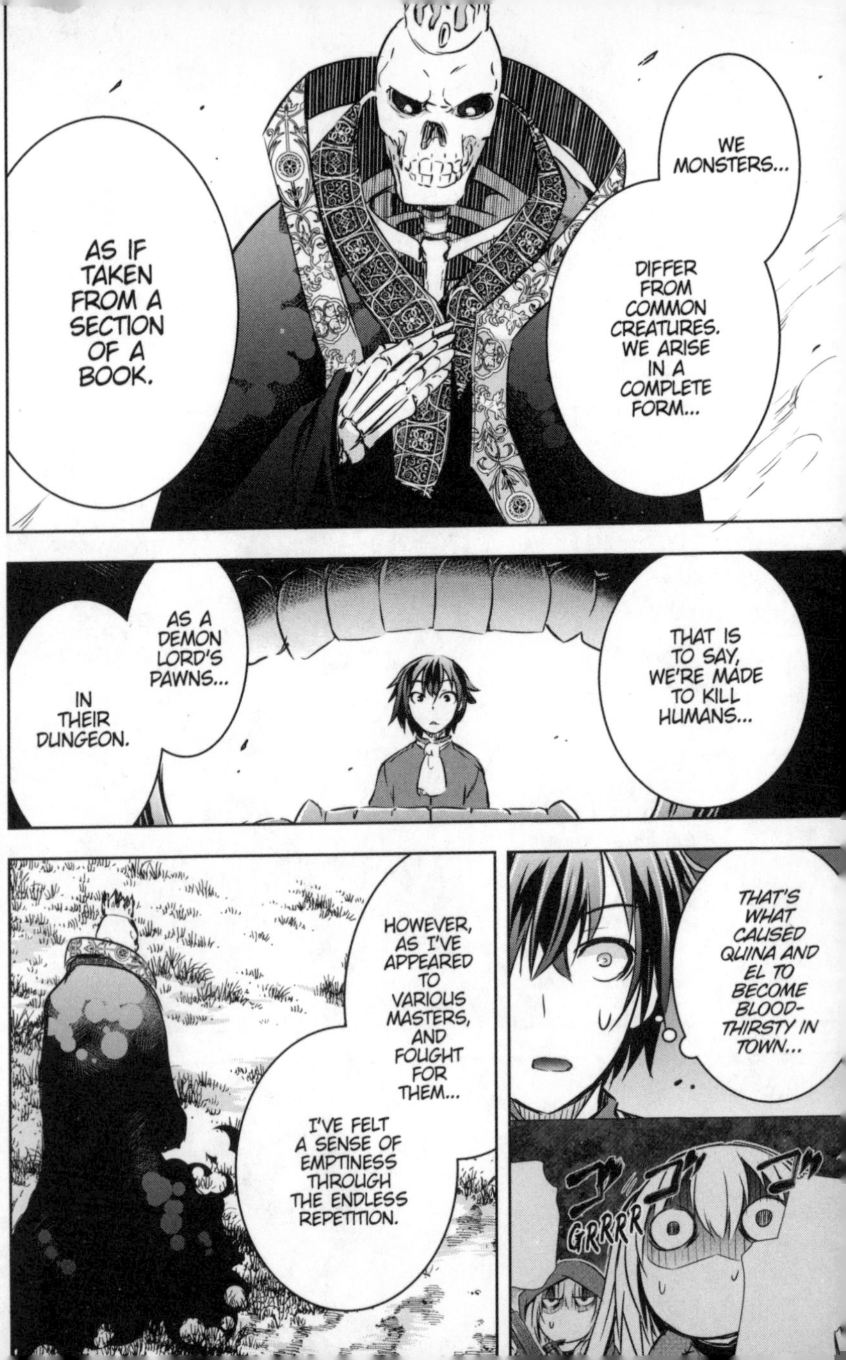
WE MONSTERS...
DIFFER FROM COMMON CREATURES. WE ARISE IN A COMPLETE FORM...
AS IF TAKEN FROM A SECTION OF A BOOK.
THAT IS TO SAY, WE'RE MADE TO KILL HUMANS...
AS A DEMON LORD'S PAWNS...
IN THEIR DUNGEON.
THAT'S WHAT CAUSED QUINA AND EL TO BECOME BLOOD-THIRSTY IN TOWN...
ゴゴゴ
GRRRR
HOWEVER, AS I'VE APPEARED TO VARIOUS MASTERS, AND FOUGHT FOR THEM...
I'VE FELT A SENSE OF EMPTINESS THROUGH THE ENDLESS REPETITION.

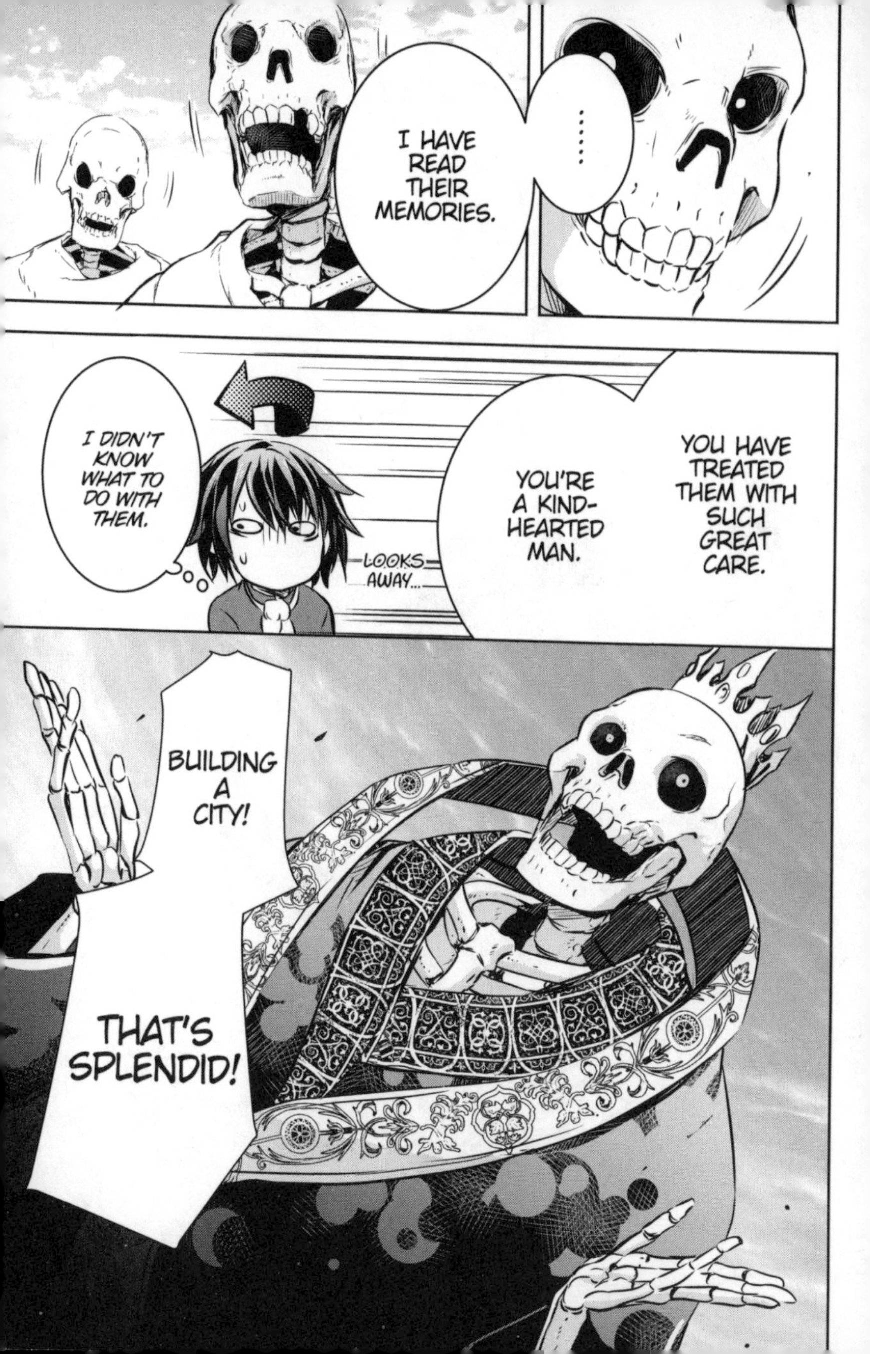
......
I HAVE READ THEIR MEMORIES.
YOU HAVE TREATED THEM WITH SUCH GREAT CARE.
YOU'RE A KIND-HEARTED MAN.
I DIDN'T KNOW WHAT TO DO WITH THEM.
LOOKS AWAY...
BUILDING A CITY!
THAT'S SPLENDID!

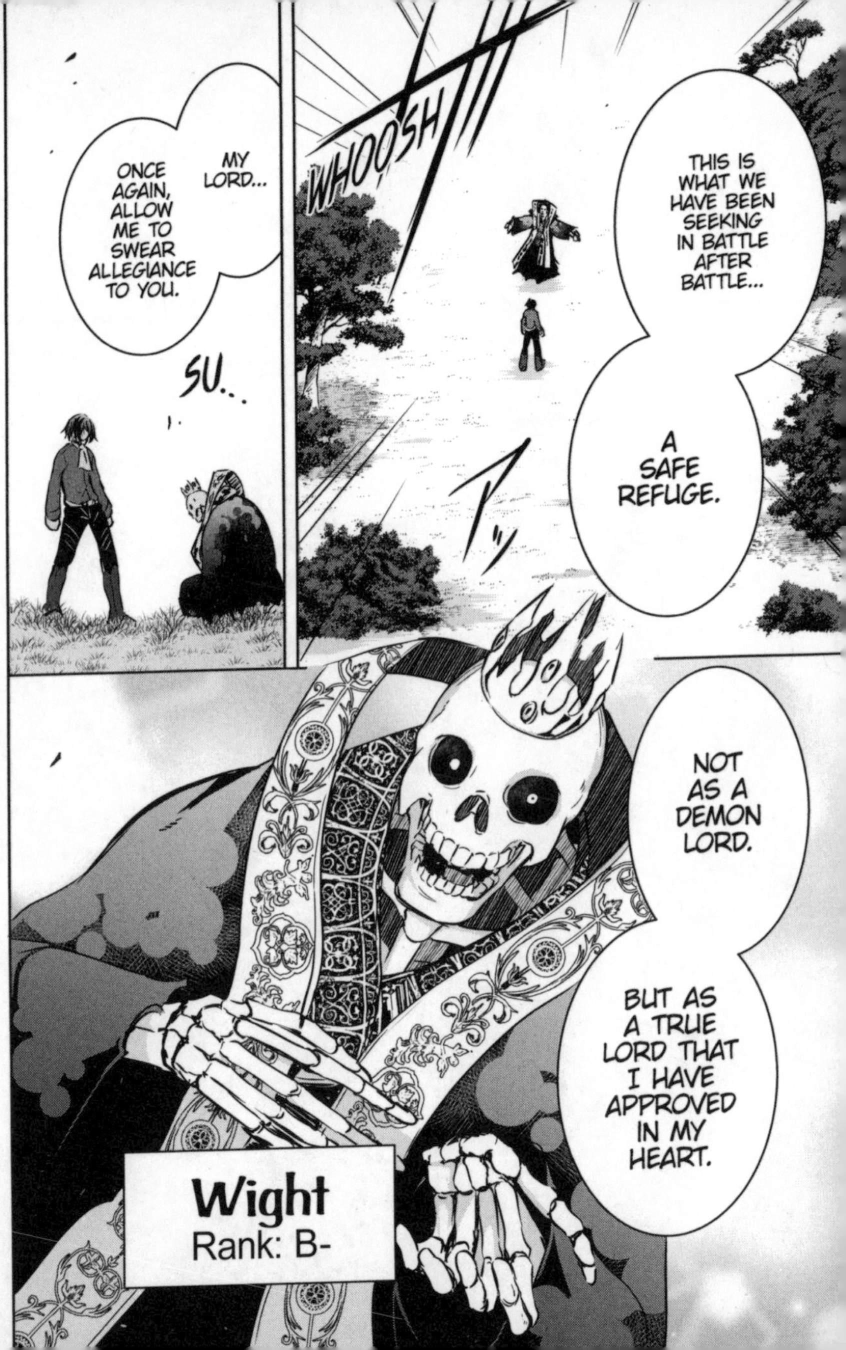
WHOOSH
THIS IS WHAT WE HAVE BEEN SEEKING IN BATTLE AFTER BATTLE...
A SAFE REFUGE.
MY LORD...
ONCE AGAIN, ALLOW ME TO SWEAR ALLEGIANCE TO YOU.
SU...
NOT AS A DEMON LORD.
BUT AS A TRUE LORD THAT I HAVE APPROVED IN MY HEART.
Wight
Rank: B-

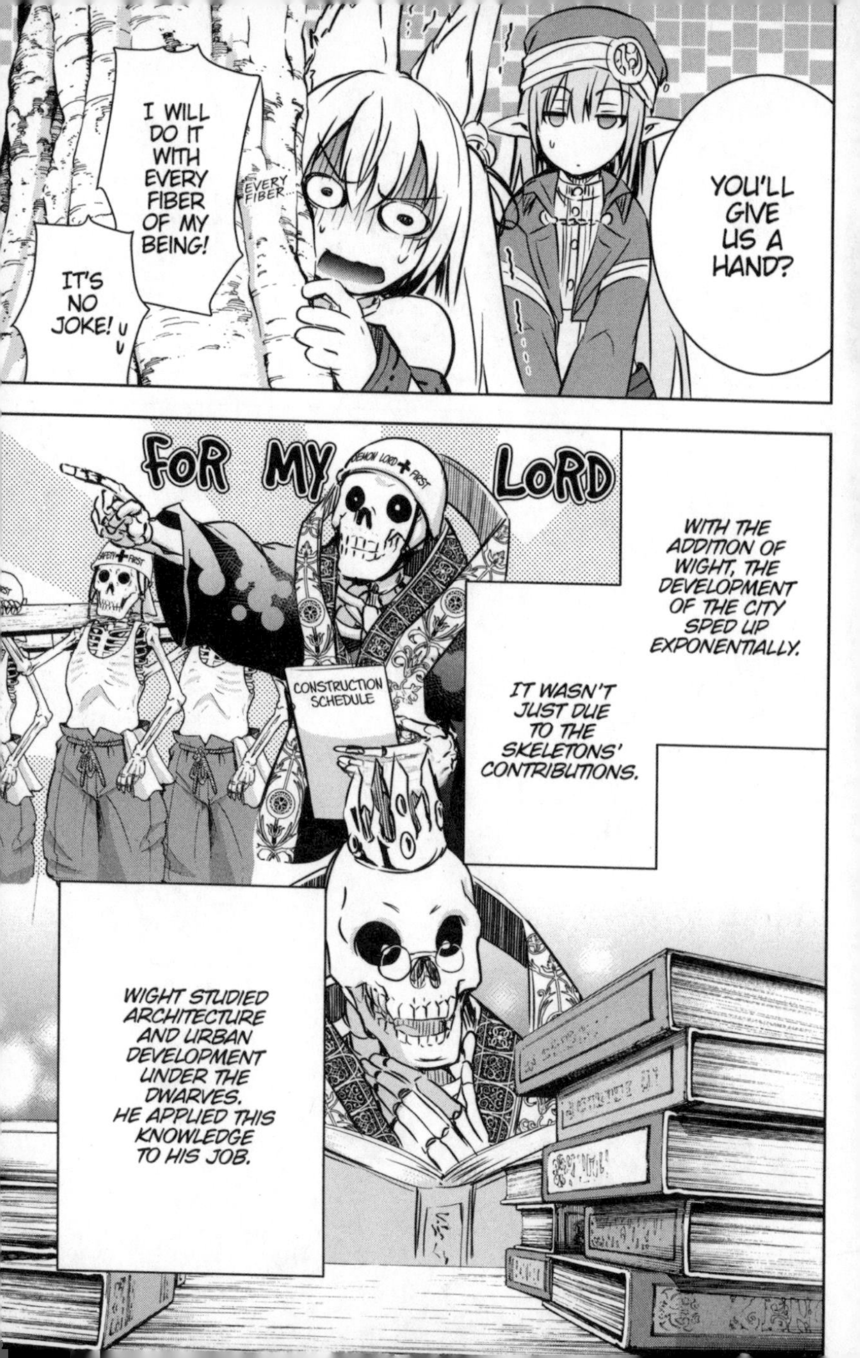
YOU'LL GIVE US A HAND?
I WILL DO IT WITH EVERY FIBER OF MY BEING!
EVERY FIBER...
IT'S NO JOKE!
WITH THE ADDITION OF WIGHT, THE DEVELOPMENT OF THE CITY SPED UP EXPONENTIALLY.
FOR MY LORD
DEMON LORD FIRST
IT WASN'T JUST DUE TO THE SKELETONS' CONTRIBUTIONS.
CONSTRUCTION SCHEDULE
SAFETY FIRST
WIGHT STUDIED ARCHITECTURE AND URBAN DEVELOPMENT UNDER THE DWARVES. HE APPLIED THIS KNOWLEDGE TO HIS JOB.

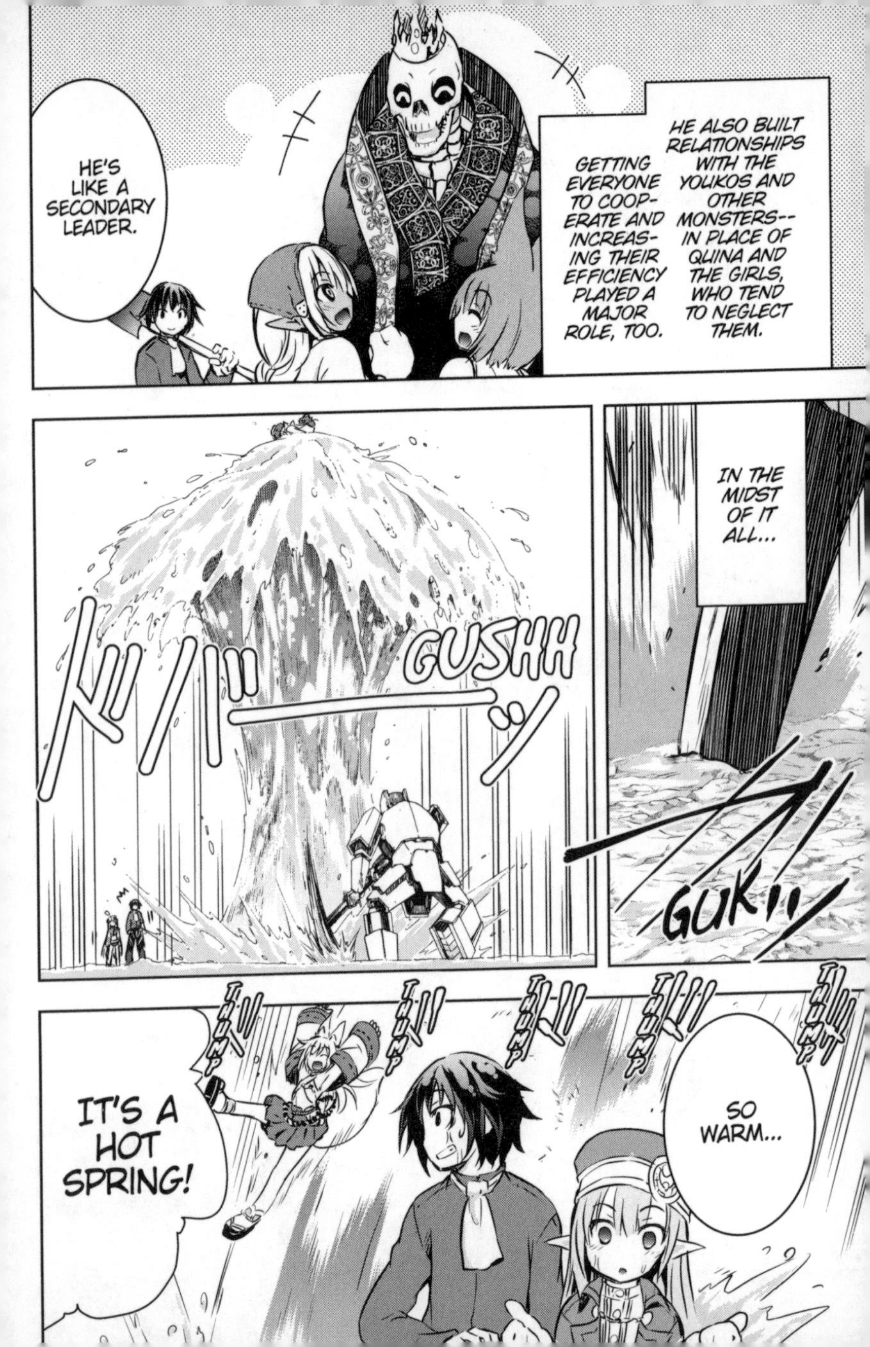
HE ALSO BUILT RELATIONSHIPS WITH THE YOUKOS AND OTHER MONSTERS-- IN PLACE OF QUINA AND THE GIRLS, WHO TEND TO NEGLECT THEM.
GETTING EVERYONE TO COOP-ERATE AND INCREAS-ING THEIR EFFICIENCY PLAYED A MAJOR ROLE, TOO.
HE'S LIKE A SECONDARY LEADER.
IN THE MIDST OF IT ALL...
GUK!!
GUSHH
ドバーッ
THUMP
THUMP
THUMP
THUMP
THUMP
SO WARM...
IT'S A HOT SPRING!

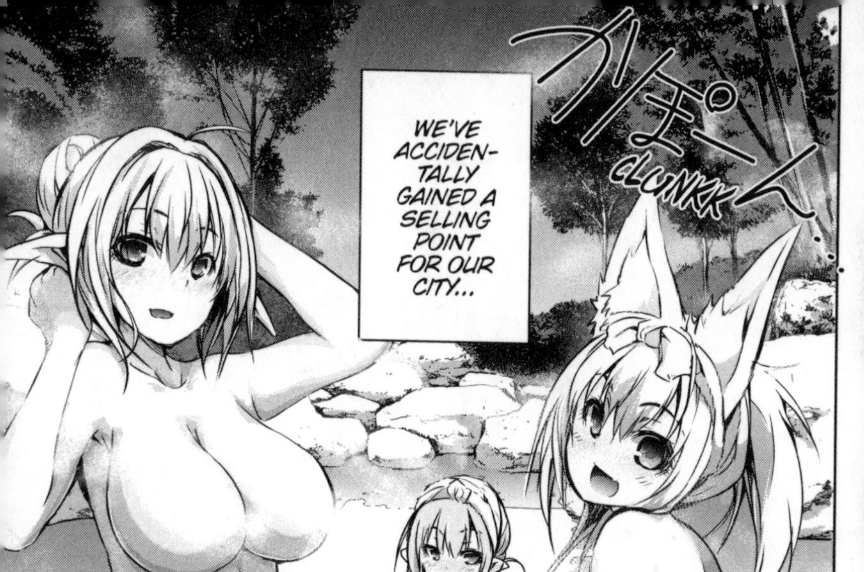
カポーン
CLUNKK
WE'VE ACCIDEN-TALLY GAINED A SELLING POINT FOR OUR CITY...
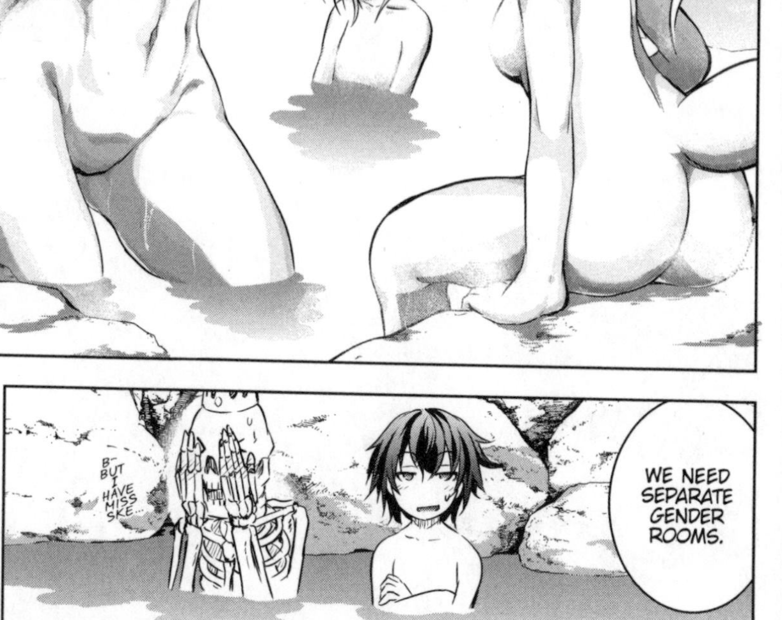
WE NEED SEPARATE GENDER ROOMS.
B-BUT I HAVE MISS SKE...

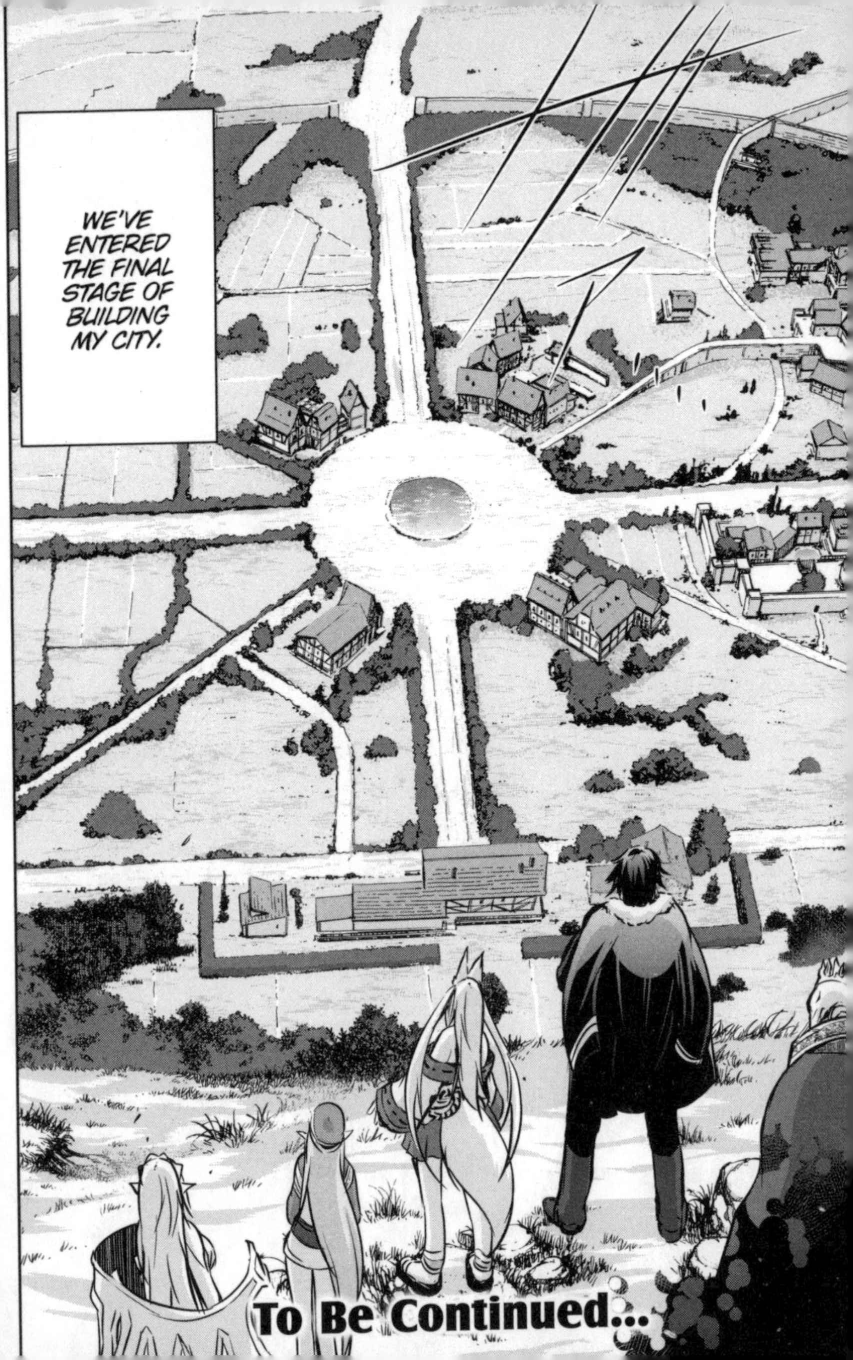
WE'VE ENTERED THE FINAL STAGE OF BUILDING MY CITY.
To Be Continued...

Bonus Manga: **The Melancholy of Astaroth**

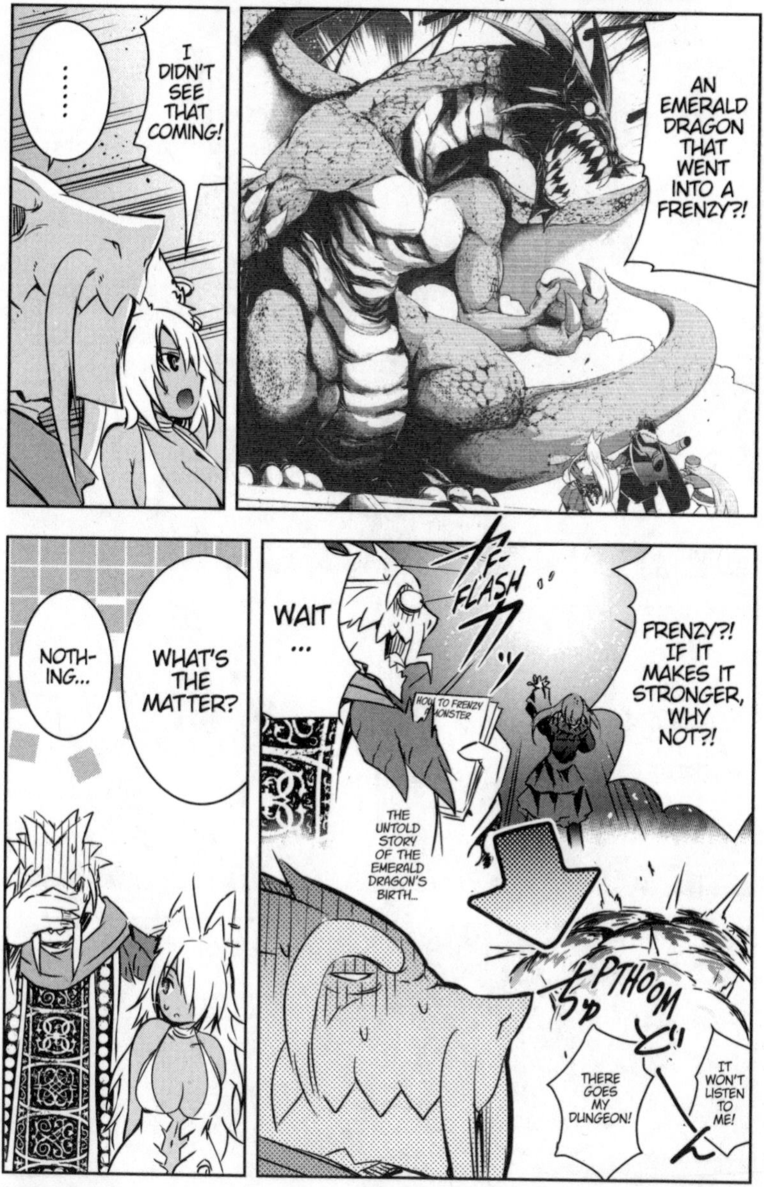
AN EMERALD DRAGON THAT WENT INTO A FRENZY?!
I DIDN'T SEE THAT COMING!
......
WAIT ...
F-FLASH
FRENZY?! IF IT MAKES IT STRONGER, WHY NOT?!
HOW TO FRENZY A MONSTER
THE UNTOLD STORY OF THE EMERALD DRAGON'S BIRTH...
PTHOOM
IT WON'T LISTEN TO ME!
THERE GOES MY DUNGEON!
WHAT'S THE MATTER?
NOTH-ING...

Bonus Manga: **Miss Stolas is Angry**

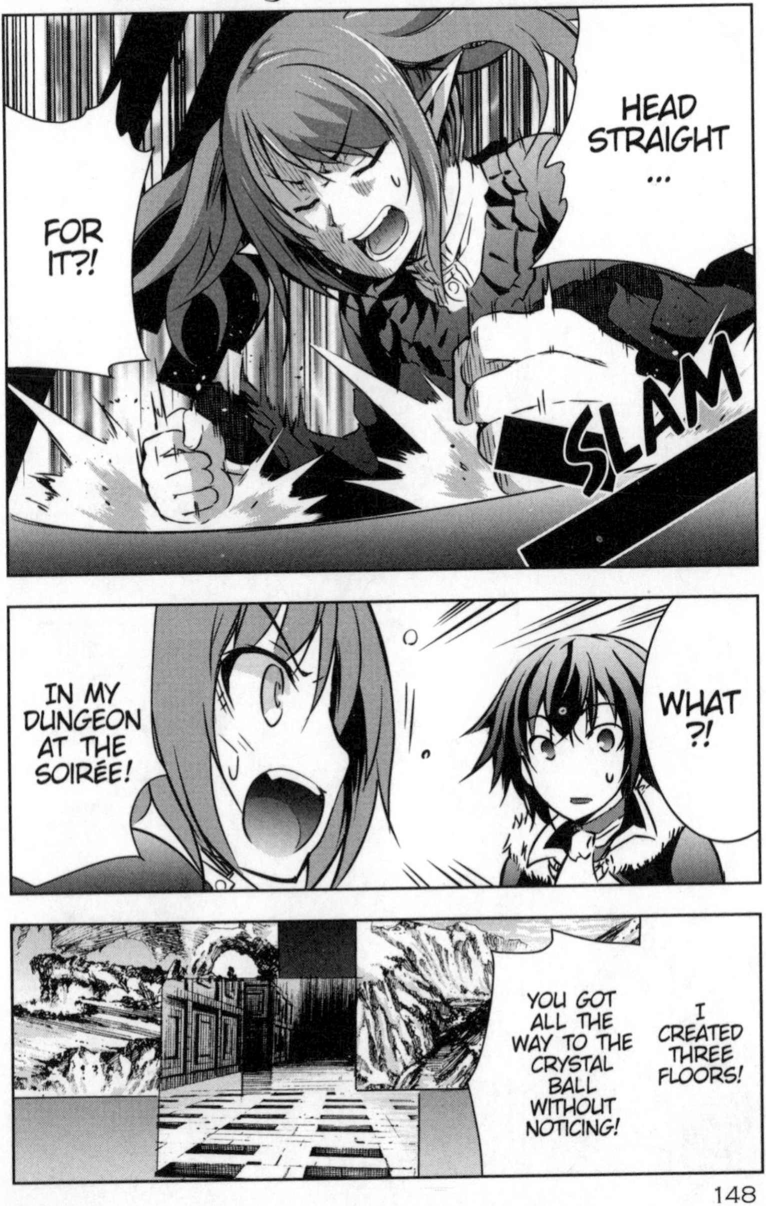
HEAD STRAIGHT ...
FOR IT?!
SLAM
WHAT ?!
IN MY DUNGEON AT THE SOIRÉE!
I CREATED THREE FLOORS!
YOU GOT ALL THE WAY TO THE CRYSTAL BALL WITHOUT NOTICING!

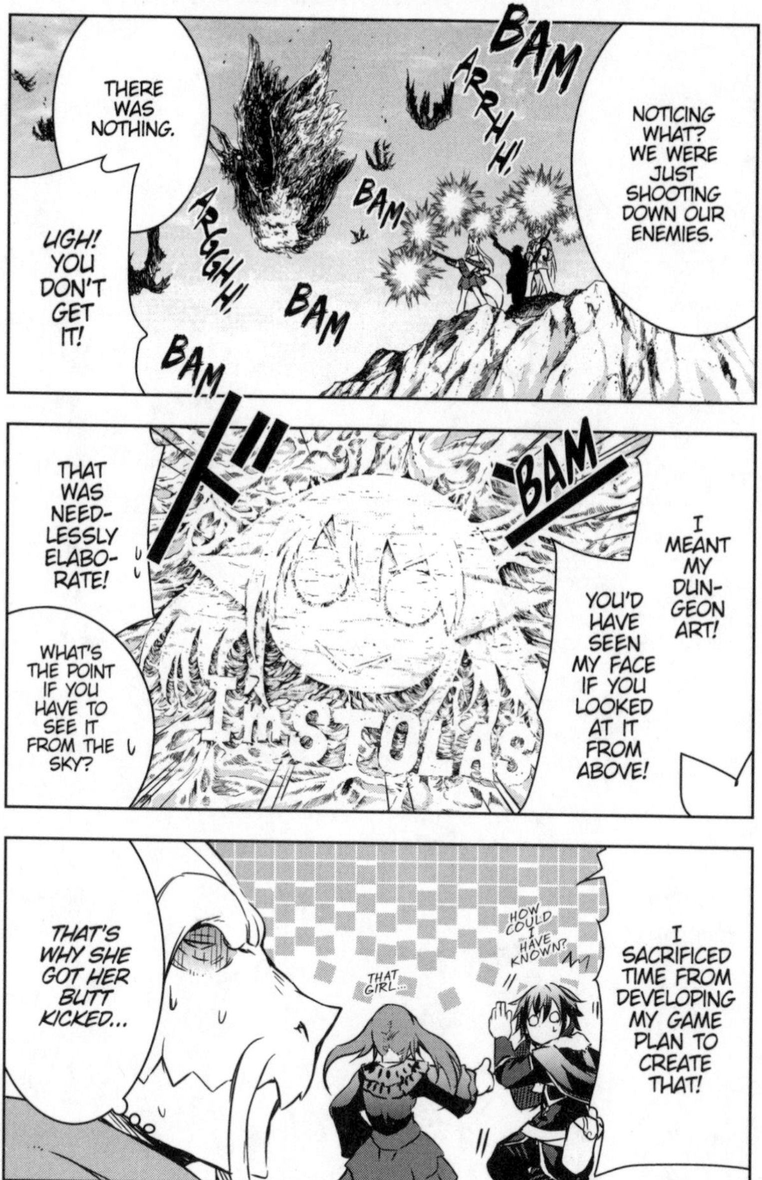
NOTICING WHAT? WE WERE JUST SHOOTING DOWN OUR ENEMIES.
BAM
ARRHH!
BAM
ARGGHH!
BAM
BAM
THERE WAS NOTHING.
UGH! YOU DON'T GET IT!
I MEANT MY DUN-GEON ART!
YOU'D HAVE SEEN MY FACE IF YOU LOOKED AT IT FROM ABOVE!
BAM
I'm STOLAS
THAT WAS NEED-LESSLY ELABO-RATE!
WHAT'S THE POINT IF YOU HAVE TO SEE IT FROM THE SKY?
I SACRIFICED TIME FROM DEVELOPING MY GAME PLAN TO CREATE THAT!
HOW COULD I HAVE KNOWN?
THAT GIRL...
THAT'S WHY SHE GOT HER BUTT KICKED...

Bonus Manga: **The Demon Lord's Meal**

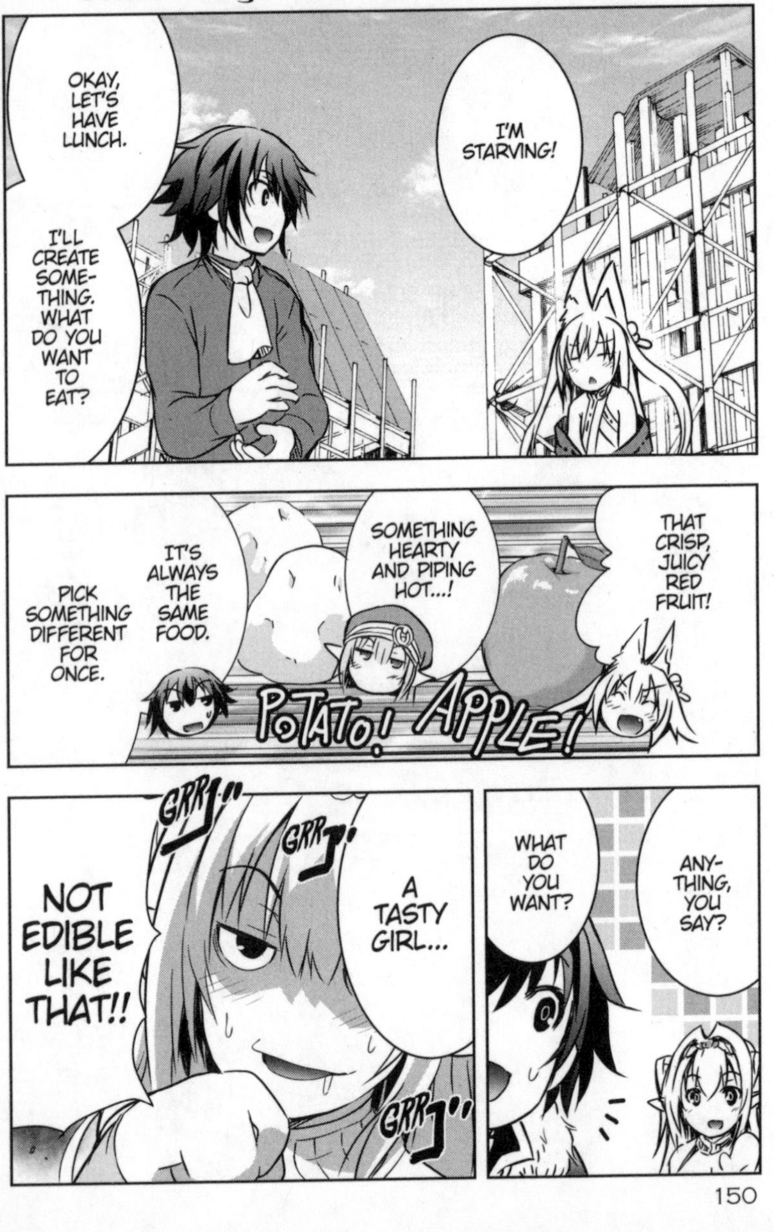
I'M STARVING!
OKAY, LET'S HAVE LUNCH.
I'LL CREATE SOME-THING. WHAT DO YOU WANT TO EAT?
THAT CRISP, JUICY RED FRUIT!
SOMETHING HEARTY AND PIPING HOT...!
IT'S ALWAYS THE SAME FOOD.
PICK SOMETHING DIFFERENT FOR ONCE.
APPLE!
POTATO!
ANY-THING, YOU SAY?
WHAT DO YOU WANT?
GRR
A TASTY GIRL...
GRR
NOT EDIBLE LIKE THAT!!
GRR

Bonus Manga: **Ancient Elf is Trouble**

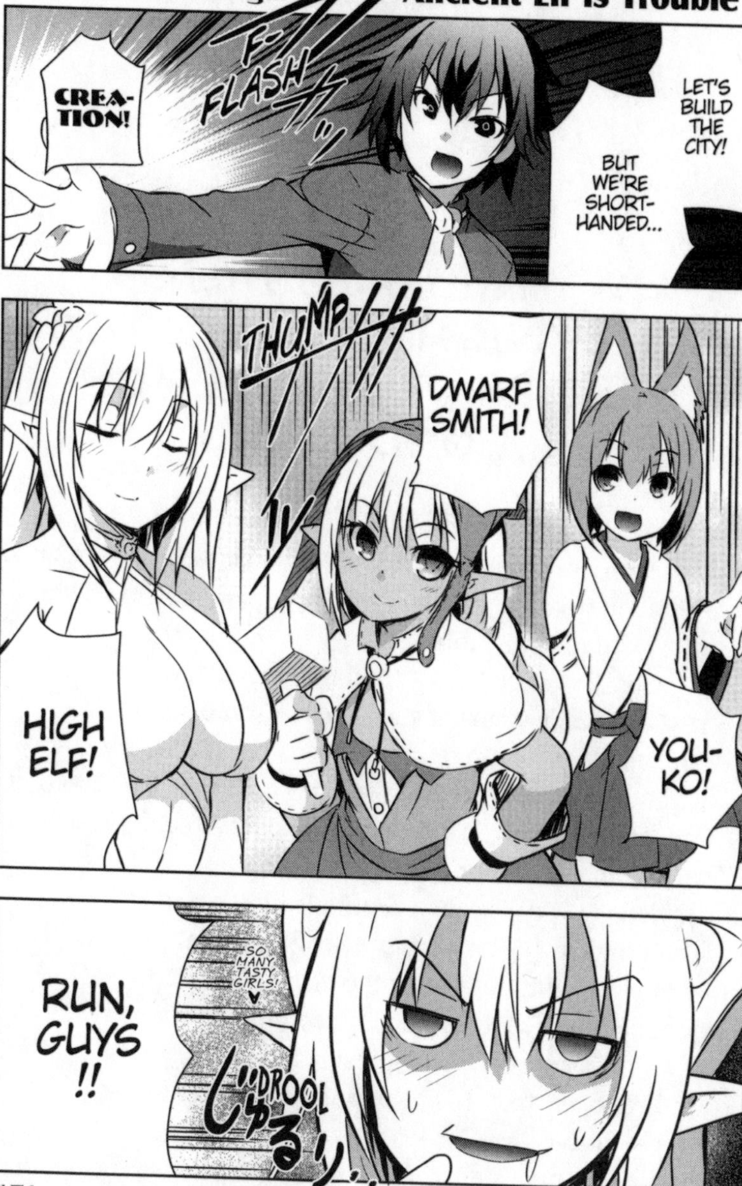

LET'S BUILD THE CITY!
BUT WE'RE SHORT-HANDED...
F-FLASH
CREATION!
YOU-KO!
DWARF SMITH!
THUMP
HIGH ELF!
SO MANY TASTY GIRLS! ♥
じゅるり
DROOL
RUN, GUYS !!

THE NIGHT BEFORE THE BIRTH OF THE DEMON LORD'S CITY

We have been making good progress in building my dungeon—my city, I mean—ever since we left Marcho's dungeon. Before we can allow people in, however, we first need to create a box.

Comfort is our focus, and that includes sanitation matters. Under current standards in some cities, it is acceptable for people to dump waste from their window without any concern. We could do the same. The thought crossed my mind, but I wouldn't approve of the practice, and neither would my monsters.

This is why I want a futuristic city, complete with water and sewage systems. This may not all be feasible at the moment, but laying the groundwork now will be beneficial in the long run. The completed water and sewage systems are being inspected.

"Yeah, perfect. It's been built according to the specifications."

Receiving a stamp of approval from the silver-haired

elder dwarf girl, the dwarf smiths share in their joy.

The elder dwarf is an S-ranked monster and the world's best alchemist, abilities that make her irreplaceable. To make use of her talents, I created the dwarf smiths to wait on her, hand and foot. The elder dwarf creates the design, and the dwarf smiths carry it out to her specifications.

My plan was a success. None of this could have been completed if the elder dwarf had to do it all by herself. Her ability to work on other designs while the dwarf smiths built the systems was ideal.

"What we have to do is cultivate some land with the high elf, maintain irrigation channels, pave a residential area, and build the necessary houses. I've completed the designs. Take care of the rest." The dwarf smiths are in good spirits. They're proud of their work. The elder dwarf was happy to leave it in their capable hands.

She had never done that before. The elder dwarf typically wouldn't do anything more than the designs, but she has always checked and followed the progress of her projects. She would often come to the worksite and watch out of the corner of her eye as she worked on other things. There was no need for this anymore. She could provide a blueprint, and she trusted her subordinates to complete the tasks they were assigned. This was an acknowledgement of the capabilities of the dwarf smiths.

"We've got a spacious farm with water channels, paved roads, houses, and water and sewage systems. It's starting to look more like a city."

"Uh-huh. Once the city is finished, we just need to build a protective wall around it. From the way things are looking, we'll have it done in no time. And take a look at this."

"Oh, it's the sword we're going to sell."

"I've modified the blade so it can be mass-produced." I receive a document from the elder dwarf.

"It's great that it's so easy to produce, but we have too many. I'll think about cutting down the production volume for now." We'll adjust the quantity. Producing as many as we can sell could have consequences. Our reason for producing swords is strictly to increase visitors and settlers in our city. Let's say a visitor comes to the city to purchase a sword and leaves for good... It's preferable to have him return because it's sold out. However, stock that is *too* low will make him give up, and a good first impression is important for word of mouth. I'll ask Wight for his advice. He's very good at things like this. Now that I mention it, I want to check on the progress of his work, too. I've finished inspecting the water and sewage systems. I'll go over there.

I go to see Wight. I left the elder dwarf in charge of hardware aspects, such as housing and infrastructure, but Wight is responsible for other things, like lodging.

My city will provide farms and housing to attract farmers to settle here, and serve as a hub to adventurers by taking advantage of its close proximity to the popular dungeon. We could bring lodging businesses from other cities when we see some success, but first we need our own tavern. I left Wight in charge of that.

The tavern overlooks a residential area and a farm, and it can easily accommodate over a hundred travelers. I enter the tavern.

"Oh, my lord. Thank you for coming all this way. I would have come to see you if I had known," says Wight, as he bows gracefully, like a gentleman. It suits him to make such gestures, in spite of being a bony monster.

"I wanted to check out your tavern anyway." Most of it is already finished. The price list is up, and the interior is coming together. It's sleek and stylish.

"Do you have enough workers?"

"Yes, the Youkos are all brilliant. They're quick to catch on, and they work efficiently. But most of all, they're quite lovely."

"Was that last part important to mention?"

"Why, of course. I would prefer to be served by lovely girls than by anyone else."

I suppose he's right. Youkos are monsters that are ranked two levels below Tenko. Since they "transform" into humans at times, I created them to be service attendants. They're busy running around. I notice a pretty girl with fox ears amongst them.

"Hey, it's Daddy! Guys, say hi!" Quina, the Tenko, is my contracted monster.

"Quina, I didn't know you were helping out."

"Yeah! The uniforms are so cute!" Quina and the girls are wearing maid uniforms that were designed to be comfortable.

"How did you get that style?"

"I fell in love with it when I saw it in the anime you got for me. I had El-chan make it for me." I have the ability to use "Creation" to generate anything from my memory.

As a newly arisen Demon Lord, I shouldn't have any memory, but somehow I have the knowledge of a ruined civilization. That's why I was able to create this.

"Daddy, how do I look?"

"It looks great on all of you."

"Yay! ♪ " Quina and the others are excited.

More new visitors show up. They're blonde elves with gorgeous bodies—the ancient elf and her subordinates, the high elves.

"Master! Just the person I was looking for. Ta-da! We have new fruits and vegetables. We're going to have a tasting party, and we'd like to know what you think."

"You've prepared so much."

"Yes, we obtained every seed from a neighboring town and modified each to adapt to our soil and water."

If the dwarves are in charge of artifacts, the elves are responsible for nature. They bless the soil and water for purification. They do a wide range of tasks, like controlling the climate. With the elves' powers, the climate will be on my city's side.

"I can see from all that produce in the basket that the adaptation was a success."

"Thank you, but we still have to taste them! We won't know if it was a success until we try them."

The crop growth is mainly influenced by environmental factors, such as soil, water, and the climate. That's why I use the elves' powers to adapt them to this city. The growth of the modified seeds can be enhanced with the elves' help, which allows for quick inspection. With the already-blessed soil and water, growing enhanced crops will guarantee a rich harvest. That will satisfy the migrated farmers and lead them to settle here permanently. A good food infrastructure is necessary for the prosperity of the city.

The dwarf team joins us at the tasting party after work. There's the Tenko and her subordinates, the Youkos, the elder dwarf and her underlings, the dwarf smiths, and the ancient elf and the high elves. It becomes lively with Wight and the skeleton squad, turning into more of a banquet. They arrange a large dining hall to accommodate everyone, and serve dishes that the ancient elf prepared with their vegetables.

"This steamed potato with butter is awesome."

"The tomato is so sweet! Quina loves this."

"Nice, crisp lettuce."

"I recommend the corn. It tastes best when it's freshly boiled."

Every vegetable is delicious. Since they're larger than normal size, I expected them to taste bland, but they taste superb.

"I'm surprised. You've grown them well, and I can't believe how great they taste."

"I may not look it, but I'm the oldest and most

powerful elf. Of course I can make them grow well. These are tasty, nutritious vegetables. Eating a lot of good food is very important."

That makes sense. Having a good, hearty meal will soothe the soul. Infrastructure is important, but food is important, too.

As everyone parties, I decide to get some fresh air. I open a window to see vacant houses and a whole field stretched out in front of me. This is still an empty box. It's taking shape, but it isn't a city yet. Soon, we'll have many people come, and the city will be established. And then it will grow.

"I can't wait," I blurt out, even though I wasn't talking to anyone.

"Yay! Quina can't wait, either!"

"It'll be interesting if we get a lot of people to come. People will bring a lot of technology with them. I'll get to build many things. I'm excited."

"I'll do my best, too. I'll show people what true abundance is." Everyone is so positive. The gate to Avalon will be open to people in a few days. I just can't wait for that moment!

THE END

Comment by: Rui Tsukiyo
Art by: Hideaki Yoshikawa

Afterword

Thank you for reading *Dungeon Builder*, Volume 2. I'm the author, Rui Tsukiyo. The dungeon building has finally begun! Feel the excitement rise as the city develops. Both the manga and the city will get more and more interesting.

It's great that the manga shows the kind of motion you can't fully enjoy in its original written form, but I also recommend reading the light novel, too. It reveals more details and backstories that aren't in the manga. It's currently available from GA Novel!

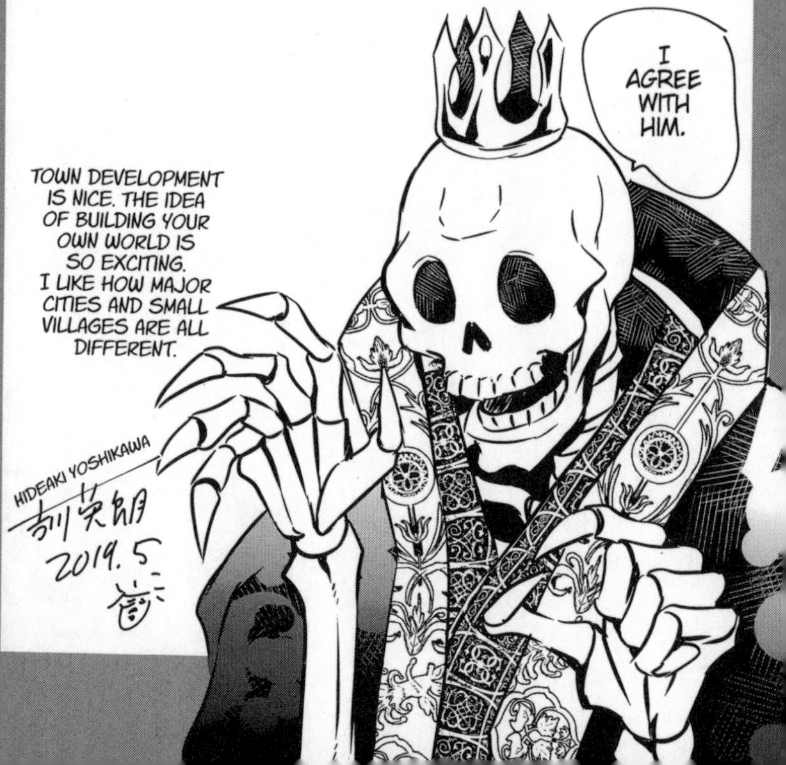
I AGREE WITH HIM.
TOWN DEVELOPMENT IS NICE. THE IDEA OF BUILDING YOUR OWN WORLD IS SO EXCITING. I LIKE HOW MAJOR CITIES AND SMALL VILLAGES ARE ALL DIFFERENT.
HIDEAKI YOSHIKAWA
吉川英朗
2019.5

DUNGEON BUILDER:
THE DEMON KING'S LABYRINTH IS A MODERN CITY!

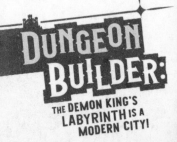

SEVEN SEAS ENTERTAINMENT PRESENTS

DUNGEON BUILDER:
WITHDRAWN
THE DEMON KING'S LABYRINTH IS A MODERN CITY!

story by RUI TSUKUYO   art by HIDEAKI YOSHIKAWA   VOLUME 2

TRANSLATION
Elina Ishikawa-Curran

ADAPTATION
Julia Kinsman

LETTERING
Roland Amago
Bambi Eloriaga-Amago

COVER DESIGN
KC Fabellon

PROOFREADING
Kurestin Armada

EDITOR
Peter Adrian Behravesh
Shanti Whitesides

PREPRESS TECHNICIAN
Rhiannon Rasmussen-Silverstein

PRODUCTION MANAGER
Lissa Pattillo

MANAGING EDITOR
Julie Davis

ASSOCIATE PUBLISHER
Adam Arnold

PUBLISHER
Jason DeAngelis

MAOU-SAMA NO MACHIZUKURI! SAIKYOU NO DUNGEON WA KINDAI
TOSHI VOL. 2
© 2019 Hideaki Yoshikawa
© Rui Tsukuyo/OVERLAP
Originally published in Japan in 2019 by OVERLAP Inc., Ltd., Tokyo.
English translation rights arranged with OVERLAP Inc., Ltd., Tokyo.

Seven Seas press and purchase enquiries can be sent to Marketing Manager
Lianne Sentar at press@gomanga.com. Information regarding the distribution
and purchase of digital editions is available from Digital Manager CK Russell
at digital@gomanga.com.

Seven Seas and the Seven Seas logo are trademarks of
Seven Seas Entertainment. All rights reserved.

ISBN: 978-1-64505-447-4

Printed in Canada

First Printing: May 2020

10 9 8 7 6 5 4 3 2 1

FOLLOW US ONLINE: www.sevenseasentertainment.com

READING DIRECTIONS

This book reads from *right to left*, Japanese style.
If this is your first time reading manga, you start
reading from the top right panel on each page and
take it from there. If you get lost, just follow the
numbered diagram here. It may seem backwards at
first, but you'll get the hang of it! Have fun!!

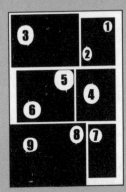